BRICK, CONCRETE, STONEWORK

MONTE BURCH

CREATIVE HOMEOWNER PRESS® A DIVISION OF FEDERAL MARKETING CORPORATION, 24 PARK WAY, UPPER SADDLE RIVER, NEW JERSEY 07458

BRICK, CONCRETE, STONEWORK

PROJECTS LIST

Learn the Basics	Page
Determine the Amount of Material you Need	12
Learn to Mix Concrete	13
Learn to Pour Concrete	16
Learn to Finish Concrete	17
Learn to Cut Edges & Joints	17
Create Unusual Finishes in Concrete	18
Add Color to Concrete	21

Working with Concrete	Page
Excavate a Site	23
Build the Form	23
Add Footings	24
Build a Concrete Walk	25
Build Concrete Steps	27
Build a Concrete Patio	30
Build a Concrete Driveway	34
Build Concrete Retaining Walls	36

Working with Brick Masonry	Page
Set up Batter Boards	39
Build a One-Wythe Wall	46
Learn to Cut Bricks	47
Build a Brick Screen	51
Build a Two-Wythe Wall	51
Lay a Brick Patio or Walk	57
Apply a Brick Veneer — Exterior	61
Apply a Brick Veneer — Interior	63

Working with Stone Masonry	Page
Learn to Cut Stone	68
Dry Lay a Stone Patio or Walk on Sand	69
Construct a Mortared Stone Wall	72
Create Stone Veneer	76

Working with Concrete Block Masonry	Page
Work with Concrete Block: Determine What you Need	80
Build a Concrete Block Foundation	82
Waterproof Foundation Walls	87
Apply Stucco to an Exterior Wall	89

Projects for Combined Materials	Page
Add a Sunken Tub to your Bathroom	94
Build a Brick Barbecue	102
Build a Stone Fireplace	105

Repair & Maintain Concrete & Masonry	Page
Learn to Repair Concrete	119
Learn to Repair Brick & Block	125
Replace Brick & Block	126
Repair your Chimney — Exterior	127
Repair your Chimney — Interior	128
Learn to Patch Stucco	130
Stain a Concrete Surface	132
Stop Erosion along your Walks & Driveway	133

Manufactured in United States of America

Current Printing (last digit)
10 9 8 7

Editorial Director: Shirley M. Horowitz
Editor: Gail Kummings
Art Director: Léone Lewensohn
Designer: Paul Sochacki
Illustrator: Norman Nuding

Technical Adviser: Frank Randall
Engineer, Portland Cement Association

Cover photograph: Philip Graham

ISBN: 0–932944–30–2 (paperback)
ISBN: 0–932944–29–9 (hardcover)
LC. 81–66575

CREATIVE HOMEOWNER PRESS®
BOOK SERIES

A DIVISION OF FEDERAL
MARKETING CORPORATION
24 PARK WAY,
UPPER SADDLE RIVER, NJ 07458

FOREWORD

Masonry and concrete are special materials. Inside and outside your home, they create long-lasting projects that are relatively low in cost—especially when compared to the prices of many other materials.

The average homeowner need not spend years practicing and perfecting concrete and masonry skills in order to master them. They are basic and are easily learned. In fact, the major requirement is patience. Once you master the skills, you have a wide variety of textures, colors and finishes at your disposal. Concrete can be either troweled smooth or left rough; it also can be colored, stained or left plain. Brick and stone also come in a variety of finishes and colors, from the highly formal appearance of polished face brick or ashlar stone to informal and rustic used brick and fieldstone. All of the materials have far more versatility than may be perceived at first.

The projects and techniques in this book are directed toward homeowners with a wide range of masonry skill levels—both those with no previous experience and those with considerable concrete and masonry knowledge. Therefore, the masonry projects include the very simple, such as brick walkways laid on sand beds, and more complex undertakings, such as a garden fountain. A broad selection of concrete jobs also are offered.

We hope that the consumer will find *Masonry & Concrete* an extremely helpful guide and instruction manual and that its use will result in both savings and increased enjoyment of the time spent at home.

CONTENTS

1 CONCRETE BASICS   8
Ingredients, proportions, mixing methods; guidelines for placing the mix; various techniques for finishing a pour for design and safety.

2 CONCRETE PROJECTS   22
Form-building procedures; means of preventing cracking and creating drainage and pitch; projects ranging from sidewalks to patios.

3 WORKING WITH BRICK MASONRY   38
Materials, tools, mortar, basic bricklaying techniques and patterns; one- and two-wythe walls, veneering, walks, and patios, and a barbecue.

4 WORKING WITH STONE MASONRY   64
Types, mortar, tools; techniques for dry-laid and mortared constructions; projects include walks, patios, walls, veneers, small structures.

5 WORKING WITH CONCRETE BLOCK MASONRY   78
Methods for laying concrete block foundations and walls; projects include retaining walls, patios, screen walls, foundations.

6 PROJECTS THAT COMBINE MATERIALS   92
Stone or concrete block barbecue, stone or brick fireplace, sunken concrete tub, garden fountain and furniture.

7 CONCRETE AND MASONRY REPAIRS   119
Repair cracks in concrete slabs; crumbling mortar between bricks, stone, and concrete block; water-damaged foundations; sunken walks.

8 MAINTENANCE OF CONCRETE & MASONRY   132
Removing grease, dirt and stains from concrete and masonry surfaces; caulking seams; attaching special fasteners.

METRIC CHARTS   139
CONTRIBUTORS, PICTURE CREDITS, ADDRESSES   142
INDEX   142

SELECTED PROJECTS

The projects given below represent a partial listing of the projects covered in this book. Consult the index for additional topics and projects.

BARBECUES   brick 103, stone 104, concrete masonry 104
BASEMENTS   concrete block 86–87
DRIVEWAYS   concrete 34–35, concrete block 87
FIREPITS   brick 60–61
FIREPLACES   stone 105–116, brick 117–118
FOUNDATIONS AND FOOTINGS   concrete 11–18
GARDEN FOUNTAINS AND POOLS   concrete with ceramic tile 101
GARDEN WALLS   brick 44–50, 51–56, stone 70–76, concrete block 81–86, 89–90
INTERIOR WALLS   concrete block 88, brick 66
PATIOS   concrete 31–33, brick 56–60, stone 68–69, concrete block 90–91
PLANTERS   brick 56, stone 64
RETAINING WALLS   concrete 36–37, stone 76–77
SCREEN WALLS   brick 51, concrete block 91
SIDEWALKS   concrete 25–26, brick 56, 60, concrete block 90–91
SMALL STRUCTURES   stone 77, concrete block 81–86, 88–89
STEPS AND RAMPS   concrete 26–60, stone 72
SUNKEN TUBS   concrete with ceramic tile 94–101
TERRACE WALLS   brick 56–60, stone 72
VENEERING   brick 61–63, stone 76
WALKS   concrete 25–26, brick 56–60, stone 67–69

1 CONCRETE BASICS

To achieve a rugged surface in an outdoor setting, outlines of the form boards used to cast this concrete wall were not smoothed away.

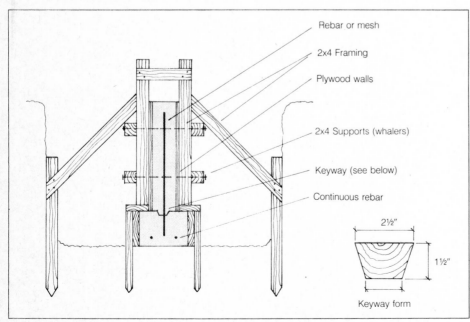

Rebar or mesh

2x4 Framing

Plywood walls

2x4 Supports (whalers)

Keyway (see below)

Continuous rebar

2½"

1½"

Keyway form

The forms used to cast concrete must be strong and well braced in order to support the weight of the material. In most cases use 2 in. thick lumber; construct the forms carefully.

Although concrete work is predictable and easily learned by most homeowners, there are a few precautions. Handling concrete is back-breaking work, so don't overdo it, especially the first day or two. Also, since concrete is so heavy, you must build forms strong enough to hold the semi-liquid material in place until it sets up. If this aspect is neglected, you can end up with a busted form and a yard full of expensive concrete, not to mention possible injury, particularly skin burns.

TOOLS NEEDED
Form-building Tools

There are several tools required. First, you will need some standard carpentry tools for constructing the forms. These can be hand tools such as a good solid hammer, hand cross-cut saw, square, and level. You will need a crowbar for tearing down forms. A portable electric saw will help speed the chore of cutting form boards. In addition, you probably will need a small sledge for driving the form stakes that hold the forms in place.

Concrete Preparation Tools

Shovels and hoes are necessary for moving the material around in the forms, as well as a garden hose and water supply for cleaning tools. You should also have a pair of rubber hip boots for wading around in the material. If you do any large jobs at all, like a patio or floor, sooner or later you are going to have to get right in the "mud." Always be careful not to let your skin come in contact with wet cement; it can cause skin burns. There are also a few specialty tools: some of them you may wish to purchase, some you may wish to rent, and some you can make yourself.

Building a measuring box. One tool you can make quite easily is a measuring box. This is actually a bottomless box that has handles on its sides. It measures 12x12x12 inches on the inside to provide a measured cubic foot of material.

Wheelbarrow and mortar box. You will need a wheelbarrow to move the material to the form. A small garden wheelbarrow is not good enough; you need a large, sturdy contractor's wheelbarrow, preferably one that has wooden handles and a large pneumatic tire. If you mix the material yourself and plan on

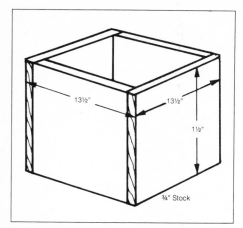

To measure out the correct proportions of cement, sand and gravel, build a frame. The box measures one cubic foot of material.

Mix concrete in a mortar box. A concrete hoe is especially made to mix materials without separating the ingredients from the water.

Screeds level the surface of concrete and force large aggregates down into the concrete slab. Use a straight, level 2x4.

mixing only small batches, you can do the task in a wheelbarrow, a special mixing tub, or even on a flat level surface, such as a concrete patio or driveway. Or you can use a mortar box. These come in several different sizes, the smaller ranging from an 11x23x42-inch box that holds 6 cubic feet of material to one that is 11x35x82 inches and holds 15 cubic feet. For hand mixing, you will also need a mortar hoe.

Power mixers. A much faster method is to utilize a power mixer, which will be required if you are adding an air-entraining agent. (An air-entraining admixture is mandatory in areas with severe winters and frost heave.) Mixers come in a range of sizes, from a small 1½-cubic-foot wheelbarrow size that can be rolled to the job to a large 6-cubic-foot mixer that is pulled behind your automobile. You can rent mixers from most tool rental yards in larger cities. Most mixers come equipped with an electric motor, but you can also find them with gasoline motors for use in more remote locations. Incidentally, if you rent a gasoline-powered unit, make sure you have the rental people start the motor to see that it operates easily.

If you live some distance from a larger

city, or if you plan on doing quite a bit of concrete work, you may prefer to purchase your own mixer. A unit that will do most home jobs quite well holds 2½ cubic feet. The stationary type costs just a little over $300. A portable trailered unit, which can be towed behind an automobile, will cost around $500. (These costs are based on January, 1981, prices.) This tool can become an invaluable item for anyone who plans to do considerable amounts of masonry work, especially since it can be used to mix mortar as well as concrete. Just one large job, such as a fireplace, will more than pay for the time saved in mixing mortar.

Tools for Placing the Concrete

You should use a special concrete hoe or a square-ended shovel for placing the concrete in the forms. Use a concrete rake for tamping down small jobs and a vibrator for very large jobs. (Do not use ordinary garden tools when you work with concrete—they can separate the water from the rest of the mixture and ruin the project.) You will also need 2x4 boards to use as screeds or strikeboards. These pull the excess concrete off the forms. The boards should be straight and

Power mixers

Power mixers can be small enough to wheel by hand or large enough to serve industrial needs.

lightweight and should measure about 1 to 2 feet longer than the width of the form.

Finishing Tools

You will need several tools for finishing concrete. These include floats and darbies, which you can purchase or make out of wood. Floats provide an even but fairly rough finish. The final smooth finish is applied with metal trowels, which will have to be purchased—several different kinds and designs are available. You will also need an edger for finishing the edges of walks and patios, as well as a groover for cutting the control joints. The blade on the groover must be one inch deep (or one fourth of the thickness of the slab). In the event you need to trowel a large area, you can usually rent a power trowel. Broomed finishes require the use of a stiff-bristled shop broom or a special concrete broom, which you can buy.

MATERIALS

Concrete is actually a mixture of sand, gravel or other aggregates, and portland cement (this is not a brand name, but a type) mixed with enough water to form a semi-fluid state. This mixture is then poured into a form to harden.

Cement

Cement isn't the same as concrete; cement is one of the ingredients used in concrete. Portland cement is actually a mixture of burned clay, lime, iron, silica, and alumina. This mixture is put through a kiln at 2700 degrees F. and then ground to a fine powder. Gypsum is then added. The cement comes in gray, white and some shades of buff.

There are many different manufacturers of the material, which comes packaged in 1-cubic-foot bags that weigh 94 pounds. The sacks of cement are quite heavy for their size and are a bit awkward for many folks to handle, especially if you have to lift them in and out of a deep car trunk. Take your time and do not strain yourself trying to lift them. Make sure you lift from your knees and keep your back as straight as possible.

Moisture absorption and premature hardening. One of the worst problems with cement is that it absorbs moisture quickly. Once enough water has been absorbed, the cement hardens and is completely useless. Make sure that you check the material purchased at the building supply dealer to see that none of the sacks have already hardened. Some bags may seem to be somewhat hardened around the edges, but if they loosen up after they are rolled around on the floor, they usually are all right.

Once you have the cement home, you must store the bags up off the ground; otherwise, they will absorb moisture. They also should not be stored on a concrete floor or slab, as they will take

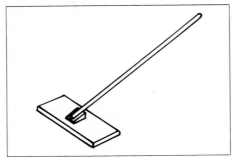

A home-made bullfloat uses a section of 1x6 fastened with wood screws to an old broom handle and an angled block of wood.

moisture from the concrete. Instead, stack the concrete sacks on wooden skids. Cover the bags with plastic or other waterproof covering if you must leave them outside.

Types of cement. There are five basic cement types. The one most used in home masonry work is Type I, which is carried by nearly all building supply yards. In some unusual cases, you may need one of the other special types, which can be specially ordered.

Type I. This is the popular, general-purpose cement commonly used in residential work.

Type II. With its moderate hydration heat, this cement is used for massive structures such as bridges and pilings and provides some sulfate resistance.

Type III. This cement hardens much more quickly than do the other two, and it generates more heat in the process. It is most commonly used on commercial structures such as smoke stacks, in which the forms are moved as quickly as the

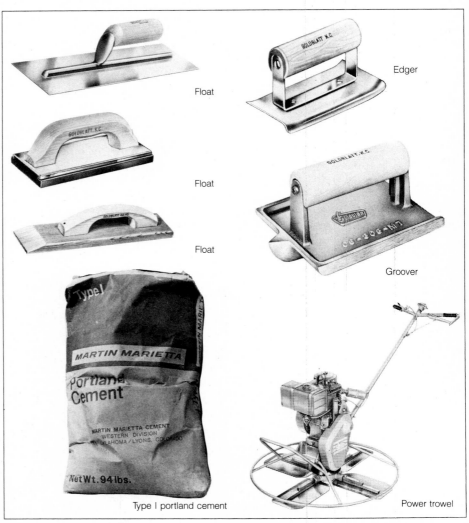

Float

Edger

Float

Float

Groover

Type I portland cement

Power trowel

Tools needed to finish a concrete slab are floats, darbies, edgers, groovers and trowels.

material sets up. It is also chosen for winter use and for rush jobs.

Type IV. A low-heat-producing cement, Type IV is used for massive structures.

Type V. Offering high sulfate resistance, Type V is used in areas with high sulfate content in the water and/or soils.

Aggregates

Sand. The second material used in concrete, aggregate, ranges in size from tiny dust-sized pieces of sand up to 2½-inch stones used as larger "fill." Ideally, aggregate combines these sizes to provide the strongest type of concrete; the small particles fill in around the larger particles. For most home masonry jobs, the aggregates used are sand and gravel or crushed stone. Do not use so-called "sharp sand" that is sometimes used for mortar. "Bank-run" sand is best, because the rounded, various-sized particles of this type of sand work to an advantage in the concrete. The sand particle size can run up to as large as ¼ inch in diameter.

Gravel or stone. The second aggregate, which is called coarse aggregate, can be either gravel or crushed stone. The stones may be as large as 1 inch. They can be screened for uniform size, or they can be bank run, which may also include some coarse sand along with the gravel sizes.

Naturally, the larger the aggregates, the more economical the material will be. The concrete will require less cement and the finished slab will suffer less from shrinkage. However, don't use aggregate larger than one quarter of the thickness of the pour. This means that if the concrete will be 4 inches thick, you can use up to 1-inch size gravel or crushed stone. A 6-inch-thick slab can include 1½-inch stones. Another consideration is the practicality of moving a mix containing the larger stones. If you have to shovel the liquid concrete some distance down a form, it is a lot harder to shovel the larger stones than it is smaller aggregates. As you can see, the type of pour makes quite a bit of difference in the aggregates that can be used.

It is a general rule to place concrete as close to its final location as possible. Excessive movement can separate the water from the cement aggregates. If you must move the concrete more than about 10 feet in the form, use ½ inch or smaller

aggregate. Larger, ¾ inch stone can be used in a flat slab where you won't have to move the material quite as far. For a large foundation, where you will be dumping directly into the forms and you won't need a smooth surface, you can use larger aggregates. Aggregate size also depends on the size of the spacing in the reinforcing bars or mesh. The stones should be no larger than three-fourths the opening between the bars, or the stones can get caught in the mesh of the bars and prevent the concrete from settling into place.

Silt testing. Any rule on aggregate sizes is fairly loose because you will probably have to use whatever types and sizes are most common in your area. Most building and masonry supply dealers will have the most commonly used sizes and materials on hand. The most important thing about the aggregate is that it should be free of silt and debris, for these can not only ruin the appearance of the job but weaken it as well. To test for the cleanliness of the aggregates, place about 2 inches of aggregate and sand in a fruit jar. Then pour water over the materials and shake gently. Allow the material to settle and the water to clear. If there is more than ⅛ inch of silt on top of the aggregate, it should be washed. This can be done quite easily—dump the aggregates onto a clean, hard surface, such as an existing concrete slab, and hose the material down. Rake the material around some to make sure all of it is clean.

Storage. When you have the aggregate material delivered, have it dumped on a clean, flat spot. You may wish to first cover the ground with plastic. Place some planks or other material around the sand to prevent it from spreading out and simply disappearing before you have a chance to work with it. Have the materials delivered as close to the work site as possible. All the substances are quite heavy, and you want to avoid moving them. If you do have to move them, try to get them placed uphill from the site rather than downhill. Then lay a cover over the aggregate to keep it clean and free of debris. Otherwise, during the fall dry leaves can quickly be blown into the pile of sand or stones. Even worse is the wandering neighborhood dog or cat who finds the sand pile to his liking. Of course, with three small kids, I'm always finding one of those tiny metal automo-

biles in my concrete or mortar mixes.

Water

The third ingredient in concrete is water. This should be free of foreign materials and impurities. One good rule is to use only water that is fit to drink.

ESTIMATING MATERIAL AMOUNTS

There are several ways to prepare concrete. You can buy the dry ingredients separately and mix them, or you can buy a dry complete mix, to which you add water. The latter is expensive, but a great way of purchasing a small amount of material for jobs such as anchoring a basketball goal or a clothesline post, or for patching a small area. If the job

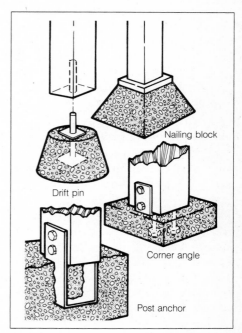

Nailing block

Drift pin

Corner angle

Post anchor

Posthole footings need no base or forms and are ideal anchors for clothespoles or fence posts. Above are examples.

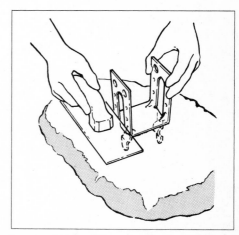

Insert anchors while concrete is still plastic; smooth concrete with a float or trowel.

requires over a yard of concrete, you might be better off using a ready-mix concrete. This is delivered to the site already mixed with water and ready to pour. Be aware, however, that most ready-mix plants today won't deliver less than ½ yard, and some won't deliver less than a yard.

Concrete Proportions and Formulas

Cement, sand, coarse aggregate and water must be present in the correct proportions to create a durable, long-lasting job. Incorrect proportions result in a slab or wall that will crack, flake or chip. There should be enough large aggregates to make an economical mix, yet enough small aggregates to fill in the spaces around the larger ones—and enough cement to hold all the materials together. In addition, there should be the right proportion of water to provide proper hydration. Either too much or too little water can be disastrous.

Adding water. Adding the correct amount of water in the mix is one of the hardest tasks in concrete preparation. It is compounded by the fact that sand contains varying amounts of water. Sand usually falls into the categories of wet, damp or very wet, and you must know the moisture qualities of the sand you are using before you add water. To test, squeeze a handful of your sand into a ball. If it holds its shape, yet leaves no noticeable amount of moisture on your hand, it is considered wet sand. Damp sand will fall apart after being squeezed together. Very wet sand, on the other hand, holds its shape *and* leaves moisture in your hand. Most construction sand is of the wet variety.

The accompanying tables give water quantities on the basis of wet sand. If you have damp sand (and are following Table 1), decrease the quantity of sand by 1 pound and increase the amount of water by 1 pound. If the sand is very wet, use 1 pound more of sand and 1 pound less of water. If you are following Table 2, it is best always to use wet sand, since water affects the bulk of sand in surprising ways.

Proportions also vary according to the size of the coarse aggregates in your particular mix, and the addition (or exclusion) of air-entraining agents.

Air-entrained concrete. Air-entrained concrete is necessary in areas in which concrete must withstand freezing and thawing temperature shifts and de-icing treatments. Air-entrainment is the process of introducing millions of microscopic air bubbles into the concrete. The air bubbles permit enough space for the absorbed water to expand when the water freezes, so the concrete slab does not crack or break apart. Air-entrained concrete is also easier to place and finish than is regular concrete, because the tiny air bubbles act as lubricants while the concrete is plastic.

Air-entrained portland cement in specially marked bags can be obtained at most building supply stores. However, if it is not available in your particular area, you can add an air-entraining admixture. This is available from the same supplier who handles other materials—sand, gravel or cement. The agents vary by manufacturer; mix according to the directions given with your particular product. Whether you buy already bagged air-entrained cement or add the agent yourself, hand mixing is ineffective for entraining air. You must use a machine mixer.

Figuring the Cubic Footage Needed

Concrete. Probably the biggest problem for most beginning masons is figuring the amount of concrete they need and then figuring the amount of materials or ingredients needed to make up the concrete. This is important when mixing the materials yourself, and equally important when ordering ready-mix concrete delivered to the job. The task of figuring the amount is not particularly hard, but it does take some basic arithmetic. Measure the inside of the form: then convert all dimensions to inches. Multiply the width times the length times the height or depth of the concrete (depending on whether the pour is a slab or wall). This will provide the cubic volume in inches. To get cubic feet, divide this figure by 1,728.

The accompanying table provides a quick way to figure the amount of concrete you will need for a given project. Multiply the length times the width of the slab you want; then refer to the amount given for the depth of the slab that you are planning. Then turn to Table 3, which gives amounts for one cubic foot. Multi-

TABLE 1. PROPORTIONS BY WEIGHT TO MAKE 1 CU FT OF CONCRETE

Maximum-size coarse aggregate, in.	Air-entrained concrete				Concrete without air			
	Cement, lb	Sand lb	Coarse aggregate, lb*	Water, lb	Cement, lb	Sand, lb	Coarse aggregate, lb*	Water, lb
⅜	29	53	46	10	29	59	46	11
½	27	46	55	10	27	53	55	11
¾	25	42	65	10	25	47	65	10
1	24	39	70	9	24	45	70	10
1½	23	38	75	9	23	43	75	0

*If crushed stone is used, decrease coarse aggregate by 3 lb. and increase sand by 3 lb.

TABLE 2. PROPORTIONS BY VOLUME*

Maximum-size coarse aggregate, in.	Air-entrained concrete				Concrete without air			
	Cement	Sand	Coarse aggregate	Water	Cement	Sand	Coarse aggregate	Water
⅜	1	2¼	1½	½	1	2½	1½	½
½	1	2¼	2	½	1	2½	2	½
¾	1	2¼	2½	½	1	2½	2½	½
1	1	2¼	2¾	½	1	2½	2¾	½
1½	1	2¼	3	½	1	2½	3	½

*The combined volume is approximately ⅔ of the original bulk.

TABLE 3. CUBIC FEET OF CONCRETE IN SLABS

Area, sq ft (length x width)	Thickness, in.		
	4	5	6
50	17	22	25
100	33	41	50
200	68	84	100
300	100	124	150
400	135	168	200
500	168	208	250

ply the proportions for each material by the amounts given in the table here. The result will give you a good idea of the needed amounts of each material.

In some cases, if you are building a large patio or a driveway, you should work in terms of cubic yards. To convert from cubic feet, divide the footage by 27. This is especially true when you are ordering ready-mix materials. It is a good idea to "think" in cubic yards when figuring the materials. Always plan for a certain amount of waste; one of the worst problems is running short of materials right in the middle. By the time you get the additional ingredients you need, the material has already set up and you may end up with a ruined project.

Always plan for more concrete than you need. The amount of extra material needed depends on the project. Plan for between 10 and 15 percent for walls and footings and 20 percent for slabs. I guarantee you will find a place for any leftover concrete you have. In fact, it is a good idea to consider small projects, such as stepping stones, to use up excess concrete.

Lumber sizes for form-building. The concrete is poured into forms built of stock lumber. These form boards will come in standard sizes, such as 2x4 or 2x10. However you estimate the amount of lumber you will need, or the size of a given project, be aware of the difference between "nominal" and "actual" sizes. A 2x4 is originally cut with dimensions that measure 2 inches by 4 inches. That is the "nominal" size of the board, but the board is smoothed and finished before it is sold. As a result, the "actual" size of a 2x4 is 1½x3½ inches. Some additional common sizes are given here. If you are not sure of the actual size of the lumber that you plan to use, check the accompanying chart or ask your building materials supplier.

LUMBER SIZES

Nominal Size	Actual Size
2x2	1½x1½
2x4	1½x3½
2x6	1½x5½
2x8	1½x7¼
2x10	1½x9¼
2x12	1½x11¼

Measurement Techniques
Once you have determined exactly how much concrete you will need, the next step is to determine how much individual materials you will need, if you are mixing the concrete yourself. Naturally, this varies with the formula or proportions of materials used. To achieve properly mixed concrete, do not merely throw the ingredients into a mixer or wheelbarrow as you guess at quantities; measure accurately. Follow the proportions for the mix you need, working either by volume or by weight.

Volume method. Probably the easiest method is to use a shovel to move the cement, sand and gravel into the mixing location and merely count shovelfuls. (This works as long as you don't forget how many shovelfuls you have put it.) If you're using a power mixer, turn the mixer on and throw the shovelfuls in—the dry materials will mix together as you go along.

Another way to work by volume, although it won't work with a power mixer, is to build a bottomless measuring box. It is made to hold 1 cubic foot of solid material. Position it in the wheelbarrow or mortar box, fill it up, and lift it up off the materials.

Weight method. If you wish to work by weight, use a specially marked bucket. Place the bucket on a bathroom scale and adjust the weight indicator to zero.

Determine a set weight, for instance 10 pounds. Weigh each ingredient separately; make an identifying mark for the correct level of 10 pounds of each material, since each will be different. Then you will just count bucketfuls as you place the correct proportions into the mixing container.

Adding the correct amount of water. Measure the amount of water you add just as accurately as the solids. Turning on the hose and adding water until you feel you have the right amount can often result in a disaster. If you get too much water and do not have enough cement to add to it to correct the situation, you can ruin an entire batch of concrete. The best bet is to fill a large tank or drum with water and dip water out of it as needed. Again, use a bucket that has a known capacity so you can accurately measure the amount of water you are using.

Probably one of the biggest problems with the ingredient proportions is the amount of water required. In fact, the strength of the concrete will depend on the amount of water used. If too little water is used, there won't be enough to provide a good fluid state that can be worked easily and will ensure that each and every solid particle is coated and bonded together. You should use as much water as possible without creating a problem with the workability and smoothness of the concrete. Too much water results in concrete that is unworkable and hard to set up. The cement particles will float up to the surface and, worst of all, weaken the slab.

In most instances, professional masons consider 6 to 7 gallons of water the correct amount of water per bag of cement, depending on the dampness of the sand and the size of the aggregate.

MIXING CONCRETE BY HAND
Years ago concrete was mixed entirely by hand, with a lot of hard work. You can do the same, but it will take time and practice before you get used to the job. Concrete mixing is hard work. You can make it easier by pacing yourself instead of rushing. Make sure you have good balance, and use your entire body to mix instead of just your arms. Do not use a shovel to lift materials more often than you have to. Use a mixing hoe instead—a large-bladed hoe with two holes in the blade. When only a shovel can do the job, do not use a shovel that is too large for you to handle comfortably.

Measure ingredients carefully by weight or volume. Mix concrete close to the site—it is heavy and difficult to transport.

Using a Mortar Box or Wheelbarrow

To hand mix concrete you need a clean, smooth, flat surface. Even a concrete driveway or floor will do—just make sure you hose down and clean up the floor after mixing the material. Usually, though, there are two basic sites for hand mixing—a wheelbarrow (if you have a fairly large one) or a mortar box. This can be rented or purchased—or you can build your own. The mortar box is usually quite a bit larger and easier to use than the wheelbarrow. However, once the concrete is ready, you still have to shovel the material up into the wheelbarrow and move it to the job. This can be an arduous task, so my favorite method is to use a large contractor's wheelbarrow as the mixing site. Whichever you use, mix no more than the container can hold. In fact, if you are using a wheelbarrow, mix only 1 or 2 cubic feet of concrete until you get the hang of it, know how to mix properly and can handle the weight of the wheelbarrow.

Wheelbarrow method. First, wash down the inside of the wheelbarrow. Place the materials in layers on top of each other, beginning with the gravel, then sand, then cement. Before you add the water, move the wheelbarrow next to the form you plan to fill—the load will be lighter than after the water is added.

Measure a gallon of water so you keep to the proportions you need. Using a mixing hoe, make a shallow depression in the center of the material and pour in a little water. Mix this in thoroughly—get clear down into the stones in the bottom of the mix. Then add more water. Pull more dry material in from the sides, and keep mixing it in thoroughly. Any dry materials will weaken the concrete.

Some masonry contractors prefer to mix all the dry ingredients before adding water because they feel they get a more thorough mix. Which method you use is a matter of personal choice, for I have seen masons use both.

Mortar box method. You mix concrete in a mortar box in much the same manner as above, except most masons place the materials in layers in about two-thirds of the box, leaving empty the areas next to the boards. The worker adds a little water in the empty end, rakes some of the material into the water and mixes the two. This process continues until the correct proportions and mix are achieved. You can mix all the dry ingredients before you add the water if you prefer, but mixing the ingredients as they are pulled into the water takes less work.

Troubleshooting Problems

Too much water, or too little. One problem that you will soon figure out is that the more water is added to the mix, the easier the mix is to work with, and also the easier it is to pour into the forms.

Testing the mix: the slump test. When you have mixed the concrete to your satisfaction, you can test to see if it is correct by making the slump test. You can use a professional tool called a slump cone, or create your own by removing both ends from a coffee can. Fill the cone in three layers. After each layer, tamp down 25 times with a stick to be certain there are no air pockets. After tamping the third layer, scrape the concrete level across the top of the cone. Then lift the cone. The concrete will settle. Set the cone beside the concrete and measure the difference between the two heights. A large slump indicates a wet consistency. A slight slump indicates a stiff consistency. The material should slump down to about half (but no less) its original height if you have the correct amount of water and ingredients.

The settling test. Another test is based on the stiffness of ridges in the concrete. Pull the concrete up in a series of ridges with the hoe. If the ridges slump back down and cannot be seen easily, there is too much water. If you cannot create distinct ridges, there is too little water.

Poor mixing. Make sure you have mixed all the ingredients properly and thoroughly, scraping them from the sides and bottom of the wheelbarrow or mixing box. The concrete mix should be an even color. Light or dark streaks indicate poor mixing.

Remedying a poor mix. If your mix is too wet, it doesn't have enough sand and aggregate for the amount of cement paste. Add 5 to 10 percent more of sand and aggregate, mix well, and test. Repeat this until the mix is correct. Keep careful notes of the added amounts; when you make the new batch, you will follow the revised figures for sand and coarse aggregate.

If your mix is too stiff, it has too much aggregate. Do not try to remedy the situation by addition of water alone. Instead, add a cement-water solution that has proportions of 2 to 1. Unfortunately, in most cases even this will not work and you will have to start all over again with decreased amounts of sand and coarse aggregate. Experiment, keeping track of the decreased proportions, until you have

To test, pull the mix into a series of ridges. They should be distinct. Too much or too little water will ruin the concrete.

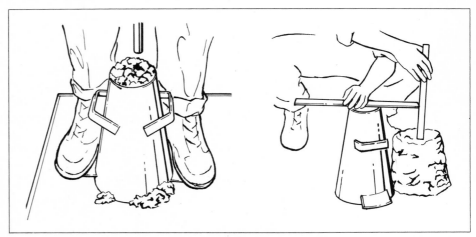

The slump cone is 21 in. high. The base diameter is 8 in. and the top diameter 4 in. Hold the cone down on a firm surface by placing feet onto cone projections. Fill cone with 3 layers of concrete; tamp each 25 times. Level off the concrete at the top. Lift the cone; allow the concrete to settle. Stand the cone next to the concrete in order to measure. A large slump indicates a wet consistency; a slight slump is due to a stiff consistency.

a satisfactory mix. You may have to prepare several batches before you produce the right mixture.

Getting Concrete to the Forms

After the concrete has been mixed thoroughly and properly, the next step is to transport it in a wheelbarrow to the form.

If the ground is soft, lay down planks to provide a stable pathway, and make sure the tire on the wheelbarrow is properly inflated.

Do not fill the wheelbarrow so full that you cannot manage the weight. Center the load, and do not rush. It is quite easy to dump a load of concrete accidentally from a wheelbarrow. In fact, I almost got fired when I worked summers as a concrete laborer back in my college days because I nearly dumped a full wheelbarrow load on my boss's new truck. You can make small, gradually inclined ramps that lead up to the edge of the form and enable you to wheel the material and dump it easily into place. As soon as the material is poured, thoroughly hose down the wheelbarrow and the mixing hoe.

USING A POWER MIXER

Mixing with a powered mixer prepares concrete much easier and faster than does hand mixing. Position the mixer close to the sand and gravel pile. With the mixer turned off, add the amount of dry ingredients needed. Then turn the mixer on and allow it to run in order to mix the dry ingredients thoroughly. Then pour in a little water, allow it to mix a few minutes, and add more water a little at a time until you have added the whole amount already decided on for the mix. Once the material has been properly mixed, turn the mixer over and dump the concrete into a wheelbarrow and start over as needed. As you can see, in this situation two people can really do a better job than one. One person keeps the mixer going while the other moves the concrete to the form, dumps it, spreads it out and gets ready for the next pour.

USING READY MIX

If you have a fairly large project, such as a driveway or a patio, the best bet is to use ready-mix concrete. This is delivered to your door already mixed and in larger quantities than you can easily or quickly mix yourself. Ready-mix or transit-mix concrete has definite advantages—it is often more economical than the total cost of the individual ingredients, and air-entrainment can be provided.

Transport and Access

There are several possible limitations, however, that must be considered before ordering ready-mix materials. The first is whether or not the truck can get to the forms. Most trucks have chutes that can be attached to enable the operator to move the concrete as much as 20 feet, but that is about the limit. If the truck cannot get close enough, you will have to move the material in wheelbarrows to the final location. If there is any doubt about your situation, and if you are dealing with a fair amount of materials, it would be wise to have the concrete dealer come out and look at your situation.

You also should be aware that concrete transit trucks are extremely heavy. Fill areas around new house construction, or even around older homes, may be too soft to support the weight. The result is often a stuck truck. More serious results would arise if the truck tipped over due to the fill. Even in dry weather and on normal ground, the trucks can sometimes tear up a yard. Try to plan a route that will cause the least amount of damage to your property.

If you will have to move the concrete some distance by hand, this must also be explained to the dealer, since his truck may be at your site longer than normal. Some dealers may even charge for this extra time. You should also specify to the contractor what you are actually building as well as the aggregate size and the maximum amount of water per cubic yard. If you wish additives such as air-entrainment, this must also be noted.

How to Order and Schedule

After determining that you can utilize the trucks to haul the material, the next step is to figure the amount of concrete needed and to order it from the dealer. If at all possible, specify the load to be brought early in the morning; this will give you plenty of time to work it properly.

In almost all instances the truck will bring a bit more than is needed. Since the truck may have to be rinsed and dumped, you should have an area available in which to dump the excess. If just a little is left over, it can be put in a wheelbarrow and kept until the pour is completed—in case you need it. After the forms are filled, you may need a shovelful or two in places that looked full during the pour.

Preparing for the Delivery

Soak the form and the subgrade with water the evening before you make the pour—or moisten the subgrade just before the pour. This will prevent dryness in the soil and the forms from pulling moisture too quickly from the concrete, which makes it stiffen too quickly. In some instances, the subgrade takes up too much water from the concrete and causes a low spot in the cured slab.

The morning the mix is to arrive, make sure that you have properly prepared the site, and that you have all tools on hand. It is a good idea to have a couple of friends for a large pour, as it takes a great deal of work to spread the large amounts of concrete required for a patio or a long sidewalk.

Since concrete is such a heavy building material, it's best to break up large jobs into smaller segments. You may take longer to build the project, but the job will definitely be easier on you. For instance, divide each portion of a patio into smaller segments that are poured one at a time. Allow one to cure; then remove the form from that section before you pour the next.

Ordering Transit Mix

An alternative to the ready-mix delivery is a U-Haul delivery of concrete. This may be available on a trailer that you pick up and haul to your home. The trailer is equipped with a device to keep the concrete mixer during transit. Or the unit

Use a wheelbarrow for mixing and/or moving the concrete. The best kind has a pneumatic tire and strong wooden handles.

may be a pickup truck that has the concrete mixer mounted on the bed. The truck is easier to handle than the trailer because a trailer loaded with concrete is difficult to back into place. Also, some of today's smaller cars may have a problem hauling the heavy concrete load. The average load for each of these is one cubic yard.

BASIC CASTING TECHNIQUE
Making the Pour

Placing the concrete. Regardless of whether you hand mix, use a portable mixer, or purchase the concrete from a transit mix company, the method of casting is the same. Start as far back in the form as you can, and spread the back area first. Move the concrete with rakes or shovels. A rake is easier to use than a shovel because you can easily pull the material in place and lift the rake out. You will have to use a shovel in some instances to lift material and move it back in odd areas. When you do this, you will soon find that not only is concrete heavy, but it also has a tendency to suck the shovel down. This makes it almost impossible to lift the shovel out unless you turn it slightly sideways and allow it to "slide" out. Again, I must repeat, you will need rubber hip boots, preferably the kind without buckles. You're probably going to have to get right in there in the mix in order to move it around.

During the pour, fill all forms to their top edges. Pay special attention to corners, along the edges of forms, or at any turns or curves in the forms. Spade the concrete in these areas.

Spading concrete. To spade, insert the shovel vertically into the concrete. Then pull the shovel up and down to remove air pockets. Do not overdo this, however. Overworked concrete will separate—the water will break away from the cement paste and aggregates and float to the surface. (This problem is also called segregation.) Use the back of the shovel to press the concrete in place along the forms. Fill the forms to their top edges.

Screeding. After you fill the forms properly, the next step is screeding. Select a straight 2x4. Examine it carefully, for if it's slightly warped, the warp must bow up rather than down. A downward bow will create a surface that will hold puddles (called "birdbaths"). An upward bow will provide drainage. If the warping is too severe, however, do not use that particular board.

Starting at the back end of the pour, move the screed towards the front to strike off excess concrete as you go. Move the screed back and forth sideways as you progress to help it "slide" through the excess concrete. Merely scraping it from the back to the front won't do any good at all. The correct process not only removes excess concrete, but also pushes the larger pieces of aggregate down just below the surface of the pour.

If you find low spots behind the screed in some areas, use the shovel to move some of the excess cement to fill these areas. Then screed again.

Tamping. After screeding the material in place, it should be tamped. This is especially important around the edges of all forms and on deep forms such as

foundations. However, it should be done throughout the entire form and pour. This will remove most of the air bubbles (which are inevitable), as well as drive large aggregates down in place and get them deep enough so they won't be a problem during the finishing of the concrete. For most home jobs, use a concrete rake, jabbing it up and down. On larger jobs you may wish to rent a mason's vibrator or construct one. Spade all edges and corners carefully and rap the forms to remove air pockets. When you take off a form and find a huge vacant spot left from an air bubble, you will see that it not only weakens the pour but looks bad and must be filled in by hand.

Finishing the Concrete

The finishing of the concrete is the easiest part of a concrete project, but the one part many folks seem to dread. It seems quite complicated, when actually it is fairly simple if you have the right tools and work in the proper sequence.

Types of finishes. There are several different finishes for concrete. The first has a slick, hard surface such as for interior floors. The surface can even be troweled slick enough to dance or skate on; this is used primarily where other flooring is to be installed over it, such as inlaid flooring, tile or carpeting.

The second type of finish is somewhat rougher and is used for patios, walks, steps and other exterior surfaces. This can be accomplished by floating or by brushing with a stiff-bristle brush. In addition, there are unusual finishes such as exposed aggregate.

Tamp or spade the concrete to remove air bubbles. This is especially important next to the form boards and in the corners.

Screed the tamped concrete surface. Fill in any low areas. One or two more screedings will be necessary to level the slab.

Remove concrete that falls outside the form during screeding. If it hardens, it will make the form boards difficult to remove.

Timing. There are several different steps used in properly finishing concrete. Not only is their sequence important, but the timing of the steps is also important. For instance, if you start finishing the concrete too soon, you will bring too much of the water in the mix to the surface. Too much cement will be floated away and the result will be a weakened pour. On the other hand, if you wait too long, the concrete will set up so firmly that you cannot work or finish it at all and then you really have a mess.

Because of the variations in humidity, climate and even the concrete mix itself, there is no way to say exactly how long you should wait. For instance, a small pour such as a sidewalk made on a 110 degree, dry summer day, can bleed and stiffen and be ready to finish in about 20 minutes. On the other hand, a large pour such as a basement floor on a cool, humid day will probably take several hours to bleed and to stiffen enough for finishing. A good rule of thumb is to start the finishing process as soon as the sheen of excess water is gone and the concrete can withstand foot pressure. Another indication is the texture; the concrete surface should feel like gritty sand under trowel pressure.

Floating the surface. The first step in finishing is floating the surface of the concrete. This can be done with a bullfloat or darby, followed by a hand float if necessary. The bullfloat is used on large surfaces, such as patios or floor slabs. The float removes excess water from the surface and knocks down the small ridges left by the screeding operation. It leaves the pour smooth and level. Push and pull the large bullfloat back and forth over the concrete. At the end of each stroke, lift the float and move it over to make another parallel stroke. When pushing it forward, tilt it a little so the front edge is raised; when pulling backward, tilt the back edge up just a little to prevent the edge of the float from digging into the concrete. This is the hardest part of the job for most first timers, but one that will come with practice.

On smaller jobs (such as sidewalks) in which you can reach across or at least to the center of the job from each side, use a darby. This is a smaller, two-handed float. It is used in a circular motion. Again, make sure you do not allow the edges or corners to dig into the wet concrete.

Cutting Edges and Joints

Edges. Surfaces of driveways or walks should be edged to provide a round, smoothed edge. This keeps the slab from chipping as badly as it would if it had sharp edges. It also is safer to walk on, and it looks better. Run a hand edger back and forth along the edges of the pour, holding the tool flat on the surface and against the wood form. The biggest problem is preventing the edger from digging into the wet concrete; still, edging is a task that is easily learned.

Control joints. Cutting control joints is actually done in much the same way as edging; however, the reasons for it are different. Not only do the grooves break up the appearance of a huge slab of concrete, but they also provide a place for the concrete to crack should it settle and shift. This sounds terrible, but a crack in one of the joints will follow the groove rather than occurring randomly. The result is a good-looking, durable surface. Without the control joint, the concrete will still crack, but the crack is liable to have a jagged, uneven appearance. The spacing of control joints will differ according to the various projects, as will be discussed in detail for each type. The depth of the joint, which is dictated by the kind and size of your project, is also very important. The rule is that the groove should be one-fourth the thickness of the concrete slab.

Tools. Control joints are cut with a grooving tool. To provide a straight line, place the tool against a 2x4 guide strip tacked across the top of the forms or a plank laid on the concrete. There are two types of groovers, a hand groover and a walking groover. The former is the one most commonly used for home masonry. You push and pull the tool along, just as

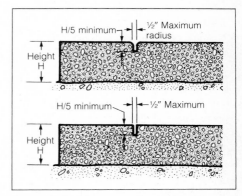

A control joint is cut to one-fourth of the depth of the slab. Cut joints in a large slab with a circular saw and masonry blade.

When the sheen of surface water is gone, float the surface to remove excess water and smooth down ridges from screeding.

An edger slices a rounded edge in the slab. As you work, do not dig into the plastic concrete. Edging prevents later chipping.

A 2x4 laid across the form guides the groover when you cut control joints. The distance between the joints varies by project.

with the edger, forcing the V-shaped bottom to cut through the wet concrete and form the joint. On large pours, the walking groover is easier to use. However, if you hand-groove, you will need to support your weight with knee pads or flat pieces of plywood on the concrete. Remove them as you progress.

An edging tool can also be used to groove, but you will have to make two passes, since it only finishes on one side at a time.

The Final Finish

After the grooving and edging operations, the surfacing usually is hand floated with a steel aluminum, magnesium or wood float. You can use a homemade wooden float for this job, but it is somewhat harder to use than a metal one. In the case of a driveway, this step may be eliminated. On pours requiring a smooth surface, float the surface by moving the tool in a circular sweep. This removes edge marks left by the sides of the edger or groover. Floating also drives the larger aggregate down below the surface. Again, on large surfaces you will have to use knee pads to prevent sinking into the concrete.

Troweling. If you want a really slick, hard finish, smooth the concrete with a steel trowel. Apply it in the same circular motion as the float, and, as with bullfloating, keep the edge lifted slightly with each pass so you do not cut into the surface of the concrete. Sprinkling the surface with a bit of water will help provide an even slicker finish, but do not overdo it. Use slight pressure on the trowel to get the best finish; trowel until the surface feels silky smooth without any gritty feel of sand.

Once the troweling has been completed, go back over the edges and grooves to lightly clean off any excess moisture and cement that might have been forced down into them. You can use a hand brush for this. Be careful to keep the edges of the tools from cutting into the freshly troweled cement.

Broomed finish. In some instances you may prefer a lightly broomed finish. The roughness resembles that of a floated finish, but a broomed finish has quite a bit more tooth. It is especially important for sloping driveways and for walkways because it provides safe walking in wet weather.

In most instances, the brooming is done after edging and floating the slab. Follow the process with a slight reworking of the edging and grooving to clean up the grooves.

Brooming may be done with almost any broom. However, a stiff bristle, push-pull, shop broom works the best. You can also purchase special concrete brooms. The hardest problem is working the broom without digging the bristles into the surface and marring it. The best method is to pull the broom across the surface. Lift it after each stroke and move to the opposite side. Pull across again. For the best results, broom the surface at right angles to the traffic pattern rather than in the same direction.

Curing Concrete

Curing of concrete involves keeping it at a favorable temperature and moisture level a certain length of time. Allow the slab to set for about 4 or 5 hours; then dampen it with a fine mist from a garden hose. If the water pressure is too high, you will wash out the finish. Cover the concrete with pieces of burlap or old newspapers or polyethylene sheets soaked with water. Keep the coverings well soaked for at least 3 days at the proper temperature. If the temperature goes below 50 degrees, continue curing for another 3 days. Most contractors like to continue the curing process for at least a week.

CREATING UNUSUAL FINISHES

There are several different, unusual finishes that can be applied to concrete to dress up its otherwise utilitarian looks. Some are more appropriate than others, depending upon the location of the slab and its ultimate purpose. Some designs are simple to make. For instance, to create the illusion of something other than a huge expanse of concrete, use the grooving tool to create small, staggered squares. (Use a 2x4 guide strip to create lines that are straight and square with each other.) A broomed surface need not only be done in straight lines. A wavy or swirled texture is a safe, attractive alternative.

Salting for a Pitted Surface

A sprinkling of rock salt over a freshly troweled concrete surface will give a pitted, weathered finish. Throw the salt out over the slab, but don't use a lot, since too much can result in a deeply pitted surface that will be weak and

A steel trowel creates a slick surface. Use curving strokes. The more you trowel, the smoother the finish will become.

A slick sidewalk is hazardous when wet. A lightly broomed surface has more tooth. Use straight or curving strokes as you work.

A variety of surfaces, such as exposed aggregate or pitted, are safer underfoot than a slick surface.

useless. The salt will immediately begin to draw moisture out of the concrete. Embed the salt, with a trowel or a float, up to the tops of the grains. Wait until the concrete has hardened; then wash the salt away and brush away any remaining residue.

One word of caution. A pitted, rock-salt surface is not recommended in any areas subject to freezing temperatures. Water settles in the holes and, when the water freezes, it can crack the level surface and ruin the entire slab.

Simulating Flagstone

You can "carve" a design into the concrete surface to make it resemble a flagstone installation. "Flagging," as the process is called, can be done in one of two ways. The first, which uses strips of wood or other material, is probably better for finishing a large slab; the second,

which uses a hand tool, is preferable for a small one. Plan your design before you begin, no matter what size slab you are finishing.

Strip method. The first method uses narrow strips of 1x2 wood or 15-pound roofing felt. First, complete the final finishing of the slab. Cut the strips to fit the lengths required by your design. (If you use wood strips, bevel the lower side to simplify removal later.) Soak the strips in water so they will not draw moisture from the concrete and will not warp. Then lay them on the surface of the slab.

Press the strips into the concrete with a trowel or a float and leave the strips in place until the concrete hardens. Once the strips are pressed in, you can color the open concrete if you desire.

Tool method. The second method involves carving the joints between the "flagstones" with a piece of ½- or

¾-inch copper tubing. Bend the tube into an S-shape. Do the first carving right after the initial bullfloating. In that way the concrete will still be plastic enough so that you can move the coarse aggregate out of the joints. When you have done the final floating, run the tool over the joints again to smooth them.

Joints. You may fill the joints with mortar or leave them open. If you use mortar, first flood the joints with water. Then wait until the water has soaked in. (It is most convenient to flood the slab the night before you plan to mortar.) Make a paste of portland cement and water; brush the paste into the joints. Have a sponge handy to wipe off any paste that mistakenly spills onto the "flagstones."

Stamped Designs

You can rent or purchase special embossing stamps from masonry supply yards. The stamps are pressed into the wet concrete surface to simulate flagstone, brick, Belgian block and a number of other patterns. If you plan to use an embossing stamper, plan to make the size of the slab a multiple of the stamper so you do not have to do a great deal of hand stamping at the edges.

Preparations. The success of the technique requires a concrete mix that contains small coarse aggregates (ask for pea gravel that is no larger than ¼ inch) and a little more sand—this assures that the stamp will go deep enough into the concrete surface to give a satisfactory design. The surface must be plastic enough to accept the stamping. Float; then, if you want, trowel the slab smooth, but don't trowel more than once. As you use the embossing tool, rinse it clean after each impression. Otherwise, the concrete will cling to the tool and mar subsequent designs.

Using the stamper. You will need at least two of the stampers. Place the first at one edge of the slab, aligning its edges with those of the form. Then stand on the tool to impress the design. You can supplement your weight with a hand tamper. The tool should sink about one inch into the concrete. Place the second stamper next to the first, step onto it, and so on. You must work quickly. At first the concrete will take the impressions easily, but as it hardens the process will become more difficult. An extra pair of hands will be helpful. To finish off the design at the

Rock salt sprinkled over plastic concrete draws water from the mix and melts. Rinse the salt away later, after the slab has set.

Create "flagstones" that are in proportion to your project. Plan large patterns for a patio, small patterns for a walk.

A mason's brush smooths joints and removes excess concrete. You may fill joints with a cement mortar paste or color the "stones."

The stamped design should be about 1 in. deep. Be careful not to stand on the wet concrete; you can stand on the pattern maker.

Press informal patterns into wet concrete to achieve subtle and unusual designs.

Spread the aggregate evenly; then tap into the slab with a hand wooden float or a straight-edge. Float again. The surface of the slab should resemble that of a normal pour.

Wait until the slab does not indent under the weight of a person on kneeboards. Then lightly brush the slab with a nylon-bristle broom to remove excess surface mortar.

Brush and fine-spray the slab simultaneously. If aggregate becomes dislodged, stop and wait a while. Continue until the water runs clear and no apparent cement film is left.

edges, use a small hand stamp that comes with the larger stampers. Also available is a hand-jointing tool to smooth the lines of the design.

Hand-pressed impressions. For a less formal stamped pattern in your concrete, use one of these: leaves, wood grain, sea shells, circles made with "cookie cutters" made of different sized cans or any other solid shape. Use a wood float or your hand to simply press the "forms" to the desired depth in the concrete. These designs can be fun, but think them through carefully—otherwise you may wonder, six months after you lay the design, what you could have been thinking about when you did it.

Exposed Aggregate

In an exposed aggregate surface, a layer of coarse aggregate covers a rough-textured concrete slab. This technique can provide a beautiful, rustic surface for walks, patios, and decorative garden walls, as well as for garden planters and many other projects. However, the beauty and color of an exposed aggregate slab will be limited by the color and attractiveness of the aggregates. The coarse aggregates should be well-rounded gravel or small stones, of a uniform size and shape, and they should display a good variation of color. Special mixes for this type of surface can usually be found at mason's supply yards or even some garden supply stores. The biggest disadvantage of an exposed aggregate surface is that it is much harder to keep clean than smooth-finished concrete, and naturally it won't

make a good run for kids with tricycles. However, its unusual and decorative appearance often is the overriding consideration.

Whole-slab method. There are two basic ways to achieve this type of finish. The first is to use decorative aggregates throughout the full thickness of the slab. Then, after the slab has been screeded and floated, carefully hose the surface layer of cement away to expose the tops of the stones. This method, however, is quite expensive because large decorative aggregate is more expensive than the common aggregate usually found in a concrete mix. (Sometimes, however, local aggregate is very colorful and is very appropriate for this installation.)

Dry-shake method. The second method is known as a dry shake. It requires a concrete mix that has quite a bit of sand in it, such as 1 part cement, 2¾ parts sand and 3 parts aggregate. The technique is as follows:

(1) make the pour as usual, but do only a small section at a time;

(2) screed off the excess concrete; complete all grooving and edging tasks;

(3) sprinkle the special aggregates across the top of the surface and use the back of a flat shovel or a 2x4 to tamp the stones down into the surface;

(4) work carefully—if the stones are too exposed they will loosen after the concrete sets;

(5) when the tops of the stones just barely show, use a 2x4 or 2x6 across the tops of the forms to level any shallow or high spots;

(6) allow the concrete to set up to the point that it can support your weight (do not wait longer than that);

(7) use a darby or float to further depress the stones and to bring the moisture and cement up around the stones;

(8) check that there are no holes or sunken areas left in the concrete surface;

(9) allow the concrete to set up almost completely before you broom off a small area with a stiff-bristle broom (you might need to experiment to get the touch);

(10) hose the surface down to expose the tops of the stones (you can rent a hose-brush combination that does both operations at the same time);

(11) stop when you achieve the surface appearance that you desire allow the concrete to cure normally;

(12) brush off a thin film of concrete and hose down the surface after it has set for 5 or 6 hours;

(13) recut grooves and smooth the edges of the slab.

If you are doing a large slab, such as a patio, you may need to add a retarder to the concrete to allow you enough time to work the stones properly. Consult with your concrete supplier about types of retarding admixtures.

COLOR IN CONCRETE

You can add color to concrete to enhance its appearance and help it blend in with your outdoor landscaping. There are four common ways to add color to concrete.

Using Coloring Agents

The first process adds a mineral pigment coloring agent to the wet concrete while mixing it. This is the easiest method, but also the most expensive because the coloring agent runs entirely through the mix. When using this system, make sure the concrete mixture contains no streaks of color.

On thicker slabs or structures such as steps, you can make a two-layer pour. Pour the first layer of regular concrete to within about ½ to ¾ inch of the form top. Tamp to level. Allow the concrete to set just until the surface water has evaporated. Then pour a second, colored layer to bond to the first. The top pour should not contain any coarse aggregate—just pigment, sand, cement and water only. Finish the pour as usual.

Adding Dry Powders

The third method lays dry powders over the concrete surface as soon as it has been floated. Spread the powder by hand or with a hand garden duster. Work carefully to get an even coating of coloring over the surface. After the dust has absorbed moisture for a few moments, use a steel float to spread the powder evenly over the surface and blend it in place. You may have to dry shake the colored powder in

place several times (float each time) to get an even color. Then allow the concrete to set sufficiently and steel trowel the surface to a slick, smooth, evenly colored surface.

Staining and Painting

The fourth and final method, applicable only to a concrete surface that is at least a year old, is to stain or paint a surface coating on the concrete. The paint or dying agents must be applied according to manufacturer's directions. In most cases, you must remove any old paint or dye before you begin. (See Chapter 7 for removal instructions.)

Curing Colored Concrete

It is more difficult to cure colored concrete than plain concrete. Curing usually requires the use of water. However, when you add water to the surface of colored concrete, the color may become splotched. You must be very careful to keep a fine and even spray. Burlap and other water-laden materials, laid over plain concrete to aid curing, also result in splotching problems with colored concrete.

COPING WITH WEATHER

Both hot and cold weather create problems for green concrete—concrete that has not had enough time to cure properly. You should try to do all concrete work during warm weather, so watch the weather reports before you initiate a project. Concrete hardens best when the temperature is between 50 and 70 degrees F. If the temperature falls below this, you can get by with heating the materials or by providing heat to the site.

Cold and Freezing Temperatures

Concrete that freezes before it reaches a strength of 500 pounds per square inch (which takes about 2 days) will be flaky, weak and, in essence, ruined.

If cold weather catches you unexpectedly, a heavy cover of straw or old blankets will hold in the heat. However, even several layers of blankets won't keep concrete's temperature high enough for it to be used a week later. The blankets must remain in place for several weeks before the slab will have hardened enough for use. After reaching 500 pounds per square inch strength, concrete can withstand temperatures as low as 14 degrees F. and continue to gain strength. The trick is to stay off curing concrete during very cold weather. You must avoid frost heave, which might crack the concrete—proper base preparation (discussed later for each project) will solve this problem.

Hot Weather

On the other hand, to alleviate most of the problems caused by very hot weather, keep the concrete wet. Spray it with a fine mist of water and keep it covered with old burlap bags, polyethylene or a spray cure compound. Otherwise, the water in the concrete will evaporate too quickly, weakening the slab.

Rain

Rain can also damage green concrete, for it will pit the surface. Try to avoid rainstorms, but if one comes along, protect the slab with tarps or old newspapers. A pitted surface resulting from a heavy rainstorm can sometimes be troweled over and smoothed—if the concrete hasn't set up too much.

Use aggregate that's close at hand. These stones are from the Great Lakes shoreline.

2 CONCRETE PROJECTS

A concrete patio may be laid in any form to complement a home and serve the needs of the homeowner. This patio adjoins the dining/family room and extends summer entertaining area.

A combination of trowel-finished concrete and exposed aggregate in these intersecting walks provides a visual break and emphasizes the different directions of the paths.

OVERVIEW OF PROJECTS

Before starting any concrete or masonry job, check your local building code regulations so you can build the project to their specifications. Building codes are designed to ensure the longevity of your project. This is especially true in areas subject to ground heave caused by freezing temperatures. An improperly prepared site will result in a cracked concrete surface. Building codes respond to these conditions, so do not ignore them.

Locating Utilities

Prior to building any outdoor project, determine the location of all underground utilities. The major concern is that deep footings will conflict with the utility service. Most often these are located from 2½ to 8 feet below grade. Water, gas, sewage and telephone lines may force you to incorporate special construction or to relocate the project. If your house is fairly new, your local building inspector probably has a copy of your utility, gas, water and sewage hookup locations. If he doesn't, check with the customer-service representatives of your local utility companies. (Once you have the information, keep it on file for future reference.) If there is a conflict, discuss your options with the service in question or your local building inspector.

Excavating the Site

Lay out the dimensions of the pour and excavate as needed. The depth and width of an excavation depends upon the project you've planned and the specifications in

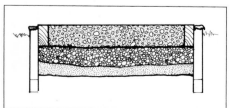

A typical sidewalk is built with a base of gravel overlaid with a bed of sand. Concrete is held by wood forms until set.

local codes. You then must prepare the subgrade on which the concrete will rest—and this is one step that is often overlooked by the first timer. Unless ,the ground is properly prepared, the concrete will settle, shift and crack.

A correctly prepared excavation has several characteristics. A uniform subgrade ensures a consistent response to temperature and moisture changes. Level the earth surface, so there are no deep holes or protruding objects. Remove all large rocks, roots and other debris from the area. Tamp the subgrade, either with a hand tamper or a mechanical one. The subgrade should follow the angle or slope of the ground.

Establishing a pitch. A concrete slab must be pitched, or set at a slight angle, to ensure necessary drainage. Pitch must angle away from a house or other structures, such as a garage. This is especially important in a patio or driveway project. A sidewalk can be pitched either along the length or across the width—again as long as the pitch is away from the house.

Determining pitch. A proper pitch is usually ¼ inch per foot, depending upon the amount of precipitation in an area. (See local codes for your particular locale.) In other words, a patio that extends out 15 feet from a house requires a pitch

of 15 feet x ¼ inch (3¾ inches). Therefore, the edge of the slab farthest from the house rests 3¾ inches below the edge nearest the house.

Creating the pitch. Once the excavation is complete determine the pitch for your particular project and regrade to the necessary slope. To establish the pitch, pound in Stake A at a corner nearest the house. On the stake, mark the proposed height of the slab. For instance, most on-grade slabs are about 2 inches above the ground. Straight out from the house, pound in Stake B at the point corresponding to the end of the slab farthest from the house. Tie a string at the mark on Stake A, and run a level string line to Stake B. Check the string with a line level. Measure down from the string to a distance equal to the required pitch. Retie the string at this point.

Pitch affects the angle of the slab, but not the thickness. A 4-inch thick slab remains 4 inches thick throughout. However, unless the slope of the ground matches the pitch of a slab, pitch will affect the amount of gap between the bottom of the form boards and top of the base materials. Ideally, the ground will slope at the same ¼ inch per foot as the slab. The form boards will sit directly on the base materials and achieve the proper pitch.

Back filling. In some cases the pitch will lower the height of the top of the slab enough so that you must dig a trench to accommodate the width of the form boards. In other situations the slope of the ground is greater than the necessary pitch of the slab. Then you must lift the boards to the correct level. To keep the concrete from filling in the space between the bottom of the form boards and the base, you must backfill, or pack in extra dirt behind and under the form boards.

Building the Base
Base materials. Base materials of sand, gravel and rock are placed at the

bottom of the excavation to prevent settling and heaving and to aid drainage. They also provide a level surface on which to pour the concrete. The depth of the base is often regulated by codes. Find how much base you need as you did for concrete, but order twice as much as your figures indicate. This is because the base materials will compress to half their original size when they are tamped.

Order of placement. First, place the gravel in at least two layers. Tamp each layer firmly so that the top of the final layer is two inches below the bottom edge of the concrete pour. Then add sand. Keep adding and tamping until you have a level layer that reaches to the top of the concrete pour. Follow this order no matter whether your installation requires a footing or not. The depth of any given layer may vary according to code. The level is checked with a special strikeboard called a dragboard. See the discussion of dragboards in the sidewalk project.

Building Forms
Concrete takes the shape of the mold in which it is placed. In most cases, the mold is made of 2x4, 2x6 or 2x8 lumber supported by 1x2, 1x4, or 2x4 stakes. The forms must be substantial or they can't support the weight of the concrete without bulging. Always set form boards

After sidewalk area is excavated a gravel base is laid and leveled.

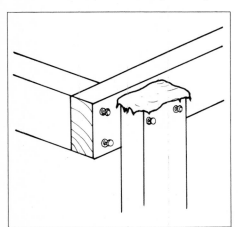

Forms are often built with 2x4 stock. They are firmly constructed with heavy, double-headed nails that allow easy removal.

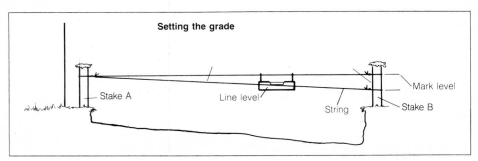

Setting the grade

Stake A   Line level   String   Mark level   Stake B

After the gravel base is leveled, it is tamped to create a firm, permanent bed.

on a true perpendicular to the subgrade. Set all stakes straight up and down so that the edges of the cured slab are plumb. If they aren't, the slab will be subtantially weakened. Forms for curved forms are discussed in detail in the patio project.

Adding Footings

In areas subject to frost heave, local codes will require a footing, which is an enlargement at the base of a foundation, wall, pier or column. The footing helps distribute the weight of the structure. Carefully follow all directions set out in local codes concerning the depth, width and position of all footings. Ideally, a footing should extend six inches below the frost line. In fact, some local codes

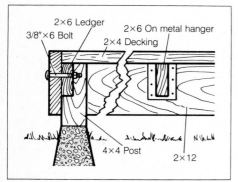

To give security to a deck, posts must be set into concrete footings. Brace posts level and plumb until concrete sets.

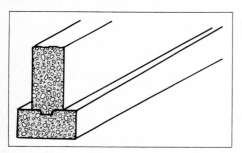

A concrete footing should contain a key into which the foundation concrete flows. This joins the two sections for security.

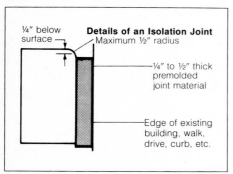

Wherever a section of concrete butts against another section or solid object, install an isolation joint to absorb pressure created when the areas expand in warm weather.

specify that the top of the footing should be below the frost line. However, in other areas this ideal would result in footings several feet below ground level, which is hardly practical. Check the requirements for your area.

Post hole footings. An economical measure that will act as footings and prevent steps from sinking is to install post hole footings. Beneath the location for the bottom tread, to the depth of a regular footing, dig two or more post holes with a diameter of from 6 to 8 inches. Do not build a form or add base materials. Simply fill the holes with concrete. In most cases, these will do the job.

Slab footing. A slab footing is usually used for the support underneath a house foundation. The foundation itself may be concrete or concrete block, but the footing is always concrete. The footing must rest below the frost line. The depth of the footing usually equals the width of the walls it will support, and the width is usually twice that of the wall.

Trench footings. In areas that have clay soils or others that stick together quite well, the footing can often merely be poured in the bottom of the excavation trench. This installation is called a trench footing. Do not pour a trench footing or a foundation directly over sandy or loose soil without compacting the subsurface first.

Pier footings. A pier footing is similar to a posthole footing except that it requires a form and base materials. If the soil is composed mainly of sand and gravel or equally dense material you can use a forming material called a Sona Tube. It is a cylindrical wax paper form that can be purchased in lengths up to 24

feet and is available in a range of diameters. The tube is cut off a little above the desired elevation and placed into the hole. The soil is then compacted around the tube to make sure that it is stable and will not shift. Then the base materials and the concrete are added to complete the pier.

Final Preparations

Isolation joints. Isolation joints are used to separate a new concrete pour from other already existing materials, such as wood, brick or old concrete. The joint is a preformed material that is about ½ inch wide. It allows for differing rates of expansion and contraction.

Construction joints. In some installations, you don't pour the entire slab at once. The forms are erected; then a section is closed off with a temporary form board called a stopboard. The section is filled with concrete, screeded and finished. Once the concrete has set, but not before it has cured, the stopboard is removed and the joint edge is oiled. Then either the rest of the form—or another portion of it—is filled.

The joint between the initial and the later sections is called a construction joint. This joint also can function as a control joint, so plan the position of all construction joints to correspond to control joint dimensions dictated by your particular project.

Adding butted construction joints. If the thickness of a slab is to be 4 inches or less, you only need a butted construction joint.

The stopboard is made in the same way as any other interior form board. Some projects, such as driveways, require tie rods that bind one part of the slab to another.

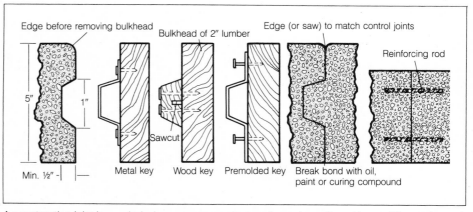

A construction joint is needed when you are pouring sections of a walk or drive at different times. A key must be created in one section or reinforcing rods installed so the later pouring of concrete will join the first sections and shift at the same rate.

Adding keyed construction joints. If the thickness of a slab is 5 inches or more, you must create a keyed construction joint. The stopboard is cut to length. Then a shaping device called a construction key is attached vertically all the way across the center of the board. The edge of the pour will take on the shape of the key, creating a groove across the edge of the slab. When the second section is poured, the pour fills the shape of the key. The resulting joint prevents the two slabs from shifting separately and maintains a level surface.

BUILDING A WALK
Probably the best project to start with is a concrete walk. It is quite simple, and you can construct it in sections to cut down on the work—as well as on any mistakes involved in your first masonry job.

Designing the Walk
The first step is to design the walk to suit your situation. You can make it as wide or narrow as you need; however, in most cases it should not be narrower than 2 feet. On the other hand, a walk does not need to be more than 5 feet wide, unless you have a wheelchair user in the family. Most municipal sidewalks that front your property are 5 feet wide, while the sidewalk to your front door is 3 to 4 feet wide.

A sidewalk is practically always 3½ inches thick, although it is called a 4-inch-thick slab. This is because the finished width of the standard 2x4 normally used for forming the sidewalk is 3½ inches. (See Chapter 1 for a discussion of nominal and actual lumber sizes.)

Excavating the Walk
The depth can vary a great deal, depending on your climate, the desired height of the walk above ground level, and the type of soil. If the soil is extremely hard and dry packed and you live in a temperate climate free of ground heave and erosion, you may wish not to excavate at all. In this case, scrape back the grass or roots and debris and then level out the area for the walk. However, contractors usually excavate to a depth of at least 2 inches, skimming off the sod and some top soil. Then, when the 2x4s are set on edge, the top edge of the form (and therefore the sidewalk) will be about 2 inches above the ground.

If, on the other hand, the soil is wet or poorly drained, it is best to excavate at least 6 to 8 inches and lay down a base of gravel or crushed stone that comes to within 2 inches of ground level. The form board will again extend 2 inches above ground. For instance, if you dug down 6 inches into the ground, you would then need 4 inches of tamped base to bring the form board up to the correct height.

To mark the walk's location, use stakes and two parallel strings. Measure the width carefully. Excavate an area that extends 6 to 9 inches farther (or more) on each side of the location of the sidewalk so you have room for the form boards. You can later fill in against the sidewalk.

Building the Base and Form
Staking the form. To build the form, position two parallel boards in the excavation so that their inside edges form the sidewalk sides. Drive stakes in place next to the ends of the form boards. Starting at the ground level's highest point, raise the ends of the boards up with their top edges approximately 2 inches above ground level. Check for level with a carpenter's level across the tops of the two form boards. Fasten the boards to the stakes with duplex head (or scaffolding) nails. (If the tops of the stakes are not flush with or slightly below the tops of the form, saw them off once the form is completed.) Raise the opposite ends of the boards up to suit, either following the contour of the ground, or raising them to match the desired pitch. Then drive stakes, spaced every 3 feet, along the form boards and

nail the stakes to the form boards. Use duplex-headed nails throughout, nailing from the outside.

Install a stake at any location where two form boards join together. Nail the stake to both form boards. Butt the two boards tightly. If the ends of the boards are angled or uneven, square them off with a saw before nailing them in place.

Stakes cut from 2x4s to brace 2x4 form boards. Stakes are driven with a sledge and then nailed to the form boards for strength.

Check forms for level or your poured concrete sidewalk may be uneven. Water may run off opposite the direction you want.

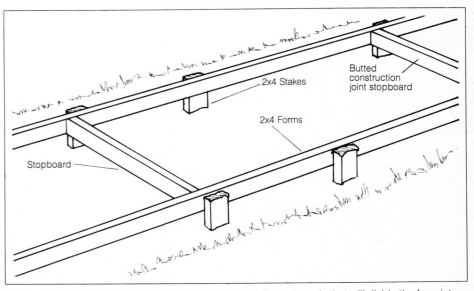

2x4 Stakes

Butted construction joint stopboard

2x4 Forms

Stopboard

If you are pouring your walk in sections, you must install stop boards that will divide the form into a smaller working space. Stop boards also brace forms for stability.

Oiling the form. Oil the form boards by painting on crankcase oil with an old paint brush. In that way the boards will not stick to the concrete or absorb water from the pour and weaken the concrete. Nail the end form boards to the side forms and drive stakes against the ends to hold them securely in place.

Tamping the ground. To check the level and depth of your excavation, cut a board equal to the thickness of the base and the slab. Center this on a 2x4 that is at least 12 inches longer than the form and nail the two boards together. This combination is called a dragboard or a strikeboard. Slide the dragboard along the forms. Fill in all low spots; excavate all

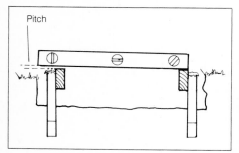

The gravel base for a concrete walk should have the same grade as the walk. To level fill, cut a drag board to fit into forms.

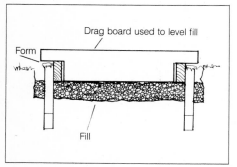

Check form boards regularly with a spirit level. If walk slopes, keep bubble indicator at the same position at each check.

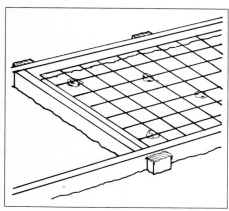

Position reinforcing mesh so that it is in the concrete rather than under it. Support the mesh with rocks during the pour.

high spots. Tamp to insure a solid subgrade.

Adding the subbase. Then install the base of crushed stone and gravel and tamp them in place. To be sure the gravel is level, create another dragboard, this one equal in height to the thickness of a 2-inch layer of sand plus the thickness of the slab.

Then add sand. At first it will sift down to fill the openings between the gravel. Keep adding and tamping until there is a two-inch layer of sand. Finally, check the sand layer with a dragboard equal to the thickness of the slab.

Adding reinforcing mesh. When set on soil that may heave or shift, the walk will require reinforcing mesh. This is also the case with a subgrade of very wet or sandy soil. The mesh won't stop the cracking, but it will hold the cracks tightly closed. The mesh is called size 6/6 and 10/10, which means it is made of welded 10-gauge wire having 6-inch square openings. The mesh comes in rolls and can be cut with large fencing pliers or electrical side cutters. Take pains to flatten the mesh thoroughly so it won't be near the top or bottom surface on the pour. Before placing the mesh, set small stones on the base to raise the mesh up about 2 inches below the top of the form—or the approximate center of the

To remove air pockets, tamp concrete firmly and evenly but not too hard or aggregate will be forced to the bottom.

concrete pour. Position the mesh on top of the rocks. Do not allow the mesh to come into contact with the form, or you will have a piece of metal sticking out the side of the concrete. This will later rust and discolor.

Placing the Concrete
Before you begin the pour, insert isolation joint material in all locations where the slab meets an existing structure. The top of the joint material should be flush with the top of the slab, or, even better, $\frac{1}{4}$ inch lower. Never have it above the slab. In some circumstances, that arrangement could be a hazard to foot traffic.

Cutting control joints. If you don't have permanent interior forms to serve as control joints, cut control joints once the concrete has been floated. The joints should fall every 5 feet in a walk that is over 3 feet wide. In a walk from 2 to 3 feet wide, set control joints every 3 feet.

BUILDING CONCRETE STEPS
Garden or porch stoop steps are constructed differently than a walk. Almost all steps must be placed on footings. The steps should be at least as wide as the sidewalk, and in some instances they can even be a little wider. Flights of more than five steps require a centered landing.

When the concrete has been tamped, screed the concrete level with the form boards. A 2x4 will work for this process.

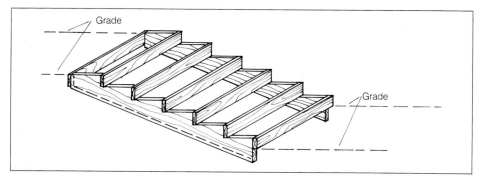

Forms for concrete steps must be built to the proper grade, tread and riser proportions. They must be securely built to withstand the pressure of the poured concrete with braces.

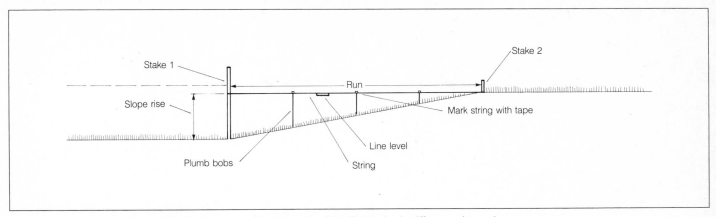

Use stakes to determine the run/rise for the steps. Run is length of the flight; rise is difference in grade.

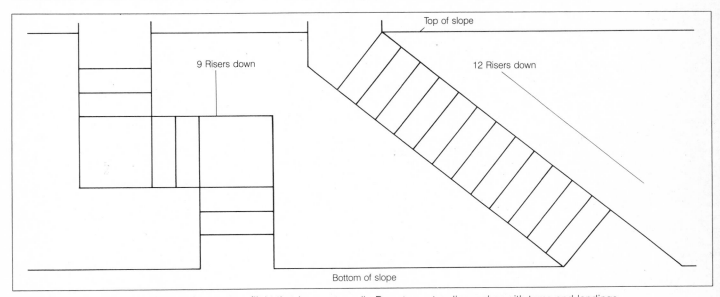

If you must run steps up a steep grade, create a flight that is easy to walk. Run steps at a diagonal or with turns and landings.

The top of a porch or stoop must be a flat landing area that is large enough to allow you to open a door outward without stepping down to a lower step. Steps that go into a sliding patio door can be made without this particular feature, although it is a good idea to make a small landing to provide ample room for turning and closing the door.

Finding the "run" and the "rise." Insert a tall stake (Stake 1) into the ground at the point where the bottom riser will meet the ground. Pound in a second stake (Stake 2) at the highest point of the top riser. If the steps adjoin a house, this second stake also will be a tall one. Leave adequate space between the house and the stake for an appropriately sized landing. If the steps are to connect different ground levels, the second stake will be much shorter than the first. The tops of both should be about level.

Tie a string at ground level (or the landing level) onto Stake 2. Run the string over to Stake 1—check with a level

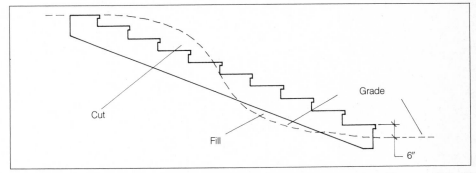

An uneven slope may require cutting and filling before steps may be added. The ground base must be adjusted to relate to the grade of the steps.

to be sure the string is level. Measure the length of the string. This is the total length of the steps' treads, or the run. On the bottom stake, measure the distance between the ground and the string. This distance equals the total height of the risers of the steps, or the rise.

Figuring the slope. To find the slope, divide the rise by the run. The slope is the angle of the steps, and it will affect your plan. In a "normal" situation, such as steps connecting a house and a walk, the

angle is about 45 degrees. If the angle is greater than 45 degrees, you may have to incorporate landings, create a series of diagonal paths for the steps, or cut away part of the slope to ease the angle.

In the last case, you will need retaining walls or other arrangements, such as ground cover or rock gardens, to prevent soil erosion. If there is a portion of the site that is quite steep, while the majority of it is flat or gently sloping, you may again need a retaining wall. If the retaining wall is to hold a steep (three feet or higher) vertical embankment, creating the structure is beyond the abilities of the do-it-yourselfer. Such a wall must be designed by an engineer and built by a contractor, in order to have the necessary horizontal and vertical strength. Shorter or stepped-back walls of boulders or railroad ties are sufficient for slope control at heights of three feet or less.

If the slope is slight, you can incorporate landings or ramps between flights, and the flight need be only one or two steps high. (See below, "Stepped Walks and Ramps.")

Tread and riser sizes. Treads and risers should relate to the average length of a person's stride. As a rule of thumb for exterior steps, the width of a tread and two risers together should equal 26 inches. The recommended height of the risers is 6 inches, and they should never be less than 3 inches or more than 7 inches. The best width for the treads is 12 to 14 inches—never less than 12 inches. Try to

stay close to the ideal, for these ratios are what most people expect, and they will be thrown off balance by odd sizes. However, do not stick to the dimensions so strictly that you wind up with one tiny step at the top or bottom—this can cause accidents.

Following these proportions, if the height of the steps is to equal 30 inches, you will need 5 risers of 6 inches each. A distance of 65 inches means that the tread will be 13 inches wide ($65 \div 5 = 13$).

Footing Excavation

Because of their weight, steps require footings. First excavate to the depth required by code. This excavation should extend at least $1\frac{1}{2}$ feet beyond all sides of the outline of the steps to provide room for the forms and bracing.

You can install a footing form, pour the footing and allow it to set before you erect the forms for the steps, but more commonly the footings and steps are poured all at once. As stated before, post hole

footings are a good choice for steps. You will need two or more post holes with a diameter of from 6 to 8 inches beneath the location of the bottom tread.

Steps without footings. If the steps run between the ground and a patio or deck that has been constructed level with interior floors, you will follow the same forming instructions given below. However, these particular steps require no footings.

Creating Forms for Steps

Purchasing lumber. Draw your plan to scale before you begin. Take the drawing along when you purchase form boards, so that you buy the correct size. To get boards for the risers that are 6 to 7 inches wide, a standard 2x8 will have to be "ripped," which is the term for making lengthwise cuts in stock lumber. A standard 2x6 will not be high enough since its actual dimension is $5\frac{1}{2}$ inches. Unless you are very experienced, do not attempt to rip lumber yourself; ask the supplier to do it for you.

Constructing the forms. Construct the forms with braces as shown. Move the tops of the riser boards outward so that they are angled by about 1 inch. The top edge of the riser supporting the front of a given tread should be about $\frac{1}{8}$ to $\frac{1}{4}$ inch higher than the bottom edge of the next riser behind the same tread. These dimensions provide a pitch for water drainage. Bevel the lower edges of each riser form board, with the high side of bevel away from the pour. This permits enough room to float the steps.

Because the weight of the concrete increases with its height, provide extra strong forming and braces for this project. Support the braces, as shown.

Making the Pour

Preparation. When you order the coarse aggregate for a step pour, use gravel that is no more than 1 inch in diameter. This will give you the best appearance.

Before you begin, insert two metal anchor bolts into the foundation wall of the house, below the location of either the top step or the landing. These will help tie the steps to the house and prevent shifting due to heaving and settling.

Fill stones. In the case of large-size steps, you can fill in some of the area with fairly large stones, but don't allow them

A flight of concrete steps must have good footings at the top and bottom of the run as well as steel reinforcing rods for added strength along the run and through each step.

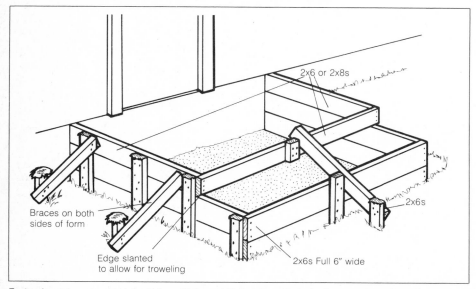

Forms for steps should be built from 2x6s and 2x4 stakes. Both the front and the sides of the forms must be braced to hold the forms secure against the pressure of the wet concrete.

to get near the sides of the forms or they will protrude out through the finished sides. Tamp the stones securely in place.

Level form boards so that your completed steps have a lean you want. Maximum pitch should be ⅛ inch per foot from back of front of tread and ¼ inch per foot to the side.

Release the concrete from the form with an edger as soon as possible after smoothing. This process simplifies the removal of the form for final finishing of the riser face.

As soon as riser forms are removed, finish the riser face and edge where tread and riser meet. Timing is critical; removing form too soon will allow concrete to slump.

Placing the concrete. Add an isolation joint between the house and the landing. Start with the bottom step. Pour, screed off the excess, and then pour the next step and screed it off level. Continue up to the landing. Tamp the concrete securely down into all corners and around all edges to prevent the concrete from honeycombing with air pockets. When you have finished the pour, again screed off the surface. This time, start with the top step or landing and work down, removing excess concrete as you go. Finish as described earlier. The best surface for steps is one that is floated or broomed.

ADDING STEPPED WALKS AND RAMPS

Ramps are indispensible for the handicapped and the elderly, and they are convenient for any wheeled equipment that must be moved from level to level. However, ramps rarely replace steps unless absolutely necessary, since people often find them hard to use.

Design and Preparation

To deal with a gentle slope, install a ramp or walk that is interspersed with steps.

The steps may have single risers, pairs, or even longer flights, depending upon the angle of the slope.

Determining the number of steps. To determine whether you need a walk with a single or a double riser—or more—stake out a level line from the top to the bottom of the slope, just as for conventional steps. Once you know the rise and run of the slope, plan your stepped walk with this rule in mind: the tread sections should equal 1 to 3 paces of an average adult (1 pace equals 26 inches). Walking an odd number of paces between steps forces people to climb first with one leg and then the other. As a result, they do not tire quickly.

No sidewalk or ramp should have a slope that is greater than 1 inch per foot. Steps compensate for the increase in slope. As the angle of a slope increases, you need an increasing number of steps. Remember that the ideal riser height is 6 inches. Therefore, if the grade changes by a height of 6 inches in the space of 78 inches, you need one step. If the change in height is 12 inches, you need two steps; for 18 inches, you need three steps, and so on.

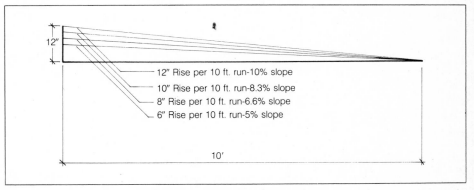

12"

12" Rise per 10 ft. run–10% slope
10" Rise per 10 ft. run–8.3% slope
8" Rise per 10 ft. run–6.6% slope
6" Rise per 10 ft. run–5% slope

10'

When a rise is not great, a ramp will be sufficient to provide access. A slope of 8.3% or more requires installation of steps to maintain a comfortable walking surface.

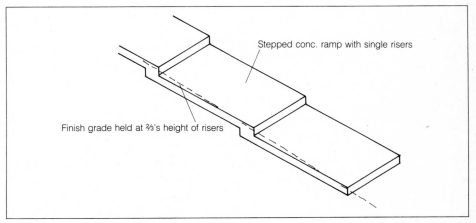

Stepped conc. ramp with single risers

Finish grade held at ⅔'s height of risers

Construct stepped ramps so that the landings allow one, three or five paces. Height of risers must be less than for a full flight of steps but high enough to be recognized as a step.

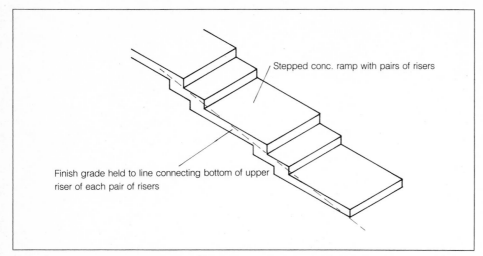

Steeper grades may require pairs of risers to allow comfortable climbing. The larger treads should allow three paces, smaller treads one. Position steps consistently for safety.

Maximums and minimums. There are several helpful guidelines:

(1) Ramps and stepped ramps should be the same width as the walks they meet when they reach ground level.

(2) The bottom and top approach to a ramp should be clear and level for a distance of at least 5 feet to allow for turning maneuvers by strollers, dollies, or wheelchairs.

(3) The minimum clear width (discounting curbs) for any ramp is 3 feet. If ramps are heavily used by pedestrians and service deliveries, provide sufficient width to accommodate both, or make provisions for alternate routes.

(4) Along the sides of ramps and landings, provide low curbs (2 inches) against which wheeled vehicles can turn their wheels in order to stop.

(5) Handrails (if included) should extend at least 18 inches beyond the top and the bottom of the ramp.

Building Stepped Ramps

Forms and footings. Build the forms for the steps and the ramp just as for other projects. The steps require footings to prevent them from sliding and to anchor the walk.

Shaping the curbs. Before you pour the concrete, make a special notched screed that will automatically form the ramp's low curbs along the sides.

On one of the 4-inch faces of a 2x4, 2 inches above one of the long edges of the face, draw a straight line the length of the

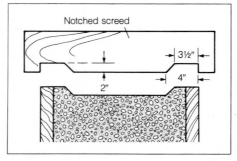

To use a notched screed after first leveling, create ramp curb and repeat after the concrete sets slightly to prevent slump.

board. Center the screed on the form. The face with the line should be toward you. At both sides of the screed, on the lower edge, place marks at the outside edges of the form boards. Then, measuring 2½ inches in from the inside edge of the form—toward the center—place two more marks. The first and second sets of marks will each be 4 inches apart. On the line you drew on the face of the stock, make an additional set of marks—two aligned with the outside edges of the form boards, and two that are 2 inches in from the inside edges of the form boards. Remove the screed and connect the 4 marks on each side to create 2 small quadrangles that are 4x2x3½ inches (see illustration). With a sabre saw, cut along the lines forming the quadrangles to create notches in the screed.

Set the screed back on the form. The form boards should fit up inside the notches, and the screed should move freely along the form. If it doesn't, remove and adjust the outer edges of the notches slightly with a chisel or a rasp.

Pouring and shaping concrete. Pour the concrete and screed with a regular

flat-edged 2x4. Then use the special screed to shape the curbs. As you pull this along the form, use a trowel to remove the concrete that builds up along the front of the screed. Repeat the operation with the special screed several times to create the shape of the ramp and the curb.

Finishing the ramp. Run the edging tool between the form and the pour. Then smooth the curb joint with your hands (be sure to wear gloves) or with a piece of ½- or ¾-inch copper tubing bent into an S-shape.

Landscaping requirements. Plantings should be located along the ramp so that shadows do not prevent the sun from melting any snow and ice on the ramp's surface. Illuminate ramps to an average maintained light level that will ensure their safe use in darkness. This is especially important at the heel and toe of a ramp.

BUILDING A PATIO

A concrete patio is an excellent project for a homeowner-mason for several reasons: it provides one of the best surfaces for family recreation; the smooth surface offers a central location for entertaining; and the kids have a smooth tricycle run. It is easy to clean—hose off dirt and debris as needed.

Design Considerations

Access to the kitchen. A patio is most often located near a kitchen area, family room or dining room. The patio should be near the largest traffic flow in the house, and the outside area affected should be one that can be easily modified without drastically changing the everyday operations of the household. Proximity to a kitchen often assures an easy flow of food and beverages.

Bathroom offshoot. Although the design is seen far less often, a small, fenced-in patio can be used as a relaxation area off of a bathroom or bedroom area. Most often, sliding doors connect the patio and the house. A gate leading to the rest of the yard can be included, if desired.

A bathroom that opens directly onto a patio is especially convenient. An end-wall of insulated glass increases the indoor-outdoor atmosphere and keeps the room filled with natural light. An eight-foot fence around the patio perimeter ensures privacy.

Control joints are necessary to prevent natural cracking of the concrete from creating an unsightly pattern. It is possible to create an attractive design with the control joints.

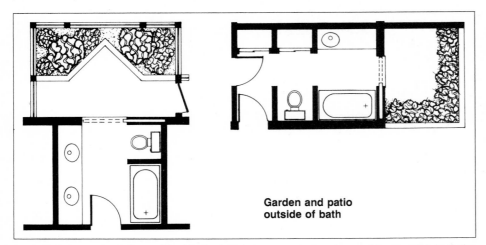

Garden and patio outside of bath

A small patio can be built outside a bath. A high fence protects privacy of those using both the patio and the bath. A small patio can be an attractive and relaxing retreat.

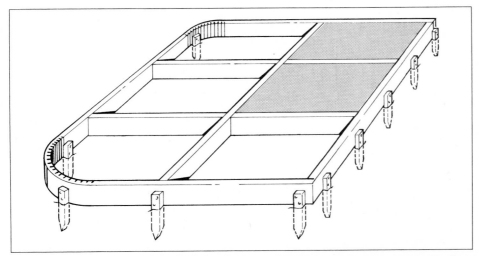

A curved patio edge is not much harder to set than a straight edge. Saw kerfs are cut into form board every ¼ inch to a depth of half the board thickness to make the form flexible.

Size. Blanket patio dimensions do not take individual needs into account. Recommended dimensions provide for 20 square feet per person—a space that is comfortable without being excessive. This converts to an area of 4 feet by 5 feet, and includes a chair and area in which to circulate. If you contemplate entertaining a group of 15 to 25 people, the corresponding size in area would be 500 square feet or an area of 20 feet by 25 feet. Keep in mind that there are limits to what a reasonably sized patio can hold. If both the patio and the immediate area surrounding it can also be used by a large group, you might find that a smaller patio will fill your needs.

Patio Shapes

Once you have decided upon the location and size of the patio, draw out your plan to scale on a piece of paper. Take the physical characteristics of your yard and your home into consideration as you plan. Then stake out the patio shape.

A square patio. To lay out a square patio, measure the width of the patio and stake out two corners along the house wall. Then measure the desired length from those marks out in the yard. Drive stakes where the two outer corners will fall. Working on the diagonal, measure between opposite corners. The two diagonal distances must be the same. If they are not, shift the outer stakes until the measurements are equal. This assures a square layout. Then run strings between the stakes, around the perimeter of the patio.

A free-form patio. A patio does not have to be square; it can be designed free form. There are several technical ways to

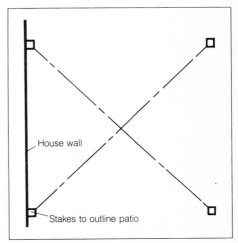

House wall

Stakes to outline patio

To lay out a square patio, drive stakes at house wall, then at outer corners. Measured diagonals should be equal.

lay out circular and curved edges, but the easiest is to "draw" the outline, right on the lawn, with a regular garden hose. Since a patio usually is quite large, irregularities in curved areas won't be noticeable. Once you like the shape of the area, set other items inside the boundaries. Walk around the area and adjust the perimeter as you please. Once you are satisfied, run a stake-and-string outline that follows the line of the hose.

Patios on Uneven Ground

A patio on a rise. A 5 to 6 percent slope is quite acceptable for a patio. If the slope is more than that you have several options, which depend in part upon the degree of slope. One possibility is to excavate into the higher portions of the lot, so that the patio nestles into the rise. In this case, the sides will require retaining walls, rock gardens, or ground cover (or a combination of these) to deal with erosion. (See the discussion of retaining walls.) If you plan to use ground cover plantings once the form has been removed, place all the topsoil you removed from the patio area along banks of the excavation. Only the most hardy plants can grow in subsoil.

A patio on a downward slope. You can extend a thickened section of the patio so that its lower edge follows the slope. The upper edge remains level all the way around the perimeter, as shown. This option is feasible only if the slope is a slight one, or if the area in which it falls away is near the edge of the slab.

Another method divides the patio into high and low areas connected by ramps, steps or both. The steps can be concrete or some other material such as brick, wood or even old railroad ties. This design will require some excavation in order to create a level slab, and cut-away areas may require retaining walls.

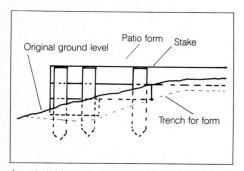

A patio laid on sloping ground requires deeper footings and forms at the lower edge in order to maintain basic level of the slab.

Elevated patios. To reach interior floor level, you may have to pour a thicker slab, or consider a raised patio. The thicker slab is expensive due to increased costs of wood and concrete. A raised patio, which requires a wooden support system for the finished patio (such as stilts), should not be attempted by the homeowner. A concrete slab is very heavy and requires a carefully constructed support system. Only a professional contractor should attempt a raised patio.

Excavation and Preparation

Once you have the outline of the patio "drawn" on the ground, move all the stakes outward at least 12 inches to allow room in which to build the forms. Excavate the patio area. If the patio surface is more than 8 inches lower than any door connecting the patio and the house, you will need a step (or steps) there. The step will require a footing. Pour steps and let them cure before you work on the patio itself, so that you have space to install the

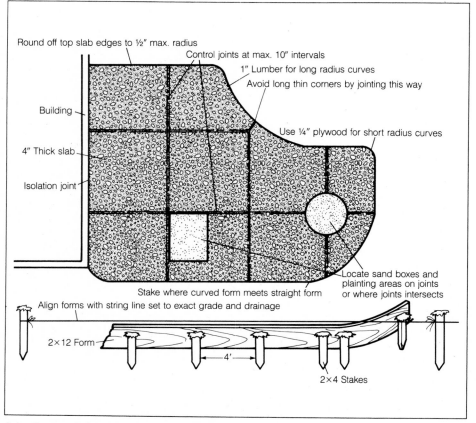

A freeform patio may be laid with properly kerfed and braced form boards. Location of control joints is determined by a combination of known stress factors and aesthetic effect.

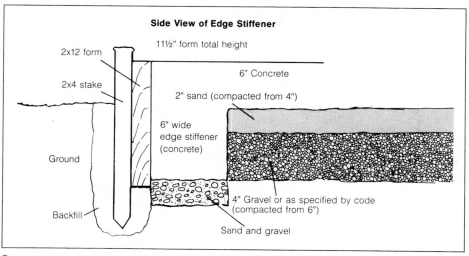

Because the edge of a slab is subject to both ground pressures and wear from use, add an edge stiffener—a thicker layer of concrete with a separate and deeper subbase.

side braces and to finish the concrete. Then install and pitch the forms. Add the base materials to the patio area and tamp.

Adding an Edge Stiffener or Beam

In areas of the country subject to severe temperatures and consequent frost heave, large slabs such as a patio need an edge stiffener or edge beam—an extra support structure along the sides of the slab. The stiffener also helps prevent chipping and breaking. It keeps the slab from sliding or shifting because of soil expansion during freezing temperatures.

Adding the concrete edge stiffener. An edge stiffener, if part of the slab itself, is easy to create. You just need an extra-thick concrete ridge, rimming and extending downward from the edge of the slab.

Install the forms and lay the base as usual. Then, right next to the inside edge of the form board, dig a 6-inch-wide trench all the way around the perimeter of the slab. Make the trench at least 8 inches deep, to allow for 2 inches of base materials and 6 inches of concrete. (The depth will vary according to code.) Check the forms to be certain that the corners are still square.

Add enough gravel to the trench to equal 1 inch when tamped. Then add a layer of sand that is also 1 inch thick when tamped. The remaining space in the trench will fill with concrete to form the edge stiffener.

Adding a wood edge stiffener. An alternative method of adding an edge stiffener is to build permanent forms rather than temporary ones. For this installation, you must use redwood or other pressure-treated wood, so the forms can hold up to the weight of the plastic concrete and to the stresses of later ground heave. Old railroad ties are especially appropriate here because of their size and their conditioning. A wooden edge stiffener can be part of a complex grid that serves as a permanent form.

Creating Permanent Forms

Materials. In a permanent form, wood strips (or other materials, such as brick or even concrete block) are installed along and across the slab. The strips in the body of the slab act as control joints and add texture and patterns. As with the edge stiffener, build the forms of redwood, cypress or cedar primed with clear wood

sealer. If you choose some other type of wood, be sure that it is preservative-treated.

Building the forms. Assemble permanent forms with care. Mitre corner joints, and neatly butt intersecting strips. Do not drive nails through the tops of permanent forms. To anchor the outside forms to the concrete, drive 16d galvanized nails in a horizontal row, from the outside, midway up the form boards. Space the nails 16 inches apart. Interior divider strips require similarly spaced nail anchors, but drive them in from alternate sides of the board. All nail heads should be flush with the forms. Stake the forms as needed to hold their shape and position; then drive the stakes at least 2 inches below the tops of the forms (or cut them off) so they

If permanent forms are used to create a pattern within the slab, cover the tops of the forms to protect them from concrete stains.

won't show once the slab is complete. Mask the tops of the boards with tape to protect them from stains and abrasions from the concrete.

Placing and Finishing the Slab

Remember to place isolation joint material where the slab meets the house or other existing structure. Place the concrete as usual. If a patio measures more than 10 feet in length or width, you will need to cut equally spaced control joints. These should never be more than 10 feet apart, but they can be closer. A permanent form does not require grooved control joints as long as the boards are spaced to these specifications, because the interior wood strips serve as control joints. Finish and cure the patio as you would a sidewalk.

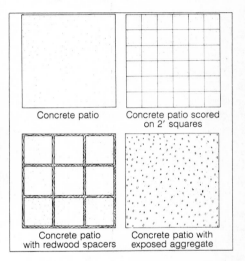

Concrete patio | Concrete patio scored on 2' squares

Concrete patio with redwood spacers | Concrete patio with exposed aggregate

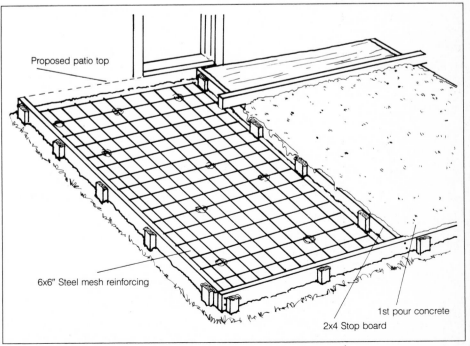

Proposed patio top

6x6" Steel mesh reinforcing

1st pour concrete

2x4 Stop board

When pouring a large patio, break the job into sections with temporary form stops. Add construction keys to form stop so two sections will unite when the second section is poured.

BUILDING A DRIVEWAY

Pouring a concrete driveway involves basically the same procedures as pouring a patio. However, because of the extra weight requirements, driveway construction is often well-regulated by local building codes. Make sure you understand all code restrictions before you begin construction. You also must have proper permits. For instance, most municipalities have strict rules governing the steepness, thickness and width of the driveway, as well as the means by which it joins the curbing.

Design Considerations

Most single driveways today are made of a single slab instead of the double-slab ramp drive that has paving only in the

areas of the wheels and grass in between. A single slab provides a wider usable surface to serve the wheel base dimensions of more car models. The trend of the times has reinforced the single slab, perhaps partly because a single slab requires less edge forming. Then, too, you do not have to mow the grass between the strips. However, the double slab (also called "double strip") is a functional, economical driveway well suited to the do-it-yourselfer. In fact, many people prefer the grassy strip as a landscape feature. Two-car driveways, on the other hand, must be of full-slab design.

Design Specifications

To unite the garage and the street. The edge of the driveway should fall

about 1 inch below the garage floor, to prevent water from running into the garage. The drive should slope downward from the garage to the street. If your garage sits downhill from the street, install a drain where the driveway meets the garage. Where the driveway meets the street, raise the edge of the drive just a little above the road to prevent water and debris from flowing from the street into the drive.

Size of the drive. In most instances, the driveway is cast so it is 2 inches above ground level. Slabs for passenger cars are 4 or 5 inches thick; however, a slab that will have truck traffic should be 5 or 6 inches thick. Some contractors make the area near the street 8 inches thick to accommodate the extra weight of trucks that might pull partly up onto the driveway for delivery or collection.

A slab for a single-car garage should be between 8 and 10 feet wide, and one for a double-car garage should be between 15 and 20 feet wide—widths up to 22 feet are common.

Pitching the driveway. The driveway should also provide a pitch of from $\frac{1}{4}$ to $\frac{1}{2}$ inch to the foot; this is considered a minimum in most areas. You can give a sideways pitch to the entire drive, but the best plan is to crown the driveway, providing pitch from the center to both sides.

To create the proper pitch from the center to the edges, the slab is poured in two stages. First, the form for the entire drive is built. Then a centered stopboard is inserted lengthwise in the form. It runs from the garage to the street, and must be high enough to create the correct pitch. If your driveway is to be 20 feet wide, the center of the pour must be 5 inches ($10 \times \frac{1}{2}$ inch) higher than the outside edges of the slab. The form boards at the garage and street must correspond to this pitch, and the top edge of the centered stopboard must be 5 inches higher than the side form boards. The center joint between the two sections of the slab will be held together with a butted construction joint.

Building Driveway Forms

Entryways. For better appearance and easier access, use curved forms to provide curved entryways on both sides where the driveway meets the street. This design is sometimes utilized at the garage

A long driveway is made attractive by use of permanent forms separating sections of exposed aggregate. The combination of curved drive, square forms and aggregate are complementary.

entryway as well. (See the section on patio construction for instructions on building curved forms.)

Joining the sections. The two sides of the slab will be held together with No. 4 reinforcing bars that are 36 inches long and are spaced about 40 inches apart. These will be held in place by the stopboard during the first pour. Bore holes in the stopboard. Oil the holes thoroughly, but do not oil the bars themselves. Pass the bars about halfway through the holes.

Base Preparation

Once the area is well excavated and smoothed, tamp it solidly. Unless the soil is extremely hard packed and well drained, lay the base as discussed earlier. Most codes will require 4 inches of gravel or crushed stone plus 2 inches of sand. Tamp the base materials.

Lay reinforcing mesh on rocks, placing it so that it doesn't touch any of the forms. Install isolation joints between the garage and the driveway and between the drive and any existing sidewalks. Asphalt impregnated cane fiber is the most commonly used material.

Making the Pour

The initial pour. When pouring a slab as big as a driveway, start at the garage and work out to the street. If you lay the length of the driveway in sections, install a stopboard at about 10 feet; it will then correspond to the placement of control joints. Place the concrete in this first section only. Tamp and spade as needed, giving special care to edges and tie bars. Screed the concrete off and place it into the .adjacent, unpoured section. If you don't screed off, some places will have a lot of extra concrete, which must be moved; other spots won't have enough. You would have to solve these problems by moving the concrete, causing possible separation and weakening of the pour.

Let the slab set up. Cut any control joints as needed, and give the driveway a lightly broomed finish.

The final pour. Once the first half of the slab is finished, remove the stopboard. This will not be easy; it is hard to slip the tie bars back through the holes in the stopboard. Repeat the entire process for the remainder of the driveway, in 10-foot sections as needed to complete the driveway.

Short curved sections of concrete forms may be made with ¼ inch plywood strips braced every 6 to 8 inches. Light forms will work when you are pouring small sections.

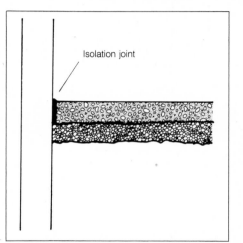

Whenever a new concrete pour abuts a solid object, you must install an isolation (expansion) joint of compressible material.

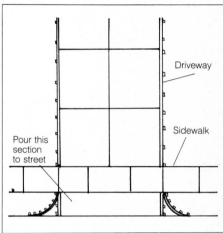

Pour new driveway and apron in sections. The apron is poured in a main section and then the two side, curved sections are added.

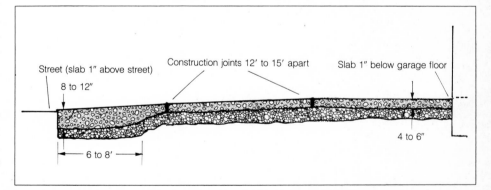

Construction joints occur because a long drive must be laid in sections. The sections should be keyed if the slab is more than four inches thick or butted if four inches or less.

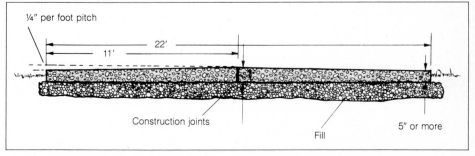

A construction strip is used at the center of a driveway pitched from the center to each side for drainage.

CONCRETE RETAINING WALLS

Concrete is quite often used for retaining walls. Because of its strength, it is naturally a very good material for this type of project. But unless some special considerations are taken, the solid mass of material can also create some problems—most noticeably, a buildup of water behind the wall, which can be dangerous. Almost all localities have strict rules governing retaining walls. Before you attempt any type of retaining (or other) wall, you must check with local code rules as to what the requirements and needs are for your particular area. In most areas, the retaining walls will also need to be inspected after the grading and forming has been done and before the concrete has been poured.

Building Terrace Walls

If the retaining wall is to be less than three feet high it is often called a terrace wall, and walls of this height or less are fairly easy to construct. Terrace walls can be used in areas where the wall height won't be over three feet and the wall won't have to support more than 50 lbs. per square foot. These walls are constructed exactly like a combination footing and foundation, although much more reinforcing is needed.

Step one: grading. The first step is to grade the slope and make the cut for the wall. Make sure you leave enough room on the earth side to build the form.

Step two: building forms. Build the form of 2x6, 2x8 (or larger) lumber. Pour the footing. Be sure it is keyed. Then build the wall form of well-braced 4x8 plywood sheet cut to size.

Step three: weep holes. To prevent water from collecting behind the walls you must provide weep holes near the bottom of the wall. To create these in the form, insert pieces of 2-inch steel pipe between the form sides. Hold them in position with heavy nails driven through the forms and the pipe ends.

Step four: the concrete pour. Make the pour, spacing No. 4 reinforcing bars 18 inches on center each way and for each face. These bars must be bent so they can fit down into the footing. Keep the bars away from the face of the wall as they will give an unsightly rusted appearance if they happen to touch the form and protrude through the finished concrete surface.

Step five: surface finish. Finish the top of the wall by first troweling it level with the tops of the form boards. Then edge the sides using an edger to give an even, smooth, rounded top.

Higher Retaining Walls

Retaining walls higher than three feet, however, are more difficult to design and to build. In most instances you will be better off having them built by a contractor.

Whether you build it, or a contractor does, make sure that the wall will have a

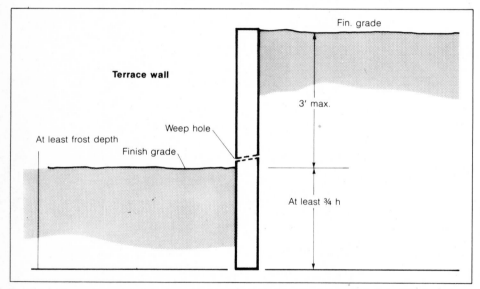

Terrace walls can be used where the difference in grade is no more than three feet and where there is no probability of the wall having to support more than 50 lb. per sq. ft. The wall should completely fill the trench, using concrete backfill if required. Earth below lower grade should be firm and dry.

REINFORCING FOR CANTILEVER RETAINING WALLS

Dimensions				Bar size & spacing	
H	W	T	A	Vertical wall rods	Horizontal footing rods
8″ Walls					
3′4″	2′4″	9″	8″	#3 @ 32″	#3 @ 27″
4′0″	2′9″	9″	10″	#4 @ 32″	#3 @ 27″
4′8″	3′3″	10″	12″	#5 @ 32″	#3 @ 27″
5′4″	3′8″	10″	14″	#4 @ 16″	#4 @ 30″
5′0″	4′2″	12″	15″	#6 @ 24″	#4 @ 25″
12″ Walls					
6′8″	4′6″	12″	16″	#6 @ 24″	#4 @ 22″
7′4″	4′10″	12″	18″	#7 @ 32″	#5 @ 26″
8′0″	5′4″	12″	20″	#7 @ 24″	#5 @ 21″
8′8″	5′10″	14″	22″	#7 @ 16″	#5 @ 26″
9′4″	6′4″	14″	24″	#8 @ 8″	#6 @ 21″

H = Height of wall; W = Width of footing;
T = Thickness of footing; A = Distance to face of wall

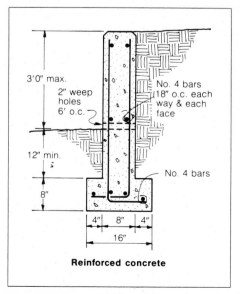

Reinforced concrete

Even a terrace wall that is less than three feet high needs reinforcement. Bend the bars so they strengthen both wall and footing.

Retaining wall illustrations, Pgs. 36–37, reproduced with permission from, MWPS, Home and Yard Improvements Handbook, 1978; Midwest Plan Service; Ames, IA 50011.

firm, solid base to rest on, below the frost line. The footing and lower part of the wall must also be low enough in the ground so there will be some soil on the front side. Because the strength of the wall is so very important, use a good quality and correctly mixed concrete, and cure it properly, as discussed earlier. The wall must be fitted with control joints every 25 feet to allow for expansion and contraction.

Types of retaining walls. There are three basic types of concrete retaining walls. The first, a gravity retaining wall, depends entirely on its weight for stability. As shown in the chart, these walls usually are constructed with a base that is three-fourths of their height. Because of the volume of material needed to construct a wall of this type, a very high wall can become quite expensive.

The second type of retaining wall is the cantilevered wall. This wall utilizes a wide, flat base and is shaped like an inverted T. One of the keys to a well-constructed cantilevered wall is the proper amount and spacing of reinforcing material (see chart).

The third type of concrete wall is the buttressed wall. This is created in much the same manner as the cantilevered wall, except the back doesn't have the wide shelf, and angled buttresses are poured in the front side of the wall to provide additional support.

Weep holes. Regardless of what type of wall is utilized, one of the most important rules is to offer an escape route for water that collects behind the wall. This can be done by adding weep holes, as mentioned for the smaller walls. For these larger walls, however, use 4-inch tile as the weep holes and place several shovels of gravel behind the weep holes during the backfilling operation. An alternative is to place a 4-inch drain tile behind the wall. However, this must lead to a surface outlet, which may not be possible in some areas.

Backfilling. During the backfilling operation, go slowly and make sure the soil is applied in a gradual manner, compacting well. Keep heavy machinery away from and off the wall.

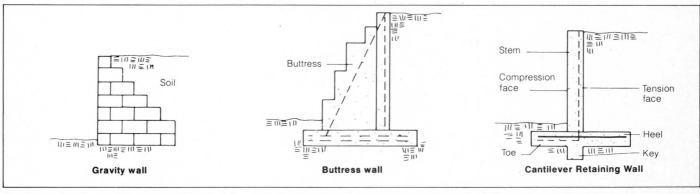

Cantilevered walls require more careful calculation and planning than do buttress or gravity walls. Soil pressure of 45 psf/ft (moderate drainage) requires 3,000 psi concrete, and 40,000 psi steel. For horizontal reinforcement, use two No. 4 bars in bond beams at 16 in. o.c. or equivalent joint reinforcement at 8 in. o.c.

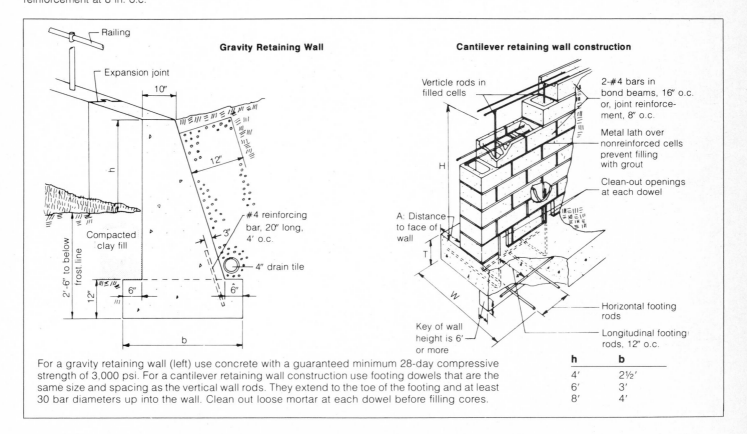

For a gravity retaining wall (left) use concrete with a guaranteed minimum 28-day compressive strength of 3,000 psi. For a cantilever retaining wall construction use footing dowels that are the same size and spacing as the vertical wall rods. They extend to the toe of the footing and at least 30 bar diameters up into the wall. Clean out loose mortar at each dowel before filling cores.

h	b
4'	2½'
6'	3'
8'	4'

3 WORKING WITH BRICK MASONRY

Brick may be used in many ways. In this installation, the house, courtyard wall and entrance walk are all brick. The house and wall have been painted; the walk is natural brick.

Brick is often used to create an attractive patio or small outdoor seating area in gardens. This brick patio is laid on a sand base, but you may lay brick on concrete or mortar.

Bricks can be used for almost any type of construction. At one time they were even used to construct high-rise buildings such as the 16-story Manadnock Building in Chicago which was built in 1889. Constructed entirely of brick, the walls were 6 feet thick at their bases and tapered to 12 inches thick at the top floor. However, the use of structural steel eliminated the use of bricks in this type of construction. Today brick is more commonly used in smaller buildings, such as wood frame homes and offices.

Brick is a very popular and important material for the do-it-yourselfer. It is still laid in place one unit at a time by hand, and it doesn't require as much physical effort as concrete block or stone. Because of this, bricklaying can be an enjoyable job. It is quite easily learned, and even the first-timer can produce a pleasing finished project. Since you do the work a little at a time, even a big job such as facing the front of a house doesn't seem so awesome a task.

Brick can be used for any number of interesting remodeling and home improvement jobs, including a new facelift for your home or the creation of an elegant and useful brick patio for your backyard. Brick can also be used for building small projects such as flower planters, low retaining walls, barbecues, and any number of other projects.

CHARACTERISTICS OF BRICK
A brick is a small individual building unit made of clay. Those made today have changed little in design and manufacture from those that were produced thousands of years ago. The main difference is that the old bricks were sun baked or dried in the sun, but today's bricks are heated in a kiln to harden them and to make them more resistant to moisture and weathering. The standard size of 2¼x3¾x8 has not changed significantly from the days when brick makers figured out that the unit was just about the right size to handle

SETTING UP BATTER BOARDS

After you have located the exact outline of the project, but before you can begin excavating, you must set up batter boards. Excavating will remove the stakes and destroy your outline. You would have to repeat the staking process several times during the construction of the footings if you did not use batter boards. These are nothing more than two long cross-pieces nailed to stakes driven parallel to each wall side. There must be a batter board on each side of each corner of the work. If the project (such as a building) outline includes an L-shape, these must also be located with placement of batter boards on the opposite sides of the building.

Normally, the batter boards are placed about 6 feet back from the preliminary outline stakes to insure that they won't get knocked down during excavation. String lines from the outline stakes are extended out to the batter boards. Nails are driven into the top of the boards and the string lines attach to these nails. A plumb bob dropped from the intersection of the crossing batter-board string lines should fall on top of the center nails of the outline stakes for the building or wall.

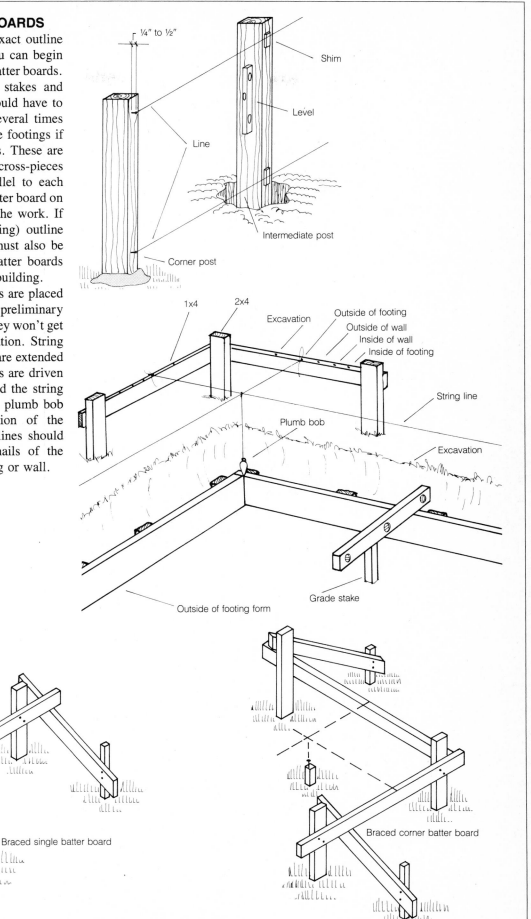

easily with one hand. Today's bricks are made of a much wider variety of clay types than the older bricks, so there are more variations in the bricks produced.

Some bricks are the natural color of the different clays after firing. They can range from gray, light tan, light or dark red, or even purple. In other cases, ceramic glazes are applied to bricks. The popularity of used brick, taken from demolished old buildings, has resulted in the manufacture of new "used" bricks that are made by adding a bit of lime and sand or cement to clay, then tumbling the finished bricks in a giant tumbler to crumble and break away their sharp edges and to give them an aged appearance.

The finish of bricks can vary from rough sand to ultra-smooth. In addition, stamping machines and embossed rollers will apply designs to the facing sides of the bricks as the bricks are cut to shape. These designs can give the effect of logs, stones, or even sculpture.

Types of Bricks

Although there are a great number of different kinds of bricks, there are four basic types used in most modern construction. Check local building codes to find what type of bricks may be used in your part of the country for particular projects.

Building or common brick. This is the most economical and popular brick. It can be used for almost any type of construction. Because the color and dimensional size of common brick varies, this would not be the choice for projects such as a fireplace front, requiring a very uniform brick. There are also more imperfections in this type of brick and some of them may be chipped, broken or warped. Still, they serve well for patios, garden walls, barbecues, or projects needing a "used" brick finish. Building or common bricks are available in three different grades.

SW. This brick will withstand severe weathering such as freezing, thawing, or rain-and-freeze conditions. These are the most expensive grade of common brick.

MW. This grade withstands modest weathering, including some rain and freezing, but cannot be used in areas of severe weathering.

NW. NW bricks can be used in mild climates where there is no danger from freezing or frost. They also are suitable for frost areas, but only if the bricks are protected from rain or moisture. The least expensive kind of common brick, they are quite commonly used for interior jobs.

Choose the most economical brick for your particular area and job. For instance there is no need to use SW bricks to face a fireplace.

Face brick. Face brick is the best quality brick; it is manufactured so that all bricks are quite uniform in color, size, texture, and face surface. The faces themselves range in style from a glazed china-like surface in a number of color choices to an imprinted pattern resembling stone or other types of materials. There are few defects in this type of brick. It is usually not any stronger than common brick, but because of the extra amount of manufacturing care, the units will usually better withstand the effects of weather than will common brick.

Paving brick. Paving brick is extremely strong and sturdy. It is made to be used without mortar for such things as courtyards or driveways. The paving brick is composed of special types of clays that are baked at higher temperatures and for a longer time than other brick types. The result is a very durable and strong brick.

Firebrick. Firebrick is made of a special clay and is heated to an extremely high temperature to make the units resistant to high heat. Firebrick is used primarily to line fireplaces, ovens and furnaces. It is a pale yellow and is installed with special fireclay mortars.

Size Variations

Nominal vs. actual size. One confusing aspect of ordering bricks is the nomenclature concerning their size. They may be referred to in nominal size or by their actual size. The nominal size, however, also includes figures for an average mortar joint. Since mortar joints can vary a great deal, the nominal figure can be misleading. I suggest that you ask for the bricks by their actual size. Then include measurements for the mortar joint in your particular project to help you figure the needs of your project quite closely.

In an ordinary run of bricks, there may be as much as ½ inch difference between brick sizes; therefore, merely measuring a brick off a pile in the brickyard won't enable you to figure the job properly. Ask your dealer for the actual sizes of the specific brick you plan to use.

Tools

The tools needed for bricklaying are fairly simple ones. Many, such as hoes and shovels, are the same used to work with concrete. First, you need a means to mix the mortar. Because of the small amounts needed at a time, the mixing can easily be done in a mortar pan or wheelbarrow. For larger jobs you may prefer to use a power mixer.

Tongs. Brick-carrying tongs can also speed the job if you have to transport units some distance to the job.

Brick masonry work often requires these tools: brick-carrying tongs, trowels, jointing tools, floats and grooves.

Mason's brush. A mason's brush is used to finish off rough spots in the joints after they have been struck.

Trowels. Brick-laying requires two trowels. The mortar is applied with a medium-sized metal trowel. You use the wooden handle of the trowel to tap the blocks in place. The other trowel is called a pointing trowel.

Story pole. Although a story pole is not considered necessary by some professionals, it makes the first job or two much easier. The pole is nothing more than a length of 1x2 on which are marked the dimensions of the blocks and mortar joints. The pole is stood up against a corner of the construction and used to gauge the brick and mortar bed thicknesses.

Mason's string. A mason's string is a device that aligns the front edges of a course and keeps the course level. At each end of a long string is an L-shaped wood block that hooks around the outside corner of the bricks. Position the blocks so that the string is barely touching the upper edges of the corner bricks.

Jointing tool. This is a tool used to clean and smooth up the mortar joints. Purchase a formed tool or shape one from a piece of $\frac{3}{8}$-inch copper tubing, as shown.

Mason's level. You will need a spirit level at least 3 feet long to level and plumb the project. Select a level that is made of metal or has metal edges to protect it from the rough surfaces of the mortar and bricks.

Brick hammer and chisel. In most instances you will need to cut some bricks, and this is done most easily using these tools. The mason's chisel has a broad cutting edge that crosses the face of the brick. The large-bodied hammer delivers the weight of the blow required to break the brick.

BRICKLAYING BASICS

Bricklaying is a simple, yet exacting craft. The job is physically easy (in most instances) and it goes fast, enabling you to realize substantial achievement by the end of a day. On the other hand, laying brick does require attention to details, especially for the first timer. Care must be exercised so that all the bricks are laid as precisely as possible. This does not mean you should fuss with each and every brick. Because the project will be seen as

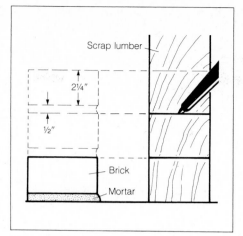

A story pole is a board marked with the desired thickness of mortar joints and the actual thickness of bricks to check courses.

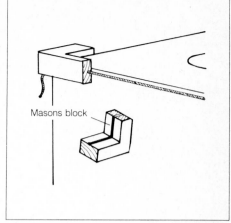

A mason's line is held in place by tension and serves as a level guide during brick masonry construction.

This attractive garden patio is laid in a running bond pattern. The closed joints have no mortar and require regular work to keep the small spaces free of weeds and grass.

This brick walk is set in a basketweave pattern with sand joints. Time, wear, and a shifting of the ground has caused a waver in joints. Use a mortar bed for permanent positioning.

Brick has an aesthetic capacity to blend with other materials. This low wall serves as a base for a wrought iron fence that divides this yard from the concrete walk.

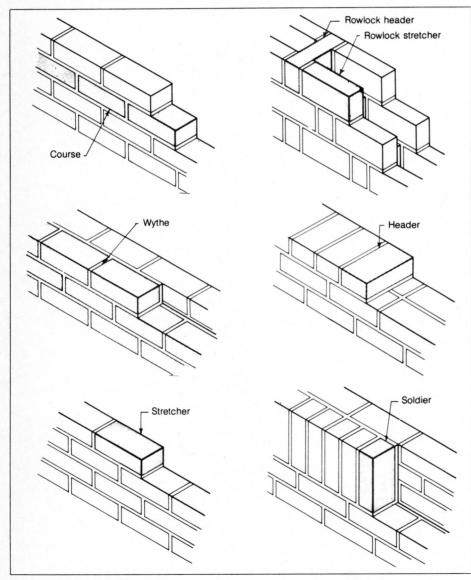

Basic terms in bricklaying indicate how a brick is laid in relation to the wall. A two-wythe wall is laid in pairs of courses and the wythes are tied together with headers. The outside faces of a two-wythe wall are even with the ends of a brick laid lengthwise.

a whole, it will permit a few poorly laid bricks. On the other hand, a sloppy job not only looks bad, it often is structurally unsound. This should not deter you from attempting brickwork, however, because about the only difference between the work of a professional and that of a beginner is the speed with which the professional works. The first-timer can often do just as good a job as the professional if he takes plenty of time and carefully watches the brick placement. Because the work is fairly repetitious, speed and skill are learned right on the job.

Terminology

Every craft has its special terminology. Bricklaying is no exception. Many patterns discussed later will be easier to follow if you learn these terms.

Stretcher. When a brick is laid so that a long, narrow side is the one that is exposed, that brick is said to be a stretcher. The long edge is horizontal.

Header. A header is a brick laid so that a small end is exposed and the wide edge is horizontal.

Rowlock stretcher. A stretcher laid so that the long, wide face is exposed.

Rowlock header. A header laid so the narrow edge of the face is horizontal.

Soldier. A brick is called a soldier when it stands vertically with the narrow, long face exposed.

Sailor. A sailor also stands on end; however, the long, broad face is exposed.

Wythe. A wythe is the term for all the vertical courses together; a brick wall may be one, two, or three wythes thick for most purposes.

Closure brick. In any course, bricks are laid from the outer edges in toward the center. The final brick, the one that fills the opening to complete the course, is called a closure brick. Often this brick must be cut to fit.

Preparation: Footings

Brick structures must be supported by concrete footings. Otherwise, the heaving of the ground due to moisture and frost heave will crack the structure and break it apart. The footing should extend to below the frost line (see local codes). In most instances, load-bearing walls must have a footing that is as deep as the wall is wide. The width of the footing should be twice the width of the wall. This means that a brick wall that is 12 inches thick requires a footing that is 12 inches deep and 24 inches wide. Walls that are not load-bearing, naturally, do not have to be as thick or as wide. A two-wythe-thick brick wall would be 8 inches thick and would require a footing 12 to 16 inches wide and 18 inches deep.

Regardless of the project, the first step is to make sure you have all the needed materials and tools on hand. Pour the concrete footing and allow it to cure for several days. Have the mortar materials on hand, and place the bricks close to the work area so you won't have to move them during the actual construction of the project.

The Mortar

Except for walks or patios made of bricks set in sand, bricks are held in place with mortar. A good, properly mixed mortar is extremely important to the quality of a finished brick project. Mortar that is too dry or too wet will not only make the job of laying the bricks harder, it also will create a finished job that is unattractive and is structurally weak.

Proportions. The mortar mix used in most instances consists of 1 part cement, ¼ part hydrated lime and 3 parts sand by volume. However, some local codes may specify a different proportion, especially in cold weather climates, so check your local code for the mortar mix required in your particular area. You can also purchase ready-mixed mason's mortar cement, which includes the lime. You merely add the sand and water. The mortar can be mixed with a powered mixer or by hand, but you should not mix more material than you can use in around half an hour. It will take a bit of practice to determine how much mortar you can mix up at a time for your particular working speed and project.

Mixing the mortar. First, mix the dry materials thoroughly. Then add a little water at a time until you get the mortar to the proper consistency. Mortar mix should be somewhat drier than a concrete mix, so here again it will take a bit of practice to determine the proper amount of material and water to achieve the right consistency. One test is to pull the mortar up in a series of ridges with the end of a hoe or shovel. If the mortar stays in sharp distinct ridges and does not slump, it has the right amount of water. If the ridges

are crumbly, you have too little water; if they slump down, you have too much water. As with concrete, it is very easy to get too much water, so add it sparingly.

It is very difficult to add dry materials in amounts that can bring the mix back up to both the proper consistency and proportion. It is always much easier to add a little more water to a dry mix than it is to add dry materials to a soupy mix.

Allow the mortar to set for a few minutes before using it. If, as you work, the mortar begins to dry out, add a very small amount of water and thoroughly remix the mortar to bring it back. However, once it starts to set up, it must be discarded. Again, this is an area which you will learn only with practice.

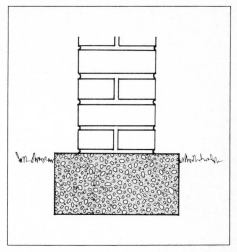

Except in the most temperate climates, masonry walls should be laid on a concrete footing or foundation wider than the wall.

Even though brick is a rectangular form, it is possible to lay it in curves or circular patterns by adjusting the joints. The pattern that is immediately visible here is circular.

This closeup shows how the circular pattern was achieved by adjusting the mortar joints and installing a few cut sections.

A good test of the consistency of a small batch of mortar is the ridge test shown. If the ridges hold, the consistency is good.

Position the mortar near at hand so you don't have to reach very far for it. If you can't get the wheelbarrow close enough to the job, use a mortar hawk and holder to hold a smaller amount close at hand.

Throwing the Mortar

Proper handling of the mortar trowel is important for brickwork because this is the most repetitious and tiring aspect of the job. Grip the trowel firmly, but do not squeeze it. Then practice "throwing" the mortar by picking up some mortar from the wheelbarrow and throwing it back in, as follows:

(1) pick up the mortar, using a slicing motion with one side of the trowel;
(2) position the trowel where you wish to place the mortar;

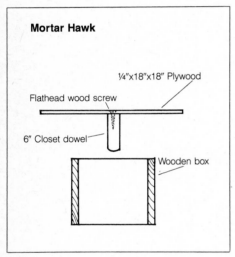

Mortar Hawk

¼"x18"x18" Plywood

Flathead wood screw

6" Closet dowel

Wooden box

Build mortarboard and hollow stand from plywood. Attach a piece of closet dowel as a handle. Box must be taller than the handle.

(3) turn the trowel sideways 90° so the blade is straight up and down;
(4) at the same time, give a slightly downward flip of the trowel.

When the mortar is thrown or flung in this manner, the mortar adheres well to the surface and settles down in any depressions. The flipping motion pulls the trowel towards you so the mortar is flung down in a line rather than in a single lump. The correct motion will cover the tops of one or two bricks.

The Dry Run

The first step is to lay out the project without mortar so you can determine the best arrangement. First, use a nail to cut scratches into the concrete footing to indicate the ends of the wall or the corners of a project. Again, you will probably have to locate these with batter boards. Use a heavy carpenter's pencil or a crayon to mark exact locations for the dry-laid bricks on the footing.

Between the corner marks, lay as many full bricks as possible, end-to-end or in the pattern chosen. Use thin wooden strips as spacers to allow for the size of the mortar joints. Note the size of the closure brick. If possible, move the wall ends or corners out so that the closure brick will be a full unit and there won't be any cutting necessary. This is especially important if you need to cut only a thin slice off the closure brick. It is much harder to cut small amounts away from a brick than it is to break away a larger piece.

After dry-laying the bricks to deter-

mine their exact positioning, snap a chalkline between the two starting points. You may prefer to place a straightedge along this line and to score the footing slightly with a nail or the edge of your trowel.

Preparing the Bricks

Brick absorbs moisture quite readily, and unless it is wetted down before it is laid, it will virtually suck the moisture out of the mortar joint. If a joint dries too rapidly, the mortar is weakened and does not properly adhere the bricks in place. You do not need to soak the brick, however. If they are dripping wet when they are laid, this also can cause problems, making the bricks hard to position and causing the mortar mix to be too wet.

Moisture check. There is a simple test you can use to determine whether the bricks are wet enough. Select the brick face that will be mortared. In a 1-inch diameter circle on the face, place several drops of water. If the moisture disappears in less than one minute, hose down all the bricks before you mix the mortar. Use a spray head on a garden hose. Continue until water runs out from the pile. By the time you get the mortar mixed and the tools in place, the surface moisture should have evaporated from the bricks and they should be ready to use.

TYPES OF BRICK WALLS

There are several different types of brick walls depending on the number of bricks used to build the wall thickness as well as the pattern or bond used in laying up the wall. The pattern in which the bricks are laid is called the bond pattern, which may be one of several types including: Flemish, English, American, Dutch, running and stack bond. Bond patterns have varying degrees of structural soundness. It's a good idea to check with local building inspectors as to what type should be chosen for your particular project, type of soil and location.

Patterns

Running bond. Running bond is most commonly used in low, single-brick garden walls or brick veneer. This type of bond pattern consists of all the bricks laid as stretchers. The bricks in one course are offset by one half brick from the bricks in courses above or below. The ends of alternate courses are completed by using

This wall built in running bond and capped by rowlock headers serves as an attractive background for base plantings. A brick wall like this is attractive in nearly any setting.

half bricks or stretchers. Most do-it-your-selfers use running bond.

Common bond. The common bond is quite similar to the running bond except it has courses of headers spaced at regular intervals—usually every 5th, 6th or 7th course. In two-wythe walls, the headers tie one wythe to another, thus strengthening the structure.

Stack bond. In stack bond all bricks are laid either as in stretchers or headers. More importantly, all joints align vertically. Stack bond is a very hard pattern for almost anyone to lay correctly because it takes extreme precision. It is also not permitted for load or structural walls, only as a veneer surface.

Flemish bond. In every course, headers alternate with stretchers. The pattern is offset by courses, so that headers center over stretchers, and vice versa. This type of bond pattern is quite often seen on Early American homes. It is also common in two-wythe walls.

English bond. English bond consists of alternate courses of stretchers and of headers. The headers are centered over the stretchers. The vertical joints of all the stretchers align.

Common bond is a simple pattern to lay. Headers tie the face and back wythes together.

A course of headers interspersed regularly among courses of stretchers forms the common bond wall.

The pattern of this Flemish bond is easy to see because the joints and brick contrast and the brick is one tone.

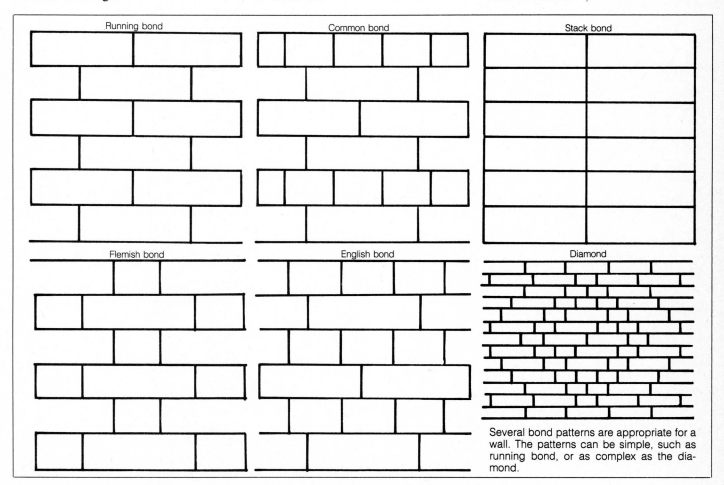

Several bond patterns are appropriate for a wall. The patterns can be simple, such as running bond, or as complex as the diamond.

BUILDING A ONE-WYTHE WALL
Building the Leads

For accurate placement and alignment, bricks are laid in a stepped-back arrangement, first building up the ends and then working toward the middle. Mortar joints usually are offset from one course to the next. If you are building a free-standing garden wall, a fireplace facing or other project that has no corners, the end bricks of the first course are laid differently than for a project such as a barbecue or a wall, which does have corners.

Free-standing Leads

Laying the first course. Starting at one end of the course, and using the trowel motion described above, throw about a 1-inch-thick bed of mortar that is long enough to seat two or three bricks and is the width of one brick. Use the tip of the trowel to furrow the mortar out, spreading it evenly along the footing. The thickness at the thickest parts should be from about ¾ to 1 inch. Lay a level on top of the brick and tap the brick down until it is level in all directions. The final mortar joint between the brick and the footing should be about ½ inch thick.

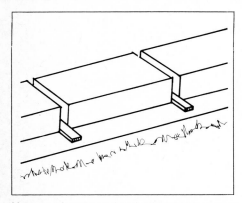

You can plan out and maintain the spacing of the bricks in a course by using spacers to indicate the joint size desired.

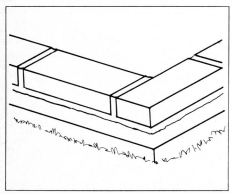

The first course of bricks is laid out with a full mortar bed on the prepared concrete foundation. Check for level.

Then proceed to the opposite end of the course and position a second brick in place in the same manner.

Run a mason's line between the two bricks; place a string level on the line and adjust the bricks until they are level with each other. This may mean removing or adding some mortar from below one brick. You cannot make extreme adjustments in this manner. If the bricks are too far out of level you may have to adjust them by spreading the adjustments out over several courses.

Filling in toward the middle. To add more bricks to the first course, first butter the end of a brick. Hold the brick in one hand, and the trowel in the other. With a flip of the wrist, turn the trowel over, dump the mortar on the brick end and press the mortar firmly in place with the trowel.

Position the brick down on the mortar bed, about 1½ to 2 inches away from the end brick. Gently push the second brick down into the mortar and against the end brick until the joints below and to the side are about ½ inch thick. Align the top front edge of the brick with the string guide, but do not let the brick touch the string. With the edge of the trowel, remove the excess mortar that has been squeezed out during placement and spread it back in the mortar box or hawk—or place it in position for the next bricks. In this manner, lay about a half dozen bricks from each end of the course towards the middle.

Laying the second course. In order to create staggered mortar joints in consecutive courses, the end bricks for the second course must be half bricks. (Cutting instructions are given below.) Lay the two end bricks, run the mason's line between them and fill in on each side until you can add no more bricks without overhanging the bricks laid in the first course. Subse-

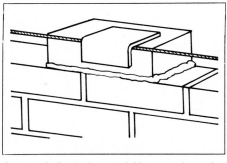

A mason's line helps a bricklayer to determine and maintain level when laying a wall so the courses will be even.

quent courses will begin alternately with full stretchers or half bricks. Complete from three to five courses to build the leads before you begin to fill in the center sections of the courses. Use the story pole to maintain the correct size mortar joint. Use a level to ensure straight and plumb sides and corners.

Laying the remaining and top courses. Continue to build up the leads and to fill in until you reach the course below the final course. The top course may be the same as those below, or you can embed a flashing layer in the mortar, or finish off the top with prefabricated capping. Some people lay a final coating of mortar across the top course. This thin layer should be smooth with rounded edges; it will help protect the mortar joints.

Leads Containing Corners

Laying the first course. Fill in the ends of one side of a multi-sided project just as you would for a free-standing lead. Then move to the adjacent side. Throw a mortar line along the footing next to the first stretcher placed. Butter the end of a brick and position the brick so that the end butts against the side of the stretcher. Place a brick at the opposite end of the course, run a mason's line, and fill in five or six bricks on each side as above. Do the same for all the connecting sides.

Laying the second course. Begin the second course at a side of a lead that includes both a header and a stretcher. Place a stretcher so that it overlaps the top and creates a flush corner edge. At the other end of this course, place a header or stretcher as needed to ensure that the joints in the two courses are not aligned. (If there is not an adjoining wall at this end, use a cut brick instead of a header.) Then fill in bricks at each side to continue building the stepped-back leads.

Bricklaying Techniques

Aligning the mason's line. Once you have built up the corner leads to your satisfaction, move the mason's line blocks to the top corners of the starting bricks of the bottom course. The top outside edges of the bricks should fall slightly in back of the string line. If the line has to reach quite a distance, it may sag. To maintain a level line, support it in the middle with temporary brick. Place a fold of sheet metal down over the brick to enclose the string. Then place a brick on top of this to hold the string in the correct, level position.

Placing the closure brick. If possible, plan the job so you don't have to cut a closure brick but can simply use a full-sized closure brick. It's a good idea to make a trial fit with this brick before applying mortar to it. Then butter generous amounts of mortar on the ends of the brick and against the ends of the bricks already in place. Carefully place the closure brick between those already in position. Try to knock off as little mortar as possible.

Cutting Bricks

Cutting a brick is actually a simple chore.

Experienced masons merely hold the brick in one hand and tap with the edge of a brick hammer to cut the brick where they wish. However, this is not only a good way for the inexperienced to break and waste a lot of bricks, but to injure a hand (or, when half the brick falls, a foot).

Place the brick on a solid surface, such as the ground or a piece of scrap lumber. Score it with a brick hammer and a brick chisel. Make sure you always wear safety goggles or glasses, as well as gloves. Hold the brick chisel in place and tap it gently with the hammer on the scored line, first on one side, and then the opposite side. In most cases, the brick

will break (snap apart) after about the second or third tap on the second side. You should follow the same procedure and precautions when cutting stone or concrete block.

Types of Mortar Joints

There are several different types of joints used for brick work. In some instances, the mortar that squeezes out as the bricks are positioned is simply left in place. The effect is supposed to be rustic. However, this joint does not shed water very well, isn't a strong joint, and it breaks away easily, which leaves an unattractive finish. To create a flush joint, merely cut away the excess mortar with the edge of the trowel.

Tooling the Joints

Tooled joints are shaped with special tools. The shaping not only prevents moisture from running back into the joints, but it also strengthens the joint because the tool compresses the mortar. In addition to the concave or rounded joint, most commonly formed with a round jointing tool, there are also several

If your wall is merely a straight section, you will have to cut bricks to fit into the ends of the walls for an even finish.

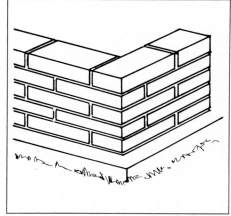

If your wall makes a right angle turn, set the bricks at the corner so its short face appears every other course on each side.

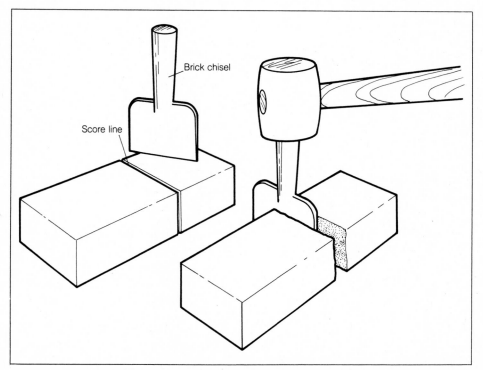

To cut a brick, first measure to locate the place for the cut, scribe a line around the brick at that point, place a brick chisel on the line, and strike the chisel with a mallet.

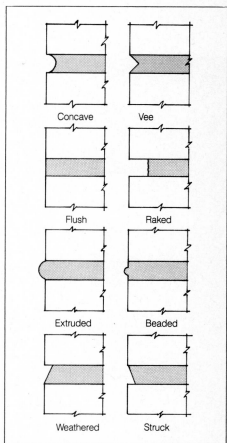

There are many ways to finish (tool) mortar joints. Raked and struck joints hold water; avoid them in areas of severe weather.

other types of brick joints, each of which has a function and an aesthetic effect of its own. Concave, vee, raked, and beaded joints are typical. Metal jointers are used to finish most joints. Flush, struck and weathered joints may be done with a trowel.

Aesthetic Effects of Joints

Concave joints make for a flat wall appearance, where this is desired. Vee joints emphasize shadows. Flush joints are acceptable in areas not subject to heavy amounts of rainfall. Raked joints leave the mortar perpendicular and recessed almost a half inch (but not more); these joints create dark shadows. Beaded joints are like extruded joints but beaded joints have a more formal appearance, achieved with a special tool. The extrusions create strong shadow lines. Struck joints and weathered joints, like the raked joint, create dark lines on the wall.

Joint types can be mixed for a desired aesthetic effect. For example, you may combine flush vertical joints and extruded horizontal joints to produce long lines of horizontal shadow. However, mixing joint styles is difficult, even for a professional.

Keep all joints tooled and cleaned as

Brick combines easily with insets of metal fencing to give an open line of sight while still providing needed protection.

you work, since the bricks absorb moisture and cause the mortar to dry out quickly. To remove any remaining mortar, lightly brush the brick faces. This is much easier now than after the mortar has set up on the brick faces.

Brick Panel and Pier Wall

One of the simplest, cheapest brick walls is the brick panel and pier wall. A pier is a column built within the wall for support; it often is thicker than the rest of the wall. (Information presented here was prepared from data provided by the Brick Institute of America.)

Designing the wall. Sketch the design, showing a pier at every corner or turn in the wall. Locate intermediate piers so that the panel spaces between the piers will be nearly equal. If the wall is tied to

the house, a pier will not be needed at that point unless desired for aesthetic considerations. When you are satisfied your plan meets your needs, add dimensions to the drawing.

Staking the location. Stake out the piers and wall foundations. In temperate areas the bricks are laid directly on the ground. In areas of extreme cold, you will have to check with your building department for local foundation underlayment standards and design the foundation to your required standards. Dig the pier holes; Table 3 shows the depths required.

Preparing the base. Prepare the earth for the base of the panels. Remove earth several inches down and scrape the excavation floor smooth and level. Remove any debris, dirt clods, or protruding stones. Tamp the earth smooth.

TABLE 1—PANEL WALL REINFORCING STEEL

Wall Span, Feet	Vertical Spacing, Inch.								
	Wind Load, 10PSF			Wind Load, 15PSF			Wind Load, 20PSF		
	A	B	C	A	B	C	A	B	C
8	45	30	19	30	20	12	23	15	9.5
10	29	19	12	19	13	8.0	14	10	6.0
12	20	13	8.5	13	9.0	5.5	10	7.0	4.0
14	15	10	6.5	10	6.5	4.0	7.5	5.0	3.0
16	11	7.5	5.0	7.5	5.0	3.0	6.0	4.0	2.5

NOTE: A=2-No. 2 bars; B=2-3/16 in. diameter wires;
C=2-9 gauge wires.

TABLE 2—PIER REINFORCING STEEL

Wall Span, Feet	Wind Load, 10PSF			Wind Load, 15PSF			Wind Load, 20PSF		
	Wall Height, Ft.			Wall Height, Ft.			Wall Height, Ft.		
	4	6	8	4	6	8	4	6	8
8	2 No. 3	2 No. 4	2 No. 5	2 No. 3	2 No. 5	2 No. 6	2 No. 4	2 No. 5	2 No. 5
10	2 No. 3	2 No. 4	2 No. 5	2 No. 4	2 No. 5	2 No. 7	2 No. 4	2 No. 6	2 No. 6
12	2 No. 3	2 No. 5	2 No. 6	2 No. 4	2 No. 6	*2 No. 6*	2 No. 4	2 No. 6	2 No. 7
14	2 No. 3	2 No. 5	2 No. 6	2 No. 4	2 No. 6	*2 No. 6*	2 No. 5	*2 No. 5*	2 No. 7
16	2 No. 4	2 No. 5	2 No. 7	2 No. 4	2 No. 6	*2 No. 7*	2 No. 5	*2 No. 6*	2 No. 7

NOTE: Italic items require 12 by 16 in. pier. All other values obtained with 12 by 12 inch pier

TABLE 3—REQUIRED EMBEDMENT FOR PIER FOUNDATION

Wall Span, Feet	Wind Load, 10PSF			Wind Load, 15PSF			Wind Load, 20PSF		
	Wall Height, Ft.			Wall Height, Ft.			Wall Height, Ft.		
	4	6	8	4	6	8	4	6	8
8	2'	2'3"	2'9"	2'3"	2'6"	3'	2'3"	2'9"	3'
10	2'	2'6"	2'9"	2'3"	2'9"	3'3"	2'6"	3'	3'3"
12	2'3"	2'6"	3'	2'3"	3'	3'3"	2'6"	3'3"	3'6"
14	2'3"	2'9"	3'	2'6"	3'	3'3"	2'9"	3'3"	3'9"
16	2'3"	2'9"	3'	2'6"	3'3"	3'6"	2'9"	3'3"	4'

NOTE: Italic items require 24 in. diameter foundation. All other values obtained with 18 in. diameter foundation

Laying the bricks. In temperate areas, lay the first course of bricks on a one-inch bed of mortar placed directly on the smooth earth. This course (and perhaps additional courses) should be below ground level. The more courses below ground, the larger the foundation will be. In areas subject to ground freeze, you must build a foundation. Check with your building department for foundation depth and preparation requirements.

The piers and the brick panels are built up at the same time; the wall courses tie into the piers as you work upward. The piers themselves are hollow-core, square columns that are part of the wall, which may connect with the pier at one side, at the center, or alternately at the front and back faces of the pier. (See the illustration for types of piers and the wall unions.)

After laying mortar for the second course, place the horizontal steel in the mortar before laying the bricks in the second course. Continue laying the brick, installing the reinforcing according to Table 1. As the panel rises, grout the center opening in the pier with mortar, to which sufficient water has been added so that it will flow readily and completely surround the vertical steel. Your local lime and cement dealer will supply grout and can tell you what mix is used in your region.

Table 3 is based on soils with an allowable bearing pressure of 3000 psi

or more. For poorer soil, additional engineering analysis of the foundation is necessary. Ask your building department to refer you to a soils engineer.

Materials for your wall. For greatest durability and strength use ASTM C270, type S brick made with 1 part portland cement, ½ part hydrated lime and 4½

parts sand by volume. Use No. 2 and larger bars of reinforcing steel with a minimum yield strength of 40,000 psi. No. 9 gauge wire and ³⁄₁₆ inch diameter wire must have a minimum yield strength of 60,000 psi.

Workmanship. Vertical (head) and bed joints must be filled solid; pack the

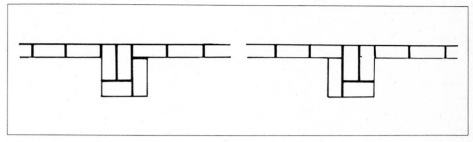

In a pier and panel wall, piers must be integral with the wall. Stagger the bond pattern of the brick course so the pier is tied into the wall from a different side in each course.

A completed wall may look more finished if the piers are capped with a coping of some kind. It is also possible to finish the tops of the piers with a mortar cap.

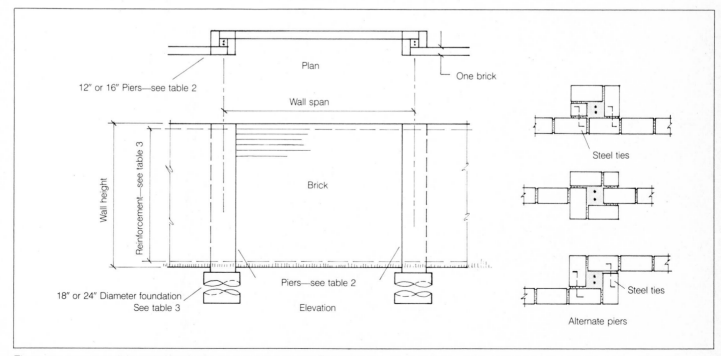

There are many possible variations in the pier and panel wall. The piers may be built hollow and reinforced with wall ties and vertical rods, then grouted full for strength. This creates a very stable wall.

joints fully and do not rake them out. The grout in the piers must surround the steel and completely fill the pier.

Constructing a Serpentine Wall

The wavering form of the serpentine wall serves a functional as well as decorative purpose: the shape provides lateral strength, allowing the wall to be built only 4 inches thick. Where the depth of the curve does not present a space problem, the serpentine wall is a relatively cheap way to build.

Determining the curve. In general, the radius of curvature of a 4-inch wall should be no more than twice the height of the wall above finished grade. This is a general rule to ensure that the curvature of the wall is not so shallow—and, therefore, weak—that the wall will topple. In other words, if the curve is too shallow it resembles a straight wall. A straight 4-inch wall that would need steel reinforcement to be stable. So, if you needed a wall 4 feet 8 inches high, your radius of curvature should not be more than 9 feet 4 inches. Another guideline is that the curvature radius should not be less than half the height. For a 4-foot 8-inch wall, the radius of curvature should not be less than 2 feet 4 inches. These limitations also seem to produce the most visually pleasing walls.

Laying out the wall. Laying out a serpentine wall calls for precision techniques. The longer the distance of the wall, the more obvious any mistakes will be. These directions are for walls that—even though they are serpentine—extend in one direction only. If the walls must jog around obstructions, the layout problems are multiplied and you would be wise to call a surveyor and have him stake out the centerline of the wall for you. (This is a good idea for any wall of this complexity.) Have a sketch to show him so that he will know what kind of wall you have in mind.

Although a serpentine wall has a less stark appearance than a high straight wall, it still ensures privacy. Hedge plantings further soften the impact of the wall.

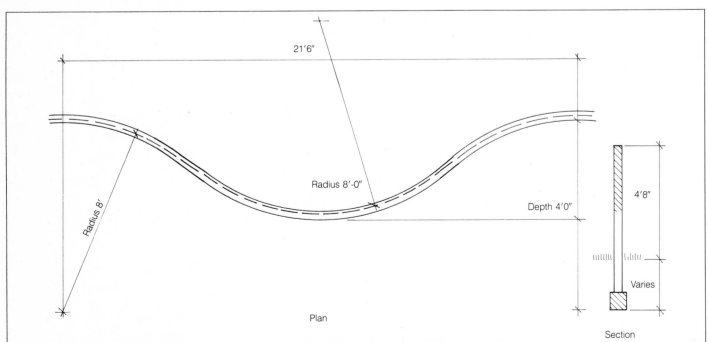

A serpentine wall acquires its strength from the internal pressures created by the curve itself. The wall is a graceful form.

BUILDING BRICK SCREENS

The brick screen wall or "perforated" wall is designed, laid out, and constructed similar to a concrete masonry screen wall and a solid masonry wall. In some designs it is easier to construct than a concrete masonry screen wall, since generally it requires less steel reinforcement. The pattern possibilities of the brick screen wall are ample, but they will all have a more squared-off quality than some of the free-form patterns available in concrete screen blocks.

Brick screen walls are commonly used as solar screens to cut off the direct rays of the sun without blocking the light completely. They are popular for setting apart activity areas. The screens help disguise air-conditioner condensing units and trash cans where you wish to enclose items but want to keep the air circulation.

Construction Methods

The brick-laying techniques for a brick perforated wall are the same as for a solid masonry wall. However, extra care must be taken to avoid putting any pressure on the screen before the mortar sets, since it has much less lateral strength than a solid masonry wall. You should also check with the building department. They sometimes have special requirements because of this lack of strength for screen walls of considerable height. Patterns are achieved by manipulating the position of brick within the courses and/or by leaving some of them out (voids or perforations). The wall may be flush, or selected bricks may be turned at right angles to the regular courses to form the voids or create deep shadows.

Creating the perforations. There are no hard rules for how much overlap (bearing surface) you need for the bricks that span perforations. However, the size of the bricks often tells you what the overlap should be. For example, if you are leaving out every other stretcher in alternate courses, and are supporting the stretcher courses with bricks turned at right angles and flat, then the stretchers should be centered over the headers—this would give you an overlap of half the width of a brick.

In general, let the brick indicate what the overlaps should be. You can use headers or rowlock headers as supports for your stretchers, but keep in mind that although perforations add pattern interest

to walls, they also weaken it. The higher the wall, the more significant this weakening effect becomes. If you use patterns with more open space than the perforations shown, or that have less overlap, you should show your sketches to an architect or get an opinion from the building department before you start.

This wall combines a two-wythe base, piers, panels, and brick screen to provide privacy while allowing some light and air passage.

Building a Two-Wythe Wall Construction

Snap a chalkline on the footing to help you accurately align the brick. Space the brick over the length of the wall to determine the joint sizes. At this point you are still laying out the bricks without mortar. Both the interior and exterior wythes

This light and airy brick screen is based on the Flemish bond pattern. The header positions, however, are left as open spaces.

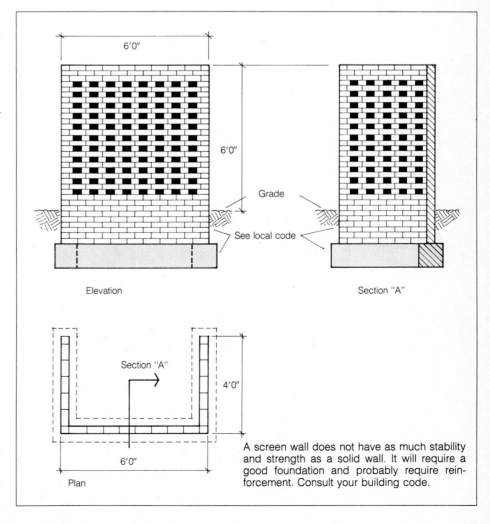

6'0"

6'0"

Grade

See local code

Elevation

Section "A"

Section "A"

4'0"

6'0"

Plan

A screen wall does not have as much stability and strength as a solid wall. It will require a good foundation and probably require reinforcement. Consult your building code.

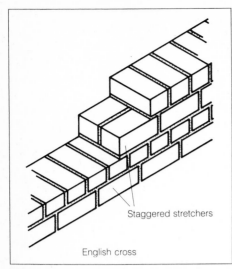

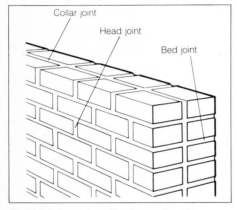

The English cross bond is very strong because both wythes are tied together with headers every other course.

Bed joints run along the base of each course; head joints run vertically. A two-wythe wall has a collar joint between wythes.

should be laid out (each line of brick is called a wythe). Keep brick moist to prevent its drawing the moisture from the mortar and weakening the bond.

Laying the base course. Starting at one corner, spread a full, thick mortar bed for the first course. Lay the exterior

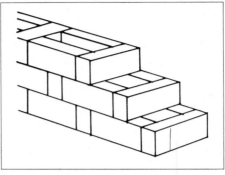

A two-wythe wall may be built with the brick on edge (rowlock). Alternate stretchers and headers in each course for strength.

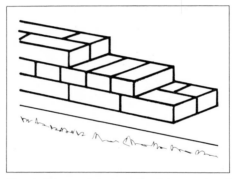

The stretcher wythes in an English cross bond should not be laid so the head joints align. Use cut brick to stagger the joints.

corner brick first, positioning it very carefully. Take another brick and "butter" the inside face. This brick is then set alongside of the first one to form the inside face of the wall. As each brick is buttered on its end, it is then brought over its final position and pushed downward into the mortar bed and against the previously laid brick. The setting motion is similar to taking a brush and scrubbing the floor. The scrubbing that takes place is what provides the bond between the bricks.

Leveling the base course. After several bricks have been laid, a mason's line is used as a straightedge to assure that they are in correct alignment. To bring to proper level and plumb, tap on the brick with the trowel handle. If a brick has receded, gently tap from behind to bring its face flush with the line. Lay the first course of masonry as accurately as possible, since subsequent courses will rely on the first course for alignment.

Building corner leads. Once the base course is down, build the corners by laying up the next several courses at the corner, keeping the corners always about 18 inches higher than the center of the wall.

Every other course must be started with a header course. This will result in the bricks being offset by one half a brick, which is the basic running bond pattern. As each course is laid at the corner, check it for plumb, alignment and level using the mason's line. At the same time, each course is checked with a level to make sure all the joints are lined up and in the same plane.

Filling in the courses. Once the corners are set, a line can be stretched between corners for each course. As you spread the mortar over the lower course, make sure the mortar is still flexible.

As each brick end is buttered and scrubbed into place, the joint between the brick—as well as the one underneath the placed brick—will ooze mortar. Simply strike off the excess with the trowel. To assure a good bond, do not spread the mortar too far ahead or it will dry out too early. Always work from the corners to the middle.

Turning a corner. First lay down two mortar lines on the foundation, just inside the chalkline. Lay the first brick on the corner, and then butter and lay up the second brick, using your steel square to

This two-wythe wall is capped by rowlock headers laid with brick slightly larger than used in the wall. This creates a overhang that protects the wall from rainwater runoff.

This installation combines old paving bricks in the drive and new bricks in the wall. A screen area is created with tile.

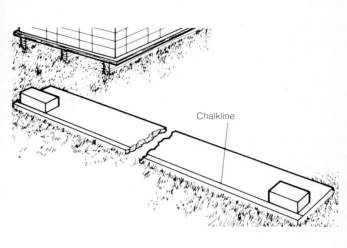

At each corner of the wall set a brick. Snap a chalkline to mark the edge of the proposed wall.

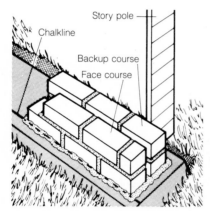

The chalk mark serves as the guideline for the run of the courses. Mark and use a story pole to provide vertical guide.

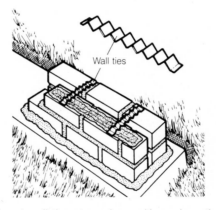

Insert wall ties at regular positions along the wall to tie the course wythe together. Stagger position along the wall.

Bend ends from alternate sides to create a vertical tie for vertical reinforcement of the two-wythe wall.

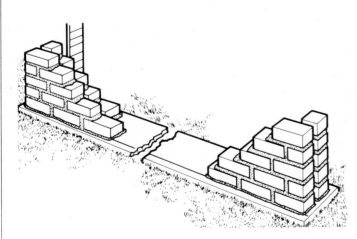

The ends of the walls are built up in "leads" to serve as guides as the wall is built. If the leads are level and plumb, the wall will be too. Guidelines run from lead to lead.

The wall is built toward the center and filled in. The leads are three courses above the center before that is finally completed with a "closure brick" in the center of each course.

ensure that the two bricks create a right angle. Now lay up the next four bricks along the chalklines, extending out from the corner, alternating placement (see illustration), until you have a six-brick corner.

Form the backup wythe in the same way, leaving enough space between this row of bricks and the first to create an exact fit for the capping course (row-locks). The bricks in this second wythe must meet at a right angle and overlap the first wythe by half a brick. In building up the second course of the first wythe, place a full brick so that it covers half of Brick 1 and half of Brick 2 (header), and the next brick over half of Brick 1 and Brick 3. Continue in this manner in succeeding courses in order to create a staggered pattern (running bond).

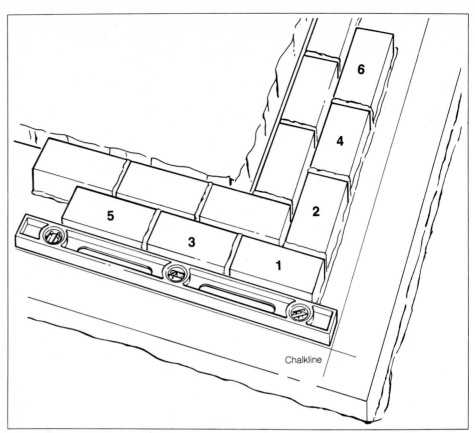

Spread two perpendicular mortar lines just inside the chalklines. Lay the first brick at the outside corner, and then work alternately from side to side, as shown. Build up six-brick corner lead. Then do the same for the other wythe.

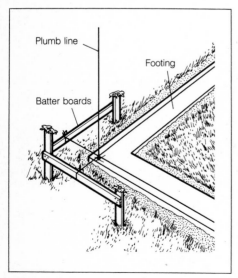

A turn in a wall is often a time to use some imagination in design. The top of this wall is finished in mitered bricks.

Begin by locating the outside perimeter of the wall from the batter boards using a plumb line and bob. Mark with a chalkline.

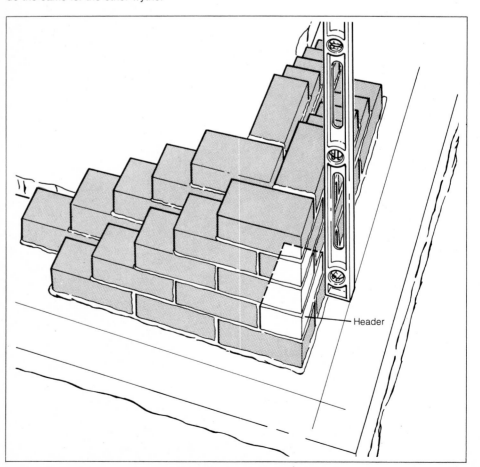

Lay header to start second course. This will offset brick and create a running bond pattern.

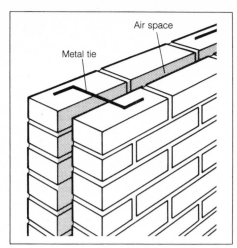

A hollow, two-wythe wall requires metal tie reinforcement to maintain full strength. Z-ties add strength to and between wythes.

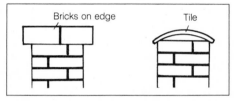

A wall may be finished at the top with bricks or with a piece of curved tile.

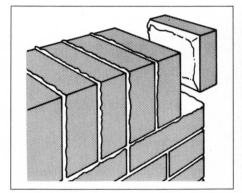

A common wall finish is a course of rowlock headers laid in a full mortar bed. Butter one broad face to create vertical joint.

If your wall turns, you will have to butt the broad face of one brick against the ends of three to make the turn.

Reinforcing. Having completed the first 6 courses (16 inches high), horizontal joint reinforcement must be set. Spread a layer of mortar about a ½ inch thick over both lines of brick (wythes). Push the reinforcing into the mortar bed until it appears fully seated. Lay the corner brick of the next course over it by buttering the bottom of the brick and placing it into position. Tap the brick until the joint is the same thickness as the others. Remove the excess mortar and repeat the operation for both the wythes. Place the ties on 24-inch centers, reaching across the two wythes to hold them together. The reinforcing will be placed every six courses vertically. After the next six courses, stagger the reinforcing horizontally so that trusses fall between the row of trusses previously set.

Tooling the joints. When the mortar is thumb hard, but not completely set, all the joints must be tooled before the mortar sets. A joint tool with a concave or vee shape edge is the simplest to use. Draw the tool along the joint while pushing in

slightly. This will cause a slight depression of the joint while at the same time smoothing it out. Do this to all the vertical joints before starting on the horizontal joints.

Flashing and capping the wall. As you approach the top of the wall, but before capping the wall, the wall should be flashed. Flashing keeps the water from entering into the wall and weakening the joints. It is a very thin metal sheet or plastic cloth that is put over the length of the wall before the capping course is installed.

Stop the coursing 4 inches below the top of the finished wall height. Place a layer of mortar about ½ inch thick over the wall and lay down the flashing. To cap, set the brick on its side with the weathering surface facing upwards; capping a wall is crucial to its strength. Place mortar on the sides of the brick that will be used for the capping course. Then place the brick on the flashing. Press down until the mortar oozes from the joint, and remove the excess. Repeat this

The piers of this wall and fence combination are finished with a mortar cap that is smoothed to a curve. The low wall is capped with rowlock headers that butt at the turn.

This pier and panel wall is finished with a course of rowlock headers. The two-wythe piers are capped with their own rowlocks. The pattern matches that of the low front walk wall.

One of the attractive qualities of brick is the fact that it blends with other materials. This solid wall offers total privacy and visual variety in the combination of materials.

This wall is finished with a curved top held by rowlock headers and a corner light.

A flight of brick steps and walk combine running bond and basketweave patterns.

This small patio area with a pond uses brick in several ways including a curved retaining wall. A retaining wall like this is not under much stress and brick is suitable.

procedure until the wall has been capped. Make sure that all joints have been struck and compressed lightly with the joint tool.

Once the wall is finished, do not clean the surface immediately. Wait for at least a week; then scrub the wall down with a brush and a solution of hydrochloric acid in ten parts water. This will etch the brick to its natural coloring. After the scrubbing, rinse the wall.

Finishing the Wall

Before filling in the area around the base of the wall, the area underneath must be treated for moisture in the ground. There are two methods that can be used.

The first method involves brushing on a bituminous coating that is composed of asphaltic tars. This can be purchased in most hardware stores. Cover the area that will be below ground. Make sure not to brush it onto any of the exposed area, since the black surface is not very attractive.

The other method is to parge (coat) the surface with a ¼-inch layer of cement plaster to form a protective shield against the moisture. This cement plaster can be purchased at any hardware store; it is troweled on as you would apply plaster. Both methods are effective. Once you have treated the below-ground face of the brick you can infill around the wall. Tamp the fill solidly. Then install the particular material you want to be the wearing surface, or spread grass seed.

BRICK WALKS, PATIOS AND TERRACES

Probably some of the easiest, most enjoyable and practical brick projects are brick walks, garden patios, terraces, or planters. In fact, once you have the materials on hand, the work is so simple that you can complete a job during a weekend.

Design Considerations

Special plantings. Be versatile when you plan your project. If the patio or terrace meets a backyard fence, leave an open area between the two. Later, fill in the area with a raised planting bed to blend the fence and the patio. Rather than removing trees or shrubs, build the patio around them. Each tree or plant will need an open area equal to at least 1½ to 2 feet in diameter. This allows an adequate amount of moisture to reach the roots and enough space to grow. For a raised patio, surround a tree with a well made of dry-laid concrete block. Then add gravel to achieve the desired height.

Materials and edgings. The patio or walk can be constructed of bricks laid in a mortar bed on a concrete footing or in a sand bed over a gravel base. Often, brick installations such as these feature permanent edging materials, such as bricks set on end, special wood beams, or even old railroad ties. The edging holds the shape of the patio and increases its longevity.

Creating edging patterns. The type of permanent edging you choose will affect the design of your project. A round or free-form patio can be edged with bricks set in a small concrete footing; a square or rectangular patio can have an edging of 2x4s or 4x4s of redwood, cypress or other wood that has been pressure-treated. Old railroad ties also make great edgings for patios. Sink them into the ground to about half their thickness so their top edges will stand only a little higher than the tops of the bricks. You can create additional designs using the wooden edging materials in interior patterns that divide the patio into smaller areas.

SAND-BED BRICK PATIO OR WALK

Laying brick in a bed of sand is by far the easiest way to create a patio, walk or terrace. If you follow the proper procedures, and if the climate is mild, the job will last as long as if laid in a bed of mortar. Pay careful attention to proper grading and installation of the sand bed, or else the project will look shoddy and haphazard. Remember, too, that no matter how carefully you work on the sand bed, it will still settle somewhat, resulting in depressions in the brick surface after the job has been completed. To remedy the problem, remove the bricks that have sunk down, place more sand beneath them, and replace them.

Excavating the Subgrade

One of the main prerequisites to creating a good-looking, long-lasting paved walk or patio is a solid, well-packed subsurface. In many instances, you need only cut away the turf to the depth necessary to accommodate 2 inches of sand and the thickness (or part of it) of the bricks. The paving material often reaches as much as 2 inches above ground level.

Brick is appropriate to many settings. It is both a formal material, as in this setting, or a rustic material in casual settings, where it provides a warm background to activities.

This formal garden patio uses brick for the walking surface, the small fountain, and fence posts. The recurring use of brick unifies the area and sets off the small planting areas.

The lines of this curved brick walk contrast with the angles of the house and the wall. Cut bricks to follow the edging.

This formal walk is laid out so it draws the eye to the tree in the center. Water drains to the roots through mortarless joints.

To finish off a low brick base topped with picket fencing, install full height brick piers. Add matching or contrasting gates.

A row of headers strengthens the front edge of brick steps. It also adds variety to the major pattern in the steps themselves.

Clear away all rocks and debris from the area and smooth it out as much as possible. In areas where the soil is not naturally well packed or does not drain well, you may need first to add a layer of well-tamped gravel or crushed stone fill. If this layer is added, adjust the depth of the excavation to suit. Even a well-packed soil surface can be improved by tamping it thoroughly before installation of the sand bed.

Installing the Edging or Form

Permanent edging. Permanent wood borders must be made of cypress, redwood or other wood that has been pressure-treated. After the excavation is complete, install the edging so that the top edge is just above, or flush with, the ground level. To anchor the edging solidly in place, install stakes made of the same material as the forms. Nail forms to the stakes with duplex-headed nails. Fill in the base and the sand bed; lay the bricks. Finish as desired. Remove the nails from the stakes. Using a wedge-shaped piece of 2x4, pound the permanent stakes below ground level. Do not hammer the edging itself. Cover the stakes with soil.

Temporary form. The edging for a patio project can be only a temporary form whose function is to hold the bricks in place until the project has been completed. Remove the form when the bricks are all in place. Pack soil around the outside edges. This installation is not as stable or long-lasting as one that has a permanent edging.

Pitching the patio. Pitch the patio, walk or terrace as discussed in Chapter 2. You may instead crown a walk by shaping the sand bed, as discussed below.

Adding the Sand Base

After the edging has been secured, place and tamp gravel fill. Then add a layer of sand that is at least 2 inches deep. Spread the sand roughly in place with a rake. With a hose set on fine spray, thoroughly dampen the sand. In a short time, the sand will settle. Fill in the spots that are obviously low, and dampen down the new fill. While the sand is still wet, pull a drag board across the edging to level the sand bed. Remove any excess sand, and fill in low spots as you go. Hose down the sand bed again after leveling. Use a fine mist only, so you don't dislodge the sand.

Crowning a walk. The paved surface must be constructed so water can run off. Although some moisture will soak down

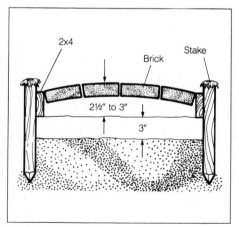

A brick walk must be crowned. This aids drainage and prevents the center of the walk from sinking after a period of time.

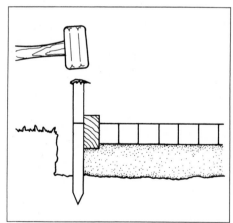

Hold a permanent edging in place with permanent stakes. Use a 2x4 wedge to pound the stakes below ground level. Cover them later.

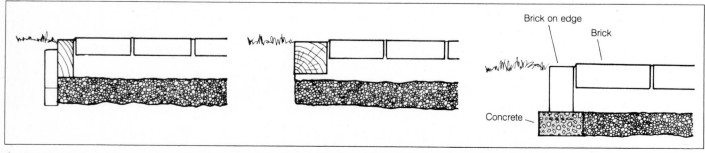

A sand-bed patio needs some type of permanent edging to hold its shape. Select pressure-treated wood, old railroad ties, or bricks set on edge.

through the cracks between the bricks, you still need a way for most of the surface water to drain away quickly. To provide the necessary pitch to a walk, the center is crowned (somewhat raised in the center). Crowning also adds another benefit to a brick walk. Since the traffic along a walk eventually will drive and pack down the center, crowning prevents the center of the walk from becoming lower than the edges.

Crown the sand by creating a dragboard that is higher in the center than at the ends. Cut the dragboard to produce the appropriate amount of pitch. (For the recommended amount of pitch in a walk, see Chapter 2.)

Setting the Brick

Start at one corner of the project. Position the brick in the desired pattern. To embed the bricks into the sand, lay a 16-inch piece of 2x6 over the bricks and hammer them down with a large hammer. Run a long level or straightedge across the surface to be sure that the finished surface is level to the edging and that the bricks are level with each other. Set the paving bricks ¼ to ½ inch higher than the desired final height of the finished surface, since the bricks will settle after a time. Butt the bricks, or allow for consistently sized joints between the pavers. You may have to tap them together in some areas. When tapping, protect the surface of the brick with a buffer board; the hammer can chip, crack or break the units.

Laying Brick Patterns

There are several patterns used in brick patios and floors, including some that aren't used in walls and other vertical structures. Two possible choices are herringbone and basketweave. The careful layout required for any horizontal brick surface is obvious in the following example, which is a discussion of basketweave.

Laying the basketweave design. A basketweave pattern, as shown, is based upon blocks of brick set on edge at right angles to each other. Each block must be of equal size. Arrange joint sizes so that the two or three bricks set in one direction equal the length of the brick.

Three-brick basketweave. Beginning in one corner, place three bricks on edge. All should run in the same direction, and there should be a ⅜-inch joint left between them. The size of the block will equal the length of the bricks (7⅝ inches), which should equal the sum of the three thicknesses and the two mortar joints (2¼+⅜+2¼+⅜+2¼) to yield a 7⅝x7⅝ inch square.

Now set the second block of three bricks at right angles to the first block. To assure the correct spacing, align the top and bottom brick with the top and bottom edges of the lengthwise brick they butt against. To complete the block, center the third brick between the two. Continue alternating blocks, working out and across the patio area. Try not to go back to an area already completed, since you may disturb the spacing.

Two-brick basketweave. If you prefer to lay the bricks flat rather than on edge, each block will contain only two bricks. Again, work on aligning outside edges to create equal squares.

Filling the Joints

Sand fill. After laying the bricks, start in one corner and spread dry sand on the surface. Sweep the sand down into the cracks between the pavers. Work on one quarter at a time, sweeping from all directions to fill all the joints completely. Then, lightly hose the surface to pack down the dry sand and clean off any excess. Repeat this process until the joints are completely filled. From time to time, you will have to sweep in more sand to keep soil and weeds from working up through the joints.

Sand-mortar fill. You can place mortar in the joints of a sand-bed patio if you wish, but the mortar joints will crack and

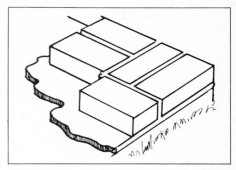

Bricks can also be laid in a mortar bed. Space them carefully for even mortar joints.

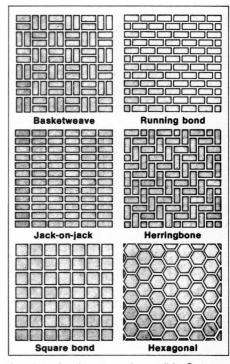

Basketweave   Running bond

Jack-on-jack   Herringbone

Square bond   Hexagonal

A variety of patio patterns is possible. Some are easier and more popular than others.

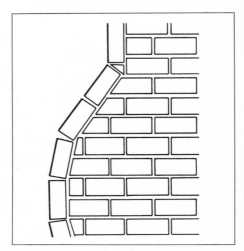

In a curved wall, adjust the mortar line between the edging bricks. This will absorb some of the roughness of the cut bricks.

A herringbone walkway fits into a traditional or a rustic setting. It must be carefully set so that the joint lines properly align.

won't look as neat as the sand-filled joints. Mortar the joints by applying a dry mix of 1 part cement and 4 parts sand. Place the dry mix in and around the bricks. Pack all joints with the dry mortar; moisten the mortar by spraying it with a garden hose. Continue the light spray for half an hour. Don't flush away any of the mortar with high water pressure. Over the next few days, dampen the surface once again. The cement will bond with the sand to form a hard joint. Repeat the process every year.

MORTAR BED BRICK PATIO
Brick may also be set in a bed of mortar over a solid concrete surface. In fact, this is one way to refurbish an old concrete patio.

Preparation
The base for the brick surface must be solid and well drained. Clean the old concrete surface as much as possible. Prepare a standard mortar mix and spread a coat that is about 1 inch thick.

Placing the Brick
Lay the bricks in the mortar in one of the patterns given above. Butter the ends and one side, position and tap each brick firmly to avoid air pockets. Leave a ½-inch wide mortar joint between each brick and between the courses. Use a level and a long straightedge to ensure that all bricks are level—high or low spots will cause water pooling. Make sure there are no air pockets trapped in the mortar below the bricks; frost will cause bricks to heave in the area around an empty air pocket.

You can trowel the joints flush with the bricks or tool the joints slightly. Tooled joints, however, should not be made too deep, or the surface will be hard to keep clean.

PATIO ACCESSORIES
Open Firepit Cooking Areas
The old-style open barbecue pit found in

some patios is really a firebrick-lined hole in the ground. Before you install a firepit, check your local fire codes since open fires are prohibited in some areas. As you design the firepit, plan both for safety and convenience. Locate the pit close enough to the patio that you can build an open fire and enjoy it, but out of the general foot-traffic pattern. Include a raised rim or ledge and a cover in the design to keep anyone from stepping into it by accident. Make sure to place the firepit so that drifting smoke won't cause discomfort. Your local National Weather Bureau office can inform you about the predominant wind direction during the summer months.

Materials. The bottom of the pit consists of a layer of coarse aggregate (similar to that used in concrete mix) and a layer of coarse torpedo sand (fine, evenly sized sand). You will need a couple of bushels of each. The sides of the pit are lined with firebrick, of which you need about 180 units. Select ones as close to the size of a common brick as possible. That will make finishing easier. If you desire, purchase additional face or decorative bricks to cover the top.

The project will require 2 bags of conventional mortar mix and 10 pounds of fire clay. To create a heatproof mortar to hold the firebrick in place, you will need 2 bags of conventional mortar mix and 10 pounds of fire clay. In some areas, you may be able to purchase premixed refractory mortar, which serves the same purpose.

Finally, you need grills. The simplest answer to this need is a grill from an old or discarded oven. Use the standard size, 16x22 inches, or special heavy-duty grills. Available at many patio centers, these come in 12-inch increments.

Excavating the pit. To build the pit, select an area 3 feet by 4 feet. Dig a 2-foot deep firepit that is 2x3 feet. Fill the bottom with a 6-inch layer of tamped aggregate. Over this, spread two inches of sand. Again, tamp firmly with either a 4x4 post or a hand tamper available at many local hardware stores. Level the base before you lay the firebrick.

Lining the firepit. The correct proportions of your mortar are 10 parts of mortar mix to 1 part of fire clay. Thus, to 40 pounds of mortar mix add four pounds of fire clay.

A double rectangle of firebrick creates

A brick barbecue is a project that is worthwhile and that adds to the utility of a patio or yard. This one features a grill that can be removed for easy cleaning. See Chapter Six.

the lining of the pit. Dry-lay first to insure that the layout has no mortar joints aligned with those in the course below.

Upon the sand base, begin laying your bricks in a double row around the pit. Start by laying a double line of four bricks at one end. Keep the mortar joints at ⅜ inch. Then, lay the sides, which also are two rows of four bricks each. Butt the ends of the initial bricks against the sides of the corner bricks. Finish the fourth side of the square with another double row of four bricks.

Build the two wythes to a total of five courses high. Lay them as described in the general procedure section. Finish off with a single-wythe sixth course of bricks set on their sides. You will have to cut bricks to fit in this course. The grills will sit on top of the fifth course. The sixth course holds the grills in position.

Curing and finishing. After the mortar has cured about a week, clean the joints at the top of the pit with a wire brush and a mixture of muriatic acid and water in the standard proportions. Use the appropriate safety precautions.

BRICK VENEER ON EXTERIOR WALLS

Brick veneer is nothing more than a single-wythe wall laid with a ½- to 1-inch wide air space between the veneer and the house sheathing or siding. A brick veneer over the frame walls of a home helps insulate it and gives an aesthetically pleasing exterior. The veneer also may be applied over concrete block walls.

Design Alternatives

Although the veneer can extend all the way up the walls to the roof, another veneering style consists of running the brick up to the level of the eaves. It is then finished off at the sides with vertical wooden siding. This combines the appeal of brick with the warmth of wood.

There are three ways to finish off the second veneering style. The first method caps the brick section with a row of single stretchers covered with flashing; then the siding is brought down over the flashing. The second method caps the wall with a row of headers cut short and laid at a downward angle. Again, the siding is brought down over the upper edges of the headers. The third system uses a special brick molding to create an even, smooth transition between the veneer and the siding.

Veneering for New Construction

Brick veneer must be supported properly on the house foundation. This is done by creating an offset foundation, which produces a supporting ledge 3 to 3½ inches wide. To allow for the extra thickness that the veneer adds to the exterior wall, order window and door frames that are made especially for use with brick veneer walls.

The sheathing required over a new construction is usually governed by local codes. The usual material required is ⅝ or ¾ inch Exterior plywood. In areas in which codes don't cover sheathing requirements, some builders use insulation board, but you will be better off using plywood. Insulation board may help keep the house warm, but it lacks the lateral strength important in a house sheathing. Over the sheathing, staple a layer of 15 pound felt. You then can begin veneering.

Wooden window trim was added to brick veneer with masonry anchors.

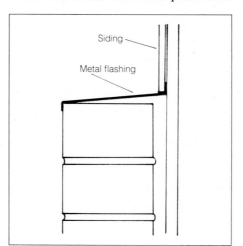

You can finish off a brick veneer exterior with siding that reaches from the eaves to the roof. Install a metal flashing first.

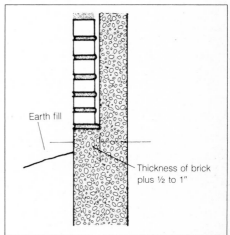

For support in new construction, create an offset foundation equal to the thickness of the brick plus the air space.

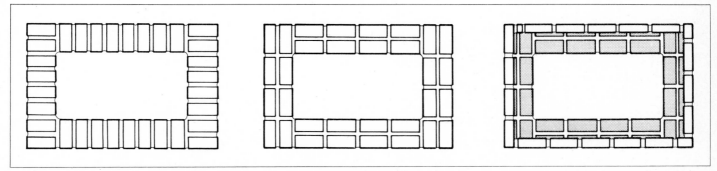

These drawings illustrate the three types of firepit courses. On the left is the layout for courses 1, 3 and 5. The middle drawing shows the headers of courses 2 and 4; these strengthen the structure. On the right is course 6, in which the bricks are set on edge.

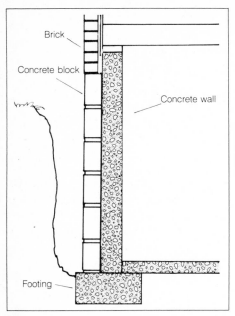

To veneer an existing house, first you must dig down to the footing and build up a concrete block support to the level of the brick.

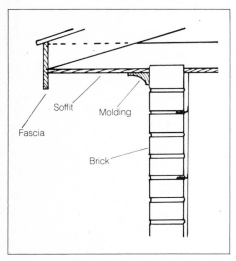

Check to see if the brick fits between the siding and the roof fascia. Cut away the soffit; extend the veneer. Finish with a molding.

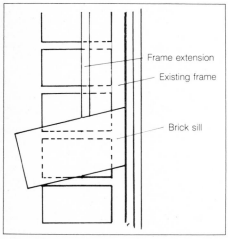

Often the window or door framing isn't wide enough to accommodate veneer. If so, attach a frame extension with masonry anchors.

Veneering for Old Construction

There are several alternatives for constructing foundation support for brick veneer applied over an existing structure. The best method is to dig down to the footing and lay up a concrete block shelf to the foundation height (or just below it). Bond the block to the old foundation with special masonry bonding materials such as Weld-Crete. The brick veneer wall is then laid on this supporting shelf.

Fitting brick to soffit and fascia allowances. At the roof line, a soffit extends outward and boxes in the ends of the rafters. The fascia encloses the space between the soffit and the roof.

If you plan to extend the veneer all the way to the roof, check to be sure that the brick will fit behind the fascia. In most instances, the eaves project far enough to allow plenty of space for the veneer. If this is the situation, first remove the existing soffit. Lay the brick up to just above the edge of the soffit, cut the soffit to fit, and re-install. Use wood molding to close the joint between soffit and veneer.

If, on the other hand, the fascia is too close to the wall to allow room for the brick, you won't be able to use the veneer without a lot of carpentry work.

Working around doors and windows. Brick veneer thickens the exterior wall of an existing home. As a result, all door and window frames must be widened. In some cases, you can build them out by nailing wood strips to them. However,

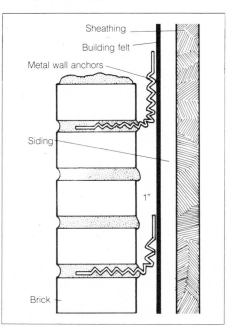

As you lay the bricks, install one end of a metal wall anchor into the mortar bed between courses; nail the other end to the framing.

this is not possible with some types of framework. In these cases you will have to replace the old frames with new ones. Cut all window sills flush with the window casings. These will be replaced after the veneering is completed.

Sheathing. For an existing structure, the sheathing itself needs no preparation or felt application. The veneer will be erected in front of the existing siding.

Laying the Veneer

The bricklaying procedures for veneering are the same as those discussed earlier. Build up corner leads, fill in, and continue the process until the veneer is as high as you desire. Leave a ½ to 1 inch space between the wall and the veneer. This air space serves for ventilation and moisture control. Don't let any mortar drop behind the bricks or protrude behind them. Use a piece of wood about the thickness of the air space to scrape away the mortar that squeezes out as you seat the bricks.

Installing a moisture barrier. A moisture barrier installed in the mortar joint between the second and third course of bricks prevents ground moisture from seeping up and saturating the mortar lines. Although the barrier is not required, it is recommended, especially in areas of the country subject to high levels of ground moisture.

The barrier is a sheet of 4 or 6 mil polyethylene cut to the width of the course. Spread a thin layer of mortar on the bricks. Lay the sheet on top of the mortar. The front edge of the sheet should fall slightly back from the front edge of the bricks so that the sheet will not be exposed when the joints are tooled. Lap cut edges by about 4 inches. Then place a layer of mortar over the sheet and seat the next course.

Adding weep holes. Weep holes must be placed in the lower brick courses. The holes provide an exit for any moisture that may accumulate between the two walls. In vertical mortar joints set in special ⅜-inch metal tubes that are long enough to reach from the outside of the veneer to the air space. Space them 2 to 3 feet apart. The metal tubes should angle downwards toward the outside of the wall. Then lay the mortar and the next course.

Using wall ties. To hold the veneer in place (and to keep it from collapsing into the yard), the structure is secured to the wooden frame wall with metal wall ties placed on 3-foot centers in every fourth course. One end of the tie is nailed in place with ring shank nails; the other is laid on the mortar bed. The next mortar application and brick course holds the tie in place. Offset the ties from one course to the next so that they do not align vertically. The ties give the veneer overall support.

Finishing window and door openings.

Window sills. When you come to a window, you can choose from at least two finishing methods for the sill. The most common treatment is to lay a series of rowlock headers, which will form a brick sill. Set the headers at about a 20 to 30 degree angle to maintain proper drainage. The sill should extend at least one header's width on either side of the window opening. The mortar will hold the bricks in position so they won't slide into the yard.

Door and window lintels. Work up the wall space on either side of the window or door until you reach the top of the opening. Throw a mortar line over the courses; then install a piece of angle iron lintel that is long enough to span the opening and extend from 6 to 8 inches beyond either side. Cover the lintel with mortar and lay the course of bricks above the lintel. Then continue working up the wall.

VENEERING AN INTERIOR

Brick can also be used to veneer an inside wall and to create an unusual and beautiful decor.

Weight Problems

The main problem with using real bricks as an interior veneer is their weight. As with exterior veneering, the brick wall must be supported directly by the house footing or by a special shelf support built up from the footing. The necessary support system can be included during the forming of the foundation in a new construction. This is true for both outer walls and inner walls.

However, the problem becomes much more complicated in an existing structure. Inner walls will most surely not have the footing support necessary. The only way to supply it is to tear out the old basement floor and to add the footing and a new floor before you install the veneer. The expense of such a project is prohibitive.

As a result, the best way to have a brick surface on a inner wall is to use one of the synthetic brick materials such as Wonder-Brix or Z-Brick, or to use partial bricks (⅓ the usual thickness).

Installation Steps

Veneering a load-bearing interior wall in a house over a slab or crawl space. If your home is built on a slab or over a crawl space, loadbearing walls are integral with the footings below the house. If the walls are masonry over a slab or crawl space, such as concrete block, use special bonding materials such as Weld-Crete to bond the veneer directly to the masonry wall as you mortar the brick in place.

Avoiding shifting in houses with basements. If, on the other hand, your house is built upon a basement, the basement floor will not be integral with the footing beneath, for the floor will have been poured after the footing was cured. As a result, the wall and the floor will shift or settle independently. In order to prevent the veneer from cracking away from the wall because of the shifting, set the veneer wall away from the existing wall and anchor it with wall anchors. Embed the ends in mortar joints, just as for exterior veneering.

An interior brick veneer wall may also be spaced away from the existing wall to provide for an insulation space. To construct the space, use special wall anchors, which are available at any brickyard. Install styrofoam insulation between the old wall and the new veneer. Then start laying the brick in the desired pattern.

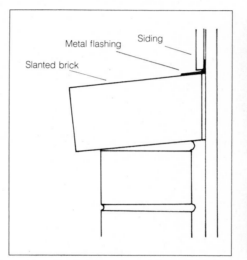

Form window sills by slanting rowlock headers for drainage. Flashing is required between the frame and the sill.

Synthetic interior brick veneer has the appearance and texture of real brick. The design can be as simple or complex as desired.

Although many people like brick interior walls, their weight requires a great deal of structural work. Instead, most homeowners choose synthetic brick such as Z-brick.

Stone comes in a variety of sizes and finishes, so it fits in any setting from formal to rustic. Walls are dry-laid or set in mortar; walks can also be cut into the soil. Your project will last for a very long time, for most stones are weather-resistant and durable.

4 WORKING WITH STONE MASONRY

Probably no other type of manual labor gives as much satisfaction as building something of stone. There is a sense of immortality in creating a stone wall or building. And rightly so; there are many, many centuries old stone buildings that are not only standing today, but just as sturdy and beautiful as they were a hundred years or more ago. Almost any type of stonework you do around your home will add to its value as well as to the beauty of your home.

Stone can be used for many different projects. It blends with almost any decor, from traditional to formal to rustic landscaping. Stone can be used to create a new patio, a garden walk, a retaining wall, or flower planters. Stonework can be used to turn a sloping backyard into a multi-leveled living area that contains a series of spaces for outdoor activities. If you're really ambitious, stonework can create the exterior walls for an entire house.

Stonework is not easy. In fact, it's back-breaking work, but work that can be accomplished by most do-it-yourselfers if they pay attention to some age-old rules

and don't try to lift too much or do too much in one day's time. Fortunately, stonework adapts well to these conditions. That's one of the real advantages of working with stone, especially for the do-it-yourselfer who may only have a couple of hours each day to spare. You can quit work almost any time you want and can continue the next day without problems. In fact, some jobs require these time intervals to insure you don't apply too much weight before the mortar sets up.

The techniques of stonework are not hard to learn, and can be acquired in a few hours. However, constructing a safe, good-looking project requires a slow, careful approach.

TYPES OF STONE
There are many different kinds of stone. The type you use depends on the project, as well as on the types of stone available in your area. Because of their great weight, it is impractical to ship stones a great distance. Those types most often chosen for use in construction projects are granite, limestone, marble, slate, flag-

stone, sandstone, gneiss and tap rock. The stones come either as quarried stone or fieldstone.

Quarried Stone
Quarried stone, cut and shaped, is used to construct more formal projects. It is cut and slabbed at the quarry, but the face of the stone is left natural. For instance, a formal patio usually is constructed of slate or flagstone, which are quarried materials.

Fieldstone
On the other hand, a rock retaining wall for an informal garden often would be constructed of fieldstone, or stones picked up from a field or dry creek bottom.

Ashlar
Another type of stonework uses ashlar, which consists of individually cut and shaped stone laid in a formal pattern. The face of ashlar is cut or faceted in a decorative manner. This is the type of faceted stone work seen most often in old commercial buildings such as college buildings and churches, as well as some older, more expensive homes.

FINDING OR BUYING THE STONES
Probably most folks will have to purchase the stone for their projects. Again, the choice of stone may depend to a great extent on the availability of the various types in your particular area. Since most purchased stone comes from quarries and natural stoneyards, visit these establishments even before you begin designing your project. Examine what they have on hand. With this knowledge you can design the project to suit the particular types of stone available.

Relative Costs
The most expensive stone naturally is cut stone. If you wish a carefully fitted,

A stone wall, dry-laid or set in mortar, provides a long-lasting, beautiful addition to your home. You can choose specially cut stone, such as flagstone, or weathered fieldstone.

formal look, this is the stone you will need. Uniformity in size and color cost even more. In most instances the quarry will have the stones graded according to color and uniformity of shape. On the other hand, rubble stone, which is the debris left from blasting and cutting the cut stone, is much more economical.

Buying the Right Amount

To figure the amount of stone you will need, figure the cubic volume of the project in feet by multiplying the length times the width, times the height. Stone is sold by the cubic yard. After determining the cubic feet you have in the project, divide the number of cubic feet in the wall by 27 to determine the cubic yards of stone needed. If you are buying selected cut stone, use this cubic volume, plus about 10 percent for breakage and waste. If, on the other hand, you are buying rubble stone, which is usually merely dumped in the back of a truck for delivery, you will need at least 25 percent extra.

Another factor is whether you plan to construct the project using a dry-laid stone, or a mortar-and-stone technique. Dry-laid stone projects will require better joint fits, since there is no mortar to help bind the stones together. We will discuss each technique later on.

Bargain Sources

You may be able to scrounge stone for your stonework, especially the more economical rubblestone and fieldstone materials. In some cases, you may get it for a much cheaper price than buying it retail at a stoneyard. In fact, sometimes you can probably get it for the cost of hauling; check first at road and building construction sites. In many instances, rock that must be removed for a building project has to be trucked away by the contractor, and you can quite often get the stone for free, if you have the equipment to take it. Another excellent spot for rubblestone is around demolition sites. Many older homes utilized rubblestone, cut stone and fieldstone foundations and you can quite often get these materials merely for the hauling. In most cases there will be some mortar adhering to the stones, but usually it is easy to scrub the mortar off. If necessary, use a brick chisel. Wear gloves and goggles.

Local farmers are another excellent source for stones in some parts of the country. Quite often, they will have outcroppings of stones or even piles of stones picked up off their fields. They may sell quite gladly, or you might offer to pick up the stones and cart them off their fields for free.

Selecting the Best Stones

When selecting natural stones, or any stones for that matter, try to pick only those that have flat, square sides. It's almost impossible to build anything with round "cannonball" shaped stones, although they can be inserted in mortared walls for a change of design if they are interesting enough in texture and color.

Naturally, the project will go faster if you use large stones. However, be careful that you don't pick stones that not only are so large they dominate the project and look out of place, but that are also too big to move very easily. The weight of a stone will fool you. Be sure you don't acquire stones that you can't easily handle

Here field stones are arranged randomly to serve as a buffer against erosion.

Although they are very long-lasting, cobblestones create a highly uneven surface.

A formal setting requires a finished surface such as flagstone. Here, specially shaped lannon stone steps join two patio levels.

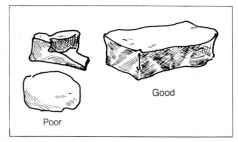

Good

Poor

For a long-lived project, select only those stones with flat sides and edges.

and get into place. In most cases, stones of 40 or 50 pounds are not only tiring for most folks to lift, but they also make it much harder to construct the project properly. Stones that weight 15 to 25 pounds at the most usually provide the most satisfying job in terms of design, as well as in ease of construction.

When selecting natural stone for fieldstone projects, you will need at least 50 percent more than the total cubic volume of the project because of the wastage in stones that just won't fit. In fact, the more stones you can have on hand, the easier the job, because you can choose the stones you need from a wider selection. You also should have a good variety of sizes and shapes when doing natural fieldstone projects. This provides the best design and construction; the small stones fill in around the larger stones.

Transporting the Stones
It doesn't take many stones to add up to a ton. Carrying stones in the back of your car is not only a great way to break down its springs, but your back as well when you try to lift them out of the trunk. The best choice is a small rented trailer or a pick-up truck. But again, the weight of the stones will fool you. Be careful for the first load to see how much you should attempt to haul at one time. Always be sure the truck's tires are properly inflated.

Sorting the Stones
Once you have a huge pile of stones in your back yard, separate them into piles. Sort out the best building stones, which are the larger tie stones used for walls. Tie stones are those large enough to lap over two stones; they should have a straight edge and sides. Then find other stones that have straight edges and sides for corner stones for walls. Then lay each of the stones out separately and flat on the ground so you can immediately survey the stone pile to find the exact stone size and shape you need. Leave about 4 to 6 feet of space between the stone pile and the proposed wall or patio, so you have room to walk through and to work properly.

TOOLS NEEDED
Stonework is one of the few crafts that requires little more than a strong back. In some instances, you may have to put down a concrete footing to hold the stone-

work, in which case you will need concrete working tools. However, for working with dry-laid stone you will need nothing more than a tape measure, a sharp-bladed shovel, a brick or stone mason's hammer and a chisel and a wheelbarrow. A large pry bar helps move larger rocks around. Wear a pair of heavy-duty leather gloves, and use safety glasses when you split stones.

Naturally, for mortared stone work you need tools for making and applying mortar, just as for concrete block or brick work. You will also need a carpenter's level, a string line, and a string level.

STONEWORK TECHNIQUES
As mentioned earlier, stones may be laid dry (without mortar) or laid with mortar. We will discuss the dry laying first because it's the easiest method.

Dry Laying a Garden Walk
There are two basic dry-laying construction systems. The first calls for cutting away the turf and dropping the stones individually in place, leaving the turf between the stones as part of the design. The second method involves laying the stones in a bed of sand, then filling in the joints between with sand.

The best method of illustration is to discuss specific projects, so the first project we will show is a garden walk. This is the easiest undertaking, yet one that can add a great deal of beauty and practicality to a backyard or garden with little expense and effort. The walkway can be laid in a formal pattern using cut flagstones or a more informal pattern of fieldstone, as shown.

Choosing the stones. The first step is to choose the stones you will use for this

Use dry-laid stone walls to outline a driveway or form retaining walls in a rustic or country setting. Stone that you gather in your locality adds uniqueness to your project.

Stone walks can be set in sand or mortar; however, they often are just laid into the ground and surrounded with sod. This installation requires little preparation or maintenance.

Set out a stake-and-string outline of the walk. The outline must be wide enough to accommodate two stones from front to back.

The initial corner stone should be wide, flat and have clean, straight faces. Set it down and cut around it with a trowel.

Use a shovel to cut away the sod. Save the sod for later use. Excavate enough dirt so the top of the stone is at ground level.

Replace the stones. They must sit securely. If they rock, cut away the dirt beneath them until they are steady.

project. Naturally, they should be as flat as possible. So they won't crack or break, the stones used for this type of project must be at least 2 inches thick. You may wish to use cut stones such as flagstone or carefully selected flat fieldstones.

Outlining the walk. Lay out the outline of the sides of the walk. This can be curved, straight, or angled. Place small stakes and connect strings to indicate the sides of the walk on the ground. It is a good idea to mow the grass down so it will be easier to work in the area. In most instances, the walk should be no less than 2 feet and no more than 3 feet wide.

Setting the stones in turf. If you are laying the stones individually in place in the turf, then merely lay one of the stones in place at one end and against the string line. Cut around it down below the sod, using a sharp bladed shovel. Keep this sod nearby; you may need some of it later on for filling in around the stones.

Lift up the stone, set it aside, and dig out the area where the stone will be placed. Place the stone back in position and check to make sure that it is fairly level and that it doesn't rock back and forth. If it does, remove the stone and dig out enough dirt to allow the stone to set level and solid. The stone should end up about 1½ inches above ground level.

When you have this stone set in place to your satisfaction, position the second stone in the same manner and place it solidly in position. Leave a bit of sod between the two if possible, but if not you can tamp dirt back in place between the stones later and then reseed the lawn.

Before replacing dirt in a deep hole, add a layer of sand.

After the last stone has been placed, remove the stakes and strings and place sod around any areas that need it. You will also probably have to place a little fill soil around each of the stones. This should be left somewhat high, as it will settle with time. You may also wish to reseed the area with grass seed, if necessary.

Laying a Dry-Laid Patio

A patio can be constructed in the very same manner, and one that has an irregular or free-form shape will really look great when constructed of fieldstone. However, a dry-laid patio does have a couple of disadvantages. The first is that it is hard to keep clean. The second is that it won't provide a very good play surface for small children.

When laying an area as large as a patio, try to vary the sizes of the stones to give a definite but interesting pattern. In most projects of natural fieldstone, you won't wish to cut the stones. You will concentrate instead on finding the right shape and then just insert it in place. However, in the case of the more formal approach of cut flagstones, you may need to cut the stones.

How to Cut Stone

Cutting the stones isn't particularly hard, but it does take practice. Plan on wasting several pieces before you learn the process.

Tools. You will need a stone mason's chisel and a heavy, short-handled sledge, as well as a pair of heavy-duty leather gloves and a pair of goggles or a safety face shield.

Scribing the cut. Position the stone on a solid spot on the ground. Mark a line with a piece of chalk where you wish to make the cut. Then hold the chisel in place on the line and lightly tap it with the hammer. As you tap, move the chisel along to score the marked line. Turn the stone over and do the same thing on the other side.

Tapping and breaking the stones. In most instances, the stone will break along the second scored line as you tap it. (Some stones such as flint won't break at all, which is why you shouldn't use them.) If the stone doesn't break, turn it back over and continue tapping on the

If you must cut a stone, use a brick hammer and chisel. Score the stone gently.

Tap one side; then the other. Usually the stone will break as you desire.

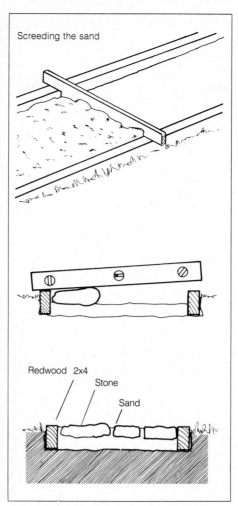

Screeding the sand

Redwood 2x4
Stone
Sand

To set stones in sand, excavate deep enough to allow for the stone plus the sand. Level the sand; then create as level a walking surface as you can. Fill the joints with more sand.

first side, deepening the groove until the stone does break.

In some cases, the stone just won't break. In other instances the stone may break, but not exactly where you wanted it to. In the latter case, don't worry too much; you can always use the smaller stones to fill in around the larger ones.

The trick when tapping is to not hit the chisel too hard with the hammer; just hit it hard enough to slightly score the stone. This takes practice, but once you get the hang of it you will be surprised at how easy it is.

Dry Laying a Patio or Walk on a Bed of Sand

The second method of laying a walk or patio with the dry technique is to lay the stones on a bed of sand. This often provides a smoother, flatter, more even surface; however, it takes more work.

Tools. You will need a shovel, raking board, broom, and carpenter's level.

Outlining with stakes and string. For either a walk or a patio, the first step is to mark the outline of the project using stakes and string.

Excavating. Use a shovel to remove all sod from the area. You will need to dig down below the ground level to a depth of 2 inches plus the thickness of the stone to allow for a layer of sand to be placed under the stones. Keep the sod aside because you will need it to fill in around the edges of the project and up against the rocks.

Try to cut the borders of the project as neatly as possible. One excellent way to create neat borders, as well as to add an unusual look, is to place redwood 2x4s as guide strips for the edging for the borders. These must be held in place with concealed stakes driven in the ground and nailed to the posts. (See Chapter Three.) These stakes are then covered over with sand. In most instances the 2x4s will provide just about the right depth for the 2-inch layer

of sand and a 2-inch-thick stone surface, allowing the surface of the walk or patio to protrude above ground level about ½ inch.

Dig down to the correct depth and level the bottom so it is as smooth as possible. Remove any large roots or gravel.

Adding the sand. Place a 2-inch layer of sand in the bottom. Rake it flat and smooth. A raking board can be made as shown to help even out the sand and make sure it doesn't have any high or low spots. Shape the sand so it is higher in the center than at the edges to help drain water away from the walk. The pitch should be very slight—about ⅛ inch per foot. After you have leveled out the sand with the board and rake, sprinkle the sand bed with water to pack it and provide a more solid surface.

Laying the stones. Start placing the stones, working from one corner and against one string line. Space the stones with about 1 inch spacing between them. Just as before, make sure they are solidly placed and won't wobble on a high area. If they do, remove them and dig away a bit of sand until the rocks are flat and evenly placed. Try to keep them placed as level as possible, using a long carpenter's level frequently to check their placement. The level can't be exact because of the nature of the stones, but you still should do the best you can.

Filling in the joints. Once all the stones have been positioned, sprinkle sand in between the joints. Fill all the joints well. Dampen the joints lightly. Wait a while and then sweep in more sand. Finally, lightly sweep excess sand from the surface. Use the sod you set aside to fill in all edges until they are as smooth and even as possible. The soil should stand a little higher than the stones at this time, to allow for settling.

Mortaring the joints. You can place mortar in a sand-bed patio if you wish, but the mortar joints will crack and won't appear as neat as sand-filled joints. If you do decide to mortar the joints, make up a dry mix of about 1 part cement and 4 parts sand. Use this instead of the sand. Place the dry mortar-sand mix in and around the stones. After making sure you have all joints packed with the dry mortar, use a garden hose set on fine spray to dampen the mortar. Gently soak the joints, but do not flush any of the mortar away with the pressure of the water.

Dry-Laying A Stone Wall

Dry-laid stone walls immediately bring to mind the rural countryside of the New England states or the Ozark mountains, with their miles and miles of stone fences and walls. Not only are these walls inexpensive (especially if the stone if free), but the walls can last for many years. Even more importantly, however, building a dry-laid stone wall is very easy to do, even for the amateur. It calls for no great amount of tools or expertise. The requirements are practice, an eye for picking the right stones, patience and a strong back.

Dry laying a retaining wall. Because there is plenty of openness in a dry laid wall, it makes a good low retaining wall. It prevents water pressure from building up behind the wall as can sometimes happen with a mortared wall. Naturally, a dry-laid wall is more rustic in appearance than a mortared wall and it can fit in quite easily with almost any garden decor. In fact, a combination of low dry-laid retaining walls and mortared garden walls can create a beautiful landscape.

Choosing suitable type of stone. In practically all instances, the stones used for this type of construction have traditionally been fieldstones. Ashlar style or cut stones could also be used, which would result in a more formal appearance. However, this would usually cost a great deal for something as rustic in appearance as a dry-laid wall.

Dimensions and guidelines for designing the wall. Naturally, as with any project, you must first plan or design the wall. A dry-laid wall can be laid out as a straight wall, or with corners, or curving—or almost any combination of these you choose. The main consideration in designing the wall is that its width must be in correct proportion to its height. The goal is to avoid building a wall that is top-heavy and thus dangerous. A general mason's rule of thumb is that a wall up to 3 feet in height must have a minimum width of 2 feet. For each additional 6 inches of height the wall width must be increased 4 inches. In most instances, low- or medium-height walls are constructed with plumb faces. However, high walls are usually constructed with a taper to the top; the top generally is about one fifth narrower than the width of the wall base. This thickness is equal to at least two stones.

Walls above 3 feet in height should have a footing that extends below frost line. Low walls that are not higher than 3 feet are usually laid without a foundation or footing and can be laid right on the grass. For the best job, however, remove the grass and turf to create a solid, smooth, flat surface upon which the first stones can rest. Most good masons will lay the bottom course below ground level.

Excavating for the wall. After deciding how high, wide and long you wish the wall to be, temporarily place wooden stakes and a cord to outline both sides of the wall. Use a good flat bottom shovel to remove the sod in the area of the wall. Then dig for the foundation, to as deep as code and weather requirements indicate.

Staking out the wall. After the general site preparation, then drive the stakes at each corner of the wall. Drive two stakes at the lowest end of the wall position.

Tie a strong mason's cord to the stakes to outline the wall. The string should be positioned about 3 inches higher than the proposed first course. With the cord in position, drive a row of stakes about 4 feet apart along the outline, allowing the cord to just touch the inside of these stakes. The cord can be tied to these stakes with a bit of fine string to insure that the string stays level and does not balloon out with the wind.

Stone selection. Dry-laid walls do require more careful stone selection than do mortared walls because you can depend on the mortar to lock the stones firmly in place. With a dry-laid wall the only thing holding the stone in place is its weight, plus the weight of the stones above it. Select stones that are as flat as possible. Make sure there are at least three flat sides, the top and bottom and one side to be used as the front. It's best if you have more than three flat sides, and six is ideal. In any event, avoid round boulders. They cause nothing but trouble in a dry-laid wall, except when used as fill stones inside openings left by the larger stones.

For the first course, choose the largest, most irregular stones you have, especially if the first course is to be below ground level.

Laying the first course. Starting with a large stone, place the flattest surface up, and the next-to-flattest surface facing out toward the string, forming the front face of the wall. You may have to dig out the ground to allow the stone to sit as flat as

possible without rocking.

The bottom layer of stones can lean inwards slightly toward the center of the wall. This will help create wall sides that are forced inwards rather than out, stabilizing the wall. If the wall butts up against a house or other similar surface, the stone face touching this area should also be as flat as possible. Lay the stones with their grain running the same way as the stones would be when found naturally.

The stone wall is actually two stones thick with fill in between. Lay the second stone behind the first, to create the back face of the wall.

Then continue laying the front and back faces of the bottom course in this manner until you reach the end of the wall. Close off the open end with three large stones to create a U shape. Fill in between the larger stones with smaller backing stones. Use a carpenter's level to keep the wall as level as possible.

Adding the second and remaining courses. With all spaces filled, you're ready for the next or second course. This is when the main rule of building a stone wall comes in: always place one stone above two, or two stones above one. This staggered effect, much like that used in brickwork, ties the wall together, eliminating vertical joints that can pull apart.

Before starting the next course, raise the string lines up about 3 inches higher than the next proposed course. The second course is laid in exactly the same manner as the first. Again, choose large stones to fit over those below them. Construct the front and back faces of the wall, filling in the center area with the smaller backer stones. Use a carpenter's level to frequently check the wall to insure that it is going up plumb.

If a stone rocks on a point or a sharp corner, you can sometimes knock off the corner to allow it to sit down more squarely. In some cases, small wedge-shaped stones can be placed in position to help hold in position those stones that are prone to rock. These small wedges should be placed on the inside of the wall and with their pointed ends facing inwards so the wedges won't be forced out of place. About every 4 to 6 horizontal feet you should install tie (also called ''bond'') stones. These are large flat stones that reach entirely across and through the wall, from the front to the back face, to tie it together.

Dry-laid stone walls can substitute for fencing or serve as low terrace walls.

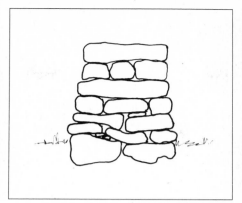

A dry-laid wall's stability depends upon the proper ratio between the width and height.

Excavate for the starting course. Set stones so they lean inward not outward.

Lay the front and back stones. Use rubble stones to fill in any open spaces.

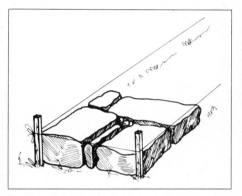

Position the stones so that you expose their most attractive faces.

Align the stones in each course with the string line to assure a level course.

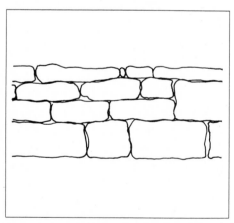

As you work upward on the wall, continue to overlap the stones in successive coursess.

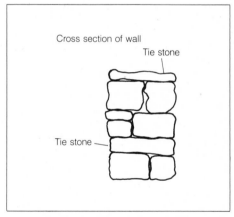

Cross section of wall

Tie stone

Tie stone

Every 3 or 4 ft., lay a tie or bond stone from the front to the back.

You need several good tie stones to finish off the corners or ends of the wall.

The top of the wall is finished off with large flat stones called cap stones.

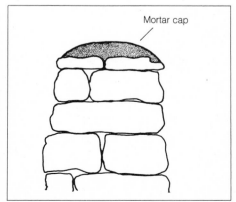

Mortar cap

Some people prefer to finish with a cap of mortar to add to the life of the wall.

Stone walls with this unusual top course can be seen in certain areas of the country.

Finishing the ends and corners. The hardest part of building a wall is finishing out the ends or corners. Save all the stones that have the squarest sides and corners for use in these areas. You also will have to use several large tie stones to bond the sides of the wall together and to form the end stones. If the wall turns a corner, the tie stones also will be needed to link the two meeting walls together. This work must be done slowly and carefully, keeping the entire wall well-tied together, not only for good appearance but for a safe, soundly constructed wall.

Topping off the wall. The top of the wall can be finished out in several ways. Usually the flattest, best-appearing stones are used to finish out the top of the wall. These "skimmers," as they are known, are often easily knocked off low walls by children and pets. One alternative is to place a 2-inch-thick layer of mortar over the top of the wall to help hold the top stones in place. This also gives a much stronger wall.

For a retaining wall, you also can bring some soil over the back edge to help hold the top stones more solidly in place.

Building Dry-Laid Steps

You can create steps in the same manner as a wall. This involves building a series of low walls, topping them off with large flat "veneer" stones. Deposit dry mortar in between the top stones. Then hose it down to dampen it and to help prevent dirt and debris from getting in between the stones.

Lay stone steps just as stone walks and walls. Some areas require a gravel base.

Constructing Mortared Stone Walls

Building a mortared stone wall is more work than constructing a dry-laid stone wall. The work progresses more slowly, but a finished wall will usually last longer and looks more formal. Of course, mortaring is required when building a fireplace wall or a small house.

A mortared wall can also be utilized when you don't have a wide selection of stones. The surface can be given a great deal of variance in appearance by using a variety of stones, as well as different colors of mortar. And, even though mortar will bond the stones, you should take the same care when choosing the proper stones for the wall.

Other than these differences, a mortared stone wall is similar in construction to a dry-laid stone wall. The major difference is that a mortared stone wall is permanent, and the only way to remove it or change it is with a big sledgehammer. Therefore, be quite sure you have properly designed and positioned it before you build it.

Foundation support. Mortared stone walls are inflexible; you must build a footing of concrete beneath it, just as for building a brick or block foundation or wall. For low walls, the footing can be dug to the width of the wall and poured of concrete. For higher walls, you will probably wish to make the footing about 4 to 6 inches wider than the wall base. The top of the footing surface should be about 2 to 3 inches below the ground level (or below frost level—check local codes) for a good-looking wall. If done in this manner, the soil can be graded back up to the

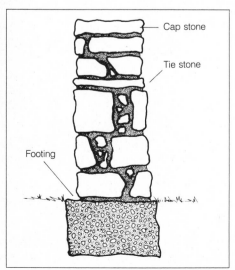

A mortared stone wall must have a footing. Check local codes for the depth required.

wall so it appears that the wall grows up out of the ground. This gives a nice, neat start to the wall.

Tools. The tools needed for creating a mortared stone wall are the same as are used for brickwork.

Preparation. Once the wall has been designed and laid out and footing dug and poured, let the footing set for at least a couple of days. As for dry-laid walls, establish the outside and inside proposed wall lines, using the cord guides and stakes. Dig to the necessary depth and width, and compact the soil.

Mixing the mortar. Mix up a batch of mortar, in the same manner as for brick or concrete block. Use a mortar mix of one part Portland cement to about four parts sand, plus a little water. Add a little bit of lime to make the batch a bit stickier and to help prevent stains. If you desire a colored mortar, you can combine a purchased mortar color with the mix. Don't mix up too much mortar at a time.

Picking out the stones. Probably one of the most important considerations in an attractive stone wall is use of a wide variety of different stone shapes and colors. Do not place too many stones all of one size in one area. The best bet for most folks is to try to select stones that fit a particular place, much in the same manner as fitting together a jigsaw puzzle. This works better than trying to cut the stones to fit.

Some people are better at fitting stones than others. My wife is an expert at selecting stones. I can look at a pile of stones for an hour and never come up with the one I need, but seemingly with one glance my wife can find just the right stone. Sometimes she just turns the stone I'm holding to the right angle position so it seems to fit perfectly. You must select

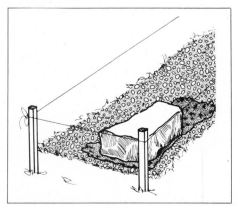

After footing cures, stake out the walk. Place the stones below ground level.

the stones carefully, tilting and turning stones, until they fit together well.

Laying the first course. It is a good idea to dry-fit the first course in a trial run. Then lay out the stones so you can just pick up the one you need as you come to its spot in the wall. This avoids the problem of mortar setting up before the stones are laid.

Starting at one corner and end of the wall footing, spread a 2- to 3-foot-long layer of mortar, about 2 inches thick, over the entire wall width. Choosing the larg-est rocks you have, position them down in the mortar. Put the broadest face downward. (Sometimes a broad stone can't be used as a base. Instead, it is tilted and used as a "veneer" stone. These often must be propped up in place with wooden sticks until the mortar around them dries and the next course is laid in place.) Lay all stones in lightly; don't drop them in place or you will knock all the mortar out from under them. If they rock slightly, place small wedge-shaped stones under them working from behind. As with the dry-laid wall, you must create two sides—a front and a back—to the wall. Then fill in with rubble or with small stones.

As you lay each stone in place, tap it slightly to knock out any air bubbles that may be in the mortar. Pack mortar in and around the stones from the face or front side (use a small trowel). Be careful not to get any mortar on the stone faces. If mortar oozes out, catch it with your trowel and dump it on top of the stone or in the center rubble area. Do not allow a

Make the mortar mix slightly thicker than that required for a brick installation.

Although the stones are heavy, carefully position them over the mortar bed.

Create the back side of the wall. Leave space for mortar between the stones.

Flip more mortar down around and between the stones to get a solid seal.

Drop in small fill or rubble stones to fill cavities between back and front.

Build up corner leads as for a brick wall. This technique insures a strong wall.

Since the mortar holds the stones in place, some can be placed on end.

Force the mortar into the joint between stones with a small pointing trowel.

Fit stones carefully. If you plan ahead, you shouldn't have to cut many of them.

lot of mortar to collect below the wall; pick it up as you go.

Do not try to lay too large a run of mortar at a time on the first course, or the mortar may set up before you can get the stone established properly. Mortar usually sets up in about 30 minutes. As with any other masonry project, the first or bottom course is very important, so position it with care.

Tips for working with mortar. The mortar will have to be forced in and around the stones as you go. The best method I have found is to sort of fling it in place with a sideways sweep of the trowel. You don't have to create a solid wall, so don't force the mortar in around the rocks; this will only cause them to slide out of position. Just throw it in place, and it will settle in to any openings. Naturally, since the mortar takes up some of the space, almost any rubble stone can be used for the backing.

Building corner leads. It's a good idea to build up one corner, and then to go to the opposite corner and build it up. Then build in between the two corners to fill in the rest of the wall. There are two advantages to this. First, you create a guide for the remainder of the wall once the two corners are finished; secondly, you make sure you use the best tie stones for the ends or corners.

Laying the remaining courses. After the first course has been laid, move the string lines up for the second course. Position them so they will be about 3 inches higher than the desired top of the second course. You can measure down from the string to check the alignment of the tops of the stones.

Lay a row of mortar about 4 or 5 feet long and 2 inches thick, covering the entire width of the wall. Then place the second course of stones, using the same stone mason's rule as for a dry-laid wall:

one stones goes over two, two stones go over one. You should never have a vertical joint of masonry. The stones should overlap each other to provide a strong, good-looking wall. Build the front and back sides to the wall and fill in between with rubble and mortar. About every 3 or 4 horizontal feet place tie stones to extend across the entire width of the wall. This bonds the two rows of stone. The practice is similar to that of a rowlock header in a brick wall.

Don't try to lay more than a couple of feet a day, as the mortar will not hold more weight than that and the wall may simply slide down onto the ground.

In most instances you will find that creating a mortared stone wall requires that you get your hands in the mortar, because quite often you will have to force mortar back under the edges of stones. This is especially true if some stones have rounded or sloping surfaces. In any case, wear gloves and keep the mortar between all the stones on each face of the wall.

Finishing and Jointing the Mortared Wall

Finishing the wall top course can be done in several ways. The top of the wall can be given a layer of cap mortar, as for the dry-laid wall. The wall top could merely be finished off with mortar between the joints, as on the wall faces. A capping or row of capping stones also can be added.

Creating different types of joints. The mortar joints on the wall can also be finished in several different ways. On a strictly utilitarian wall, the joints can merely be left as is; however, in most instances you will want to strike out excess mortar to create a sculptured look, emphasizing the texture of the stones.

Lay a bed of mortar for the second course. This should be about 2 in. thick.

As with a dry-laid wall, always place one stone over two and two over one.

Set stones carefully so that you don't force all the mortar from the joints below.

Clean away excess mortar as you go along; it will be difficult to remove later.

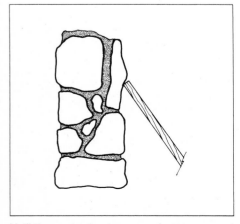

Until the mortar hardens, wood props support large, flat "veneer" stones in a wall.

This means you will remove excess mortar from the joints so they are from ½ inch to 1½ inches deep, depending on the size and shape of stones. This joint is best done using an old ⅜x6 inch round-headed bolt.

The most important factor in this particular step is timing. The mortar should be set up enough that it just barely takes a thumbprint. If it is not set up enough, you will drag most of the mortar out of the joint. On the other hand, if it has set up too much, naturally you won't be able to get any mortar out of the joint at all and the job may be ruined. This particular step takes some watching and practice before you get the timing right. On a large job, some of the mortar may have set up too much before you can get to it, so watch it carefully. Usually the time required for pointing the joints is about ½ hour after the mortar has been applied.

Once you have determined the proper waiting time, the head of the bolt is used to scrape out the excess mortar to create a mortar joint to the depth you desire. Then use a small whisk broom to finish up and smooth out the scraped joints. The surface should still be soft enough that the whisk broom will smooth it down easily. Use a steel bristle brush to remove any excess mortar that has gotten on the face of the stone. However, with a little care as you work, you can keep most of the mortar off the stone faces. If you keep this cleaned off as you go, you will not have nearly as hard a clean-up job.

You may prefer to leave the mortar joints flush with the stones. In this case, merely use the whisk broom to knock excess mortar off the faces of the stones. This will even out and smooth the joint between the stones.

Producing a Partially Mortared Wall

A mortared wall can also be constructed to look like a dry-laid wall. This is done by laying mortar only in the inside portions of the wall, keeping the mortar 4 to 6 inches away from the front faces of the wall.

Cleaning Mortared Walls

If you want a really clean wall surface, use a commercial brick cleaning solution or a mix of 1 part muriatic acid and 10 parts water. This is available at leading hardware and building supply dealers.

One way to finish off the wall is with a mortar cap. This protects the top course.

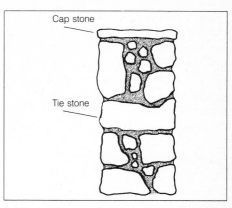
As you work up the wall, place tie stones every few feet. Finish with a capstone.

Let the mortar set until it takes a thumbprint; tool with a round-headed bolt.

A steel bristle brush refines the joints and removes excess mortar from the stones.

Smooth the surface and clean away dust and debris with a small whisk broom.

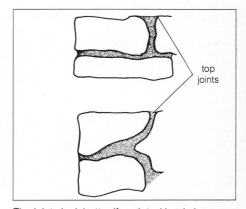
The joints look better if sculpted back; however, leave top joints nearly flush.

A partially mortared wall combines the strength of mortar with the appearance of dry-laid. The mortar fills the center but is kept at least 6 in. away from the wall's face.

Apply this acid-water solution with a wire bristle brush, scrubbing all excess mortar from the face of the stones. Then flush the stones with plenty of clean water from a hose to make sure you have stopped the etching action of the acid. Use all the precautions discussed in Chapter Three.

Creating Stone Veneer

Stone can also be veneered onto other surfaces such as concrete block, poured concrete, brick or even a wooden surface that has been strengthened with enough footing support at ground level.

In most instances, thin veneer-type stones are adhered in a bed of mortar, just like building one half of a wall. These thin stones are set up on their edges and mortar placed around and behind them to lock them securely in place. Sometimes the stones must be propped up until the mortar sets. Use wooden props until the surrounding mortar sets up. Wall anchors made of thin ribbed metal must be an-

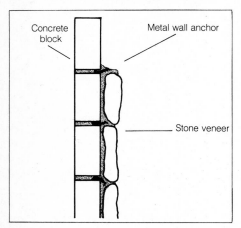

To tie two walls together, insert metal wall ties in the mortar joints as you set the block. Stagger the wall tie locations.

Once the mortar between the blocks has set up, apply the thin pieces of stone. Notice the placement of the wall ties.

chored in the supporting wall. They help anchor the mortar in place. Space them 2 feet apart both horizontally and vertically. This type of construction is a little more difficult than creating a wall entirely from stone, because it is so easy for the thin stones to tip out of the wall. Use a ½- to ¾-inch layer of mortar.

BUILDING TERRACE OR RETAINING WALLS

Stone can be used to create some beautiful and useful retaining and terrace walls. Because of the problems of water and ground pressure, and the resulting safety of the walls, many municipalities strictly govern the construction of this type of wall. You will probably have to get a building permit, as well as show the building inspector what type of wall you plan to build and the specifications for the wall. The reason for all this concern is that high walls can be dangerous if they happen to fall over or come apart. In some instances, walls have collapsed, causing injury and death. Such a collapse often occurs when soft fill dirt placed behind the wall becomes so waterlogged that the weight of the mud merely pushes the wall over. Another problem source is the freezing of moisture-laden ground, which expands and forces the wall outward. This can topple a poorly designed or constructed wall.

In most cities, walls over 4 feet high must be approved by the city engineer. In some areas, walls that are five feet high or less can be built vertically, but any higher walls must be sloped back to the hillside. In all cases, before building any type of retaining wall, check with local authorities and engineers.

Dry-Laid vs. Mortared Retaining Walls

These walls may be either mortared or

A low terrace wall of stone does not need to be mortared. In fact, a dry-laid wall suffers less from water-buildup problems.

laid dry. Mortared retaining walls must have drainage holes placed near the bottom of the wall so that excess water can escape. The 2- to 4-inch holes can be small tiles spaced about every 4 to 6 feet along the lower part of the wall. A mortared wall must also be set on a footing that extends to below the frost line. You also may use a line of 4-inch drain tile set in a 6-inch gravel base at the bottom back side of the wall. This helps divert water away from the back of the wall. In most instances, setting the top of a five-foot-high wall back about 9 inches farther than the bottom of the wall will give a good slope. The front face can be built to slope about 20 to 25 degrees, or even more for added safety if desired. The wall actually tilts, but it is supported by the earth behind it.

Dry-Laid Construction Techniques

Probably the easiest way to erect a retaining wall is to use the ancient earth-and-stone wall construction method of the Romans. This is a dry-laid wall that is laid using soil between the stones. This not only offers a fast job and easy work, but the stone and earth combination can be utilized to create an unusual rock garden along a slope.

An earth-and-stone wall is constructed in the same manner as the dry-laid and

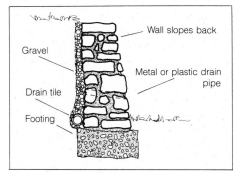

A mortared retaining wall more than 3 feet high must have footing, fill and drainage.

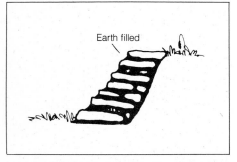

Layers of soil are between the rocks in a dry-laid wall. To set the wall at an angle, cut away the earth to the correct slope.

mortared walls in terms of choosing and positioning the correct stones. However, between each layer of stones, place a thin layer of soil. Tamp it down well, between and over the stones.

The front face of this type of wall must tilt back, just as discussed above. This is accomplished by setting the stones in succeeding courses slightly back from the front edges of the stones below. When constructing a wall with soil between, tilt the front edges of the stones upward just a little so rainwater won't wash out the soil between the stones. If the slope is gradual, dig it back for a slightly more vertical surface.

SLIP FORMING A WALL

Another type of stone construction, slip forming, is primarily used when constructing an entire building. It is one of the easiest, fastest, and cheapest methods of building.

Slip forming combines poured concrete with stone. The process involves building a long narrow form about 2 feet high, much in the same manner as for concrete, except that the formwork is not nearly so high. The construction techniques called for are those already covered in Chapters 1 and 2 for forming and pouring concrete. In slip forming, the stones will show on the outside wall but not on the inside wall, leaving a smooth inside surface to which furring strips can be attached. Then paneling or wallboard can be fastened to the furring strips.

Forming and Pouring the First Two Forms

On top of the foundation, which is built just as for any other wall or stone wall, build the front-and-back forms in pairs. Use ¾ inch plywood. You will need at least two pairs of forms. This enables you to create the corners of the building and to pour the first two wall sections at once.

Pouring the first forms. Place layers of concrete, stone and then (again) concrete inside the form. Alternate the layers as you bring the wall up within the first two forms. Be careful when placing the stones; they should be kept 2 to 4 inches away from the inside face of the wall. Place a lumber scrap inside the form to serve as a spacer.

Notes for concrete mix and placement. The concrete used is a standard concrete mix. Choose the aggregate so it is fairly small. As you make the pour, jab the concrete down to settle it around all the rocks. Then bang on the forms (but not too hard) to help the concrete run down and settle evenly along the back forms without any air bubbles or openings.

The last layer in the second form. Do not fill the top layer over with concrete. Leave it rough, with stones protruding out. Otherwise, you will end up with rows of horizontal concrete strips that show on the completed exterior of the wall.

Pouring the next form. While the lower layer is setting up you can pour the next layer. After letting the concrete cure three days, remove the bottom form and place it on top of the second form. Leave the second form in place and pour the third form. You will continue to leap-frog the forms until the wall has been completed. This is one of the reasons this type of wall is economical; you don't need to keep a lot of money tied up in form lumber. The forms used are shown.

The top of the wall. Finish the top of the wall with a coping or a layer of mortar so it is smooth, just as for other concrete surfaces. Install anchor bolts to help hold the structure's sill plate solidly in place.

Workmanship

The most irritating part of this type of construction is that you can't see the faces of the stones as you place them, so you do not know what the wall looks like until you take the forms off in a few days. With a little practice, however, you will discover what types of stones are best and how to position them.

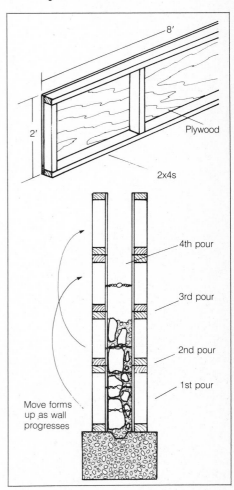

Make forms of plywood; brace them with 2x4s. Insert stone along the outside exterior side and concrete between the stones and along the interior side. Leapfrog forms to the desired height.

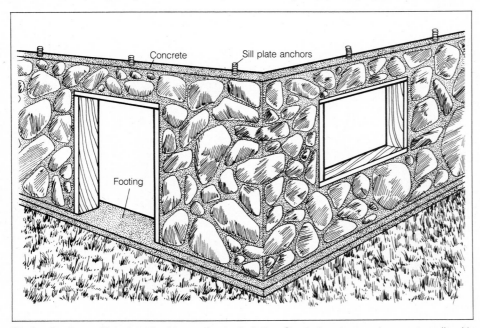

Slip forming is an efficient method to construct a building. Create the stone and concrete walls with concrete forms. Allow for the doors and windows in the framing and forms.

5 WORKING WITH CONCRETE BLOCK

Interlocking concrete pavers come in a variety of shapes and colors.

A screen wall of decorative concrete block gives privacy, ventilation and light.

One of the most practical materials, and probably the easiest for the home mason to use, is concrete block. These masonry units consist of an outside shell with a hollow center that is divided by one or two vertical ribs. Although the blocks are called concrete blocks, they may be made of several different materials including cement, sand and a variety of aggregates such as gravel or cinders.

Concrete block has several advantages. It is a cheaper material than wood. Properly constructed, a block construction can be one of the strongest and longest-lasting projects you can build. It also will be fireproof and virtually rodent-proof.

However, probably one of the greatest assets of concrete blocks—and one of the first considerations for the home mason—is their ease of use. A concrete

To accent the length of your wall and your lot, tool only horizontal joints: then paint the wall.

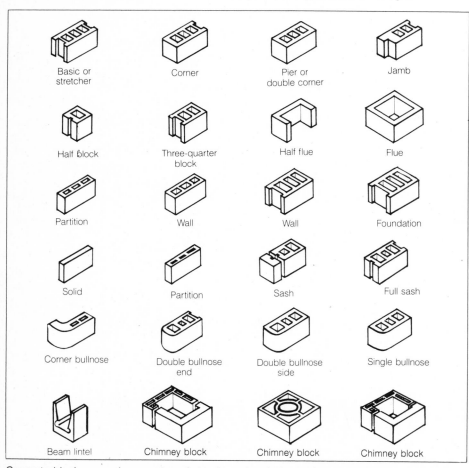

Basic or stretcher

Corner

Pier or double corner

Jamb

Half block

Three-quarter block

Half flue

Flue

Partition

Wall

Wall

Foundation

Solid

Partition

Sash

Full sash

Corner bullnose

Double bullnose end

Double bullnose side

Single bullnose

Beam lintel

Chimney block

Chimney block

Chimney block

Concrete block comes in a number of shapes and styles to assist in constructing any structure. Your block distributor will help you select the ones best for your project.

Use interlocking pavers to build a durable walk, patio or driveway.

block project doesn't require a great number of tools, and laying the blocks requires little expertise. Even the first timer can lay a passable block wall. With just a little practice almost any do-it-yourselfer can quickly learn to be a good block layer.

Another big advantage of a concrete block project is that you can work on it a little at a time. For instance, once you construct the forms for a concrete foundation you must make the pour in one continuous job. On the other hand, you can construct a concrete block foundation for a few hours each evening or on weekends. Merely work as long as you have time; then cover the project and leave it until you can get back to it. The same is true for small projects. The fact that you can break up a job into small sections makes it much easier for the first-time mason.

Of course, the work might not appear quite as neat as a professional job the first time or two that you try it. However, if you follow the proper construction steps, the building or wall you build will be just as strong and durable as a professionally constructed one. In fact, it may be a better job because the do-it-yourselfer often takes more time, adds extra reinforcing, and fills in holes and mortar joints more carefully.

CHARACTERISTICS OF CONCRETE BLOCK
Blocks for General Use
Concrete blocks are available in quite a variety of sizes and shapes. Each style serves a specific purpose. There are these types: concrete brick; solid, load-bearing block; hollow load-bearing block and hollow, nonload-bearing block. The first three types come in grade designations of N or S depending on the strength of the concrete used to make them. All blocks are constructed to be moisture-controlled or nonmoisture-controlled.

However, two basic types of concrete block are used for most home masonry jobs. The first is the basic unit, sometimes called a stretcher block. This consists of a hollow, webbed block. At both ends of stretcher blocks are flanges that join with other blocks. The second most common block is the corner or end unit. One end of the block is flanged; the other is not. The unflanged end is used to finish off a corner, a building, or a wall.

Blocks for Special Applications
Since the cost of shipping the blocks is expensive, most areas have local block manufacturing plants. You often are limited to whatever size and shape of block is being manufactured in your area.

In addition to general-use blocks, there are blocks with rounded corners for a decorative corner joint as well as solid top blocks for use in finishing out the top of a wall and even blocks that can be used to create a place for a door or window jamb. Blocks are available for creating a chimney—however, a chimney construction *must* incorporate a clay flue tile liner. Without this liner, fires and cracked chimneys are a serious risk. Finally, you can select ornamental concrete blocks for certain projects. These will be discussed later. Again, if you want some of the more exotic blocks, check first on the types available in your area.

Block Sizes
The most common size for concrete block is the standard nominal 8x8x16 inch block. The actual size of block is 7⅝x7⅝x15⅝ to allow for a ⅜ inch mortar joint between the blocks. The nominal designation simplifies the job of figuring and designing. As a result, the spacing in a project is more even.

Specially-made foundation block units may be as wide as 16 inches; wall or partition blocks usually come as 4 inches wide by 8x16 inches. You can also order half blocks, which are 8x8x8 inches. The smaller size blocks usually are used to build inside room divider walls inside a structure or partition walls; they are not recommended for load-bearing walls.

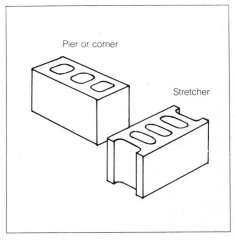

The two most commonly used blocks are stretcher and corner (or pier) block.

Block Weights
The weight of the blocks varies, depending on the type of material used to make them. For instance, cinder blocks are usually the heaviest type. They can run up to 50 pounds apiece. Lightweight blocks incorporate materials such as expanded shale, clay or slate, or pumice stone and may be as light as 25 pounds. In most instances, local building codes limit the uses of lightweight blocks, so you should check to determine where and how they can be used. The most commonly used block is made of cement, sand, and crushed stone or gravel block; it weighs about 35 to 40 pounds.

Tools Needed
Actually, you need very few tools to lay concrete block. In almost all instances you will first have to pour a good solid concrete foundation to support the block construction. This part of the project, of course, requires the tools discussed in the first chapter. Many tools used for concrete also are used for block work, for instance the mixer or mortar box, hoes or shovels.

You will need other specialized tools, most of which are the same as those needed for brick or stone work. A mortar board or hawk is helpful for carrying the mortar from the mixer to the job. Choose a good, medium-sized metal trowel to place the mortar. Use the wooden handle of the trowel to tap the blocks in place. As with brick installation, you will need a mason's string line and wooden or plastic line blocks. Since working with concrete blocks and mortar is extremely hard on your hands, you probably should wear cotton gloves.

Again as with brickwork, a story pole is a handy tool, although it is not considered necessary by some professionals. The pole makes the first job or two much easier. It is nothing more than a stick on

Decorative block can also accent differing levels of a structure.

Choose wooden-handled trowels to lay the mortar and to work on the mortar joints.

To tool the joints, buy a specially made jointer that creates the shape you want.

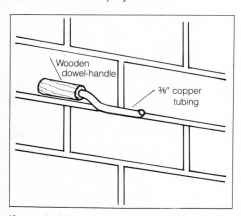

If you desire, make a jointer out of a curved piece of tubing and a wooden dowel.

The easiest way to cut concrete block is with a brick hammer and chisel.

which are marked the dimensions of the blocks and the mortar joints. It is placed against a corner of the proposed building and is used to gauge the block and mortar bed thicknesses and to check the spacing.

The necessary jointing tool for cleaning and smoothing the mortar joints can be purchased or shop-made out of a piece of ⅜-inch copper tubing. You will need a spirit level for leveling and plumbing the project. Select one that is at least 3 feet long and is made of metal or has metal edges. Metal will hold up under the rough treatment of the mortar and blocks. Finally, you will need a brick hammer and chisel in order to cut blocks to fit.

FIGURING MATERIAL NEEDS
Number of Blocks
The first step is to estimate the amount of materials you will need for your project. If at all possible, design the building so it comes out to even multiples of 8 inches in height and 16 inches or 8 inches in length and width. Measure the outside dimensions of a wall in inches; then divide this measurement by the nominal length (8x8x16) of the block to get the number of blocks in a row (course). When figuring for a building, measure the full length of each wall separately, including the corner overlap for extra blocks to allow for cutting or for breakage.

Divide the overall height of the wall by the nominal height of the blocks to find the number of courses needed to construct the wall. Then multiply the number of blocks in each course (length) by the number of courses (height) for each wall. This gives a pretty reasonable estimate of the number of blocks needed.

If there are window or door openings in the walls, first figure the amount of blocks that would fit the opening. Then subtract about half that amount from your total. In that way you allow for extra blocks. You will need to cut blocks to fit around the opening, and you must allow for waste. In most circumstances, if you describe the building, the building supply dealer can verify your totals. You also need special blocks, such as lintels for above doors or windows, or caps to finish off the tops of walls.

Mixing the Mortar
Concrete blocks are held in place with mortar, so the mortar mix is extremely important. Mortar that is not propor-

tioned properly or that is mixed to be too dry or too wet will not only make the job of laying the blocks more difficult, it will create a weaker and a less attractive project.

As is the case with all kinds of masonry projects, the make-up of the mortar is crucial to a project of any longevity at all. Basically, consider the type of mix, the type of cement, and the proportions for each. All are interrelated.

Types of mixes. Although there are actually five different types of mortar mixes, the home mason is most likely to use one of two kinds: Type M, which is best for outdoor projects, such as walls, and Type N, which is best for indoor projects, such as partitions. Type M and Type N can be made using two different types of cement.

Types of cement. There are two types of cement from which to choose. One is portland cement, the same as that used in concrete. Portland cement will create a slightly stiffer mix. The second type of cement is special masonry cement; the kind you need is called Type P. Portland cement is included in masonry cement, but hydrated lime has been added to the cement. The lime creates a mix that is best described as being ''creamier'' in texture. Both the cements create an acceptable mortar. In some instances, when masonry cement is not available, a mason will choose to add lime to regular portland cement in order to achieve the texture and consistency desired.

Proportions for mortar mix. The proportions of mortar, sand and aggregate in a mortar mix are dependent upon the type of cement you choose. The accompanying table sets out those proportions. All figures are based on volume not weight.

PROPORTIONS FOR MORTAR MATERIALS

Type	Portland Cement	Hydrated Lime or Lime Putty	Masonry Cement
M	1	¼	—
M	1	—	1 (Type II)
N	1	½-1¼	—
N	—	—	1 (Type II)

Sand proportions. Once you have decided upon the mortar mix you want, you need to figure the amount of sand needed. Remember that you still are working in terms of volume. The volume of sand is always figured in proportion to the volume of the cement *or* the cement-lime that you are using. Thus, if you are creating Type N mortar and you have 1 part portland cement and ½ part lime, you cannot determine the volume of sand that you need until you add the two dry ingredients together to equal that one-part unit. On the other hand, if you are creating Type N, which includes lime, base your proportions on the masonry cement alone. The ratio that is required for mortar for cement block is 1 part dry ingredients to 2¼ to 3 parts sand. (Usually this sand is damp. See the discussion on sand consistency in Chapter 1.)

Some local codes may specify different proportions, especially in cold weather climates, so check with code rules on the mortar mix to use in your particular area. The mortar can be mixed with a powered mixer, or by hand, but don't mix more material than you can use in a couple of hours. You will learn, with practice, to gauge the amount you can use.

Mixing procedure. First, thoroughly mix the dry materials. Then add a little water at a time until you achieve the proper consistency. Mortar mix should be somewhat drier than concrete mix, and after some practice you will learn the amount of material and water required to achieve the right consistency. One way to test the mortar is to pull it up in a series of ridges with the end of a hoe or shovel. If the ridges remain sharp and distinct, you have added the right amount of water. If the ridges are crumbly, there is too little water; if they slump down, there is too much. As is the case with all masonry mortar, it is very easy to add too much water, so proceed very carefully. It is always much easier to add just a bit more

water to a dry mix than it is to add the correct proportions of dry materials to a soupy mix.

You should allow the mortar to set for a few minutes before using it. If the mortar begins to get a little dry as you work along, you can add a small amount of water and thoroughly remix the mortar to bring it back to use. However, once the mortar starts to set up, it must be discarded. Usually mortar should be used within 2½ hours after being mixed. Again, you will learn what can and can't be done only with practice.

Block Bonds and Patterns
Lay the blocks to offset the mortar joints in succeeding courses, just as with standard brick running bond (see Chapter 3). In almost all instances, especially in home masonry, this is the pattern used, mostly because of its strength. Block can also be laid in a bond-on-bond course, but this installation takes a great deal more skill and isn't recommended for most home jobs (unless you're using certain specialized blocks). Not only is the construction of a bond-on-bond wall less structurally sound than a running bond wall, but it is almost impossible for the home mason to get the absolutely straight up-and-down mortar joints necessary to the pattern.

BASIC PROCEDURES
Storing Concrete Blocks
Bricks are always wet down before using; concrete block, however, should be used dry. Until you are ready to begin, keep the blocks covered with a tarp. Store them up off the ground after delivery on pallets or on a heavy plastic sheet—or both. If the blocks are delivered wet, allow them to dry out before you use

them. If you have to stop working on a project for a day or two, cover the tops of the installed blocks to keep rainwater from soaking down into them and down into the cores of the blocks. In addition, protect the blocks from dust and dirt, since any of these can prevent a strong bond between the mortar and the blocks.

Site Preparation
In almost all cases, concrete block projects will be laid on a supporting footing of concrete. This must be poured, screeded, floated smooth and allowed to set up thoroughly. All form boards must be removed. Then position the blocks around the perimeter of the job or (if the job is to be a building) on the inside perimeter of the job. You want them as close to the work as possible, so you don't have to carry the materials over long distances during the actual laying job. Stand the blocks up on end so you can grasp them quickly and easily.

A good example of most of the techniques involved in block laying is a foundation wall. First prepare the site and pour the footing. Then the exact corners of the building are established by using the batter board technique discussed in Chapter 3. Mark this point on the footing with a heavy pencil or with a small nail driven into the footing.

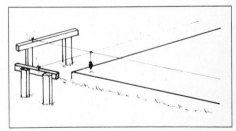

In order to keep track of the position of the footing and the wall, set out batterboards. On the boards, mark all locations.

Joints in concrete block walls are staggered in successive courses to add structural strength. This pattern is easy to set.

To lay a concrete block foundation, you must first pour a concrete footing. Dig down to the depth required for the footing. This will be governed by local codes.

Dry lay the bottom course. In that way you may be able to avoid cutting the blocks.

Because concrete blocks are heavy, the mortar mix must be thicker than a brick mortar.

Mark all corner locations. Then trowel the mortar in place for the corner blocks.

Align the first block with all corner and course markers. Then set it in place.

Position a corner block on the opposite end of the wall and run a string line.

Level both the blocks. Tap the block into position with the handle of the trowel.

To have a sturdy construction, the block must be level and plumb in all directions.

Both corner blocks must be level with each other. Use a string level to be sure.

Trial layout of block. Starting a corner block at one of the corner marks, dry lay the blocks. Place ⅜-inch wooden spacers between the blocks to leave enough room for the mortar joints. Fill the course over to the opposite corner mark. Whenever possible, adjust the wall in order to keep from cutting a number of blocks.

Chalklines. Now snap a chalkline. It can coincide with the position of the outside edge of the wall, but it will be more helpful if it is offset by about two inches so the mortar bed won't conceal it.

The mortar bed. After dry-laying the block and determining their exact location for all walls, remove the blocks and stand them up on end as close as possible to where they will be laid. Mix the mortar and place it on a mortar board or hawk. Hold the hawk above the ground with the tops of a couple of blocks or with a mortar holder. An old bucket also makes an excellent mortar hawk holder.

Place a generous amount of mortar alongside one of the chalklines. The mortar line should be long enough to lay about 3 blocks, and about 2 inches wider than the block width. The depth should be about 1½ to 1¾ inch thick. Use the edge of the mortar trowel to flatten the mortar a bit. Create a series of shallow ridges in its top surface. Do not make very deep furrows.

Building the Leads

Laying the corners. Position the first end or corner block in place. Since one side of the block cavity is thicker than the other, always set the thick side face up so you will have more space to lay the mortar line for the next course. (This also makes it easier to hang onto the block as you lift it.) Position the block, align it with the chalkline or butt it against the alignment nail. Embed the block in the mortar by tapping the top lightly with the mortar trowel. Use a level, both crosswise and lengthwise, to make sure the block is absolutely level.

Then butter the end of another block, and position it in place against the end or corner block. This is probably the hardest part of the concrete block laying. To butter the end of the block, stand it upright. Scoop up a generous portion of mortar and, using a flick of the wrist while tapping the block gently with the side of the trowel, snap the mortar in place on flanges of the block. Then, with a sliding motion, scoop off any excess mortar.

Now grasp the top web opening in the block and lift it to just over its location in the mortar bed. Keep the end that will butt the already-laid block pointed upward a little. When you get the new block into position, gently but quickly lower it in place with one smooth motion, pressing it against the adjacent block as you place the new block lightly in place. If the mortar does fall off, remove the block and try again.

Use the level to make sure the block is level and plumb. Then tap the block with the trowel handle to gently bond it with the mortar. Measure the mortar joint thickness between the two blocks and tap the block into position to ensure the correct thickness. Next, lay the third block in the same manner. Always make absolutely sure that all the blocks are installed plumb as well as level.

Checking the level of the first course. Go to the opposite end of the wall and repeat the steps given above. After these end blocks have been laid in place you can install guide string blocks over to the corner blocks in the first course (see Chapter 3). Check the line with a string level to determine if the two end blocks are level with each other. If there is only a slight difference, make the necessary adjustments in succeeding mortar joints. However, if there is a great deal of difference, lift the block that is lower and place enough mortar under it to bring it up to the level of the other end block.

Filling in the courses. Butter up the ends of two or three stretcher blocks and put them in place, making sure they almost touch the guide string. They must be level with each other as well as plumb and level in all directions. These first starting courses are very important.

Setting the closure block. Probably the hardest block to position is the last block in the course, which is called the closure block. First, carefully measure the opening to determine if a full-size block will fit the opening. If not, one has to be cut to fit. Butter the ends of the blocks that are already in place and the ends of the closure block. Slowly guide the closure block down in place between the other two blocks. Take care so that you don't knock off any more mortar than possible. If you do lose so much that the

result will be a poor seal, remove the closure block and repeat the process.

Before going any further, clean up any dropped mortar. Clean off dirt and debris.

How to Cut Concrete Block

Concrete block can be cut quite easily with a brick chisel and a hammer. Use a hammer made for striking other tools. Don't use an ordinary carpenter's hammer, because the hardened metal can chip and possibly cause an injury. Instead, use a brick or heavy ballpeen hammer. Always wear safety glasses or goggles.

It is easy to cut a block exactly in half. Most quality block is made with slight indentations in the outside shell, aligned with the center web, to aid a cut at that

location. Cutting to other sizes is a bit trickier, but can be done with practice.

Cutting procedure. With a heavy pencil or chalk, mark the location where the block is to be cut. Then hold the edge of the brick chisel on this line and with a gentle tapping motion, score one side of the block. Turn the block over and score the opposite side in the same manner. Repeat the turning and scoring until the block falls apart along the marked line. In most instances, the split will occur just after you complete scoring both sides of the block, but sometimes you must repeat it several times.

The main requirement is to take your time. If you hurry, and hammer too hard, the block will break into pieces that will not even be close to the size you wanted.

The closure block is the hardest to lay. Butter both ends of the block and the exposed ends of the blocks already in place. Then carefully slip the block into position.

It's easiest to cut blocks down the built-in score line down the center.

Tap one side of the block lightly along the scored line. Turn it over and repeat.

Face shell mortaring means that mortar is applied only to the outer edges of a block.

As you build the leads, constantly check that the corners are level and plumb.

As soon as you set the block, remove excess mortar. This can be reused.

To bond adjoining blocks, apply the mortar to the flanges at one end of a block.

With the mortared end tilted upward, set the block in place in the mortar bed.

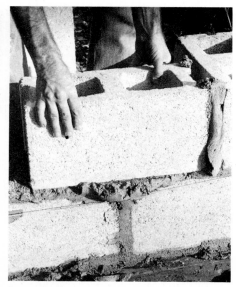

To lose very little mortar, lift and set the block with a continuous motion.

Check with a level—one end of the block must not sit lower than the other.

Build the corner leads up so that they are at least three to five courses high.

Check with a plumb level. The wall corner must not lean inward or outward.

Don't get excited if your first attempt doesn't create a clean break; you will improve with practice.

Laying the Second Course

A stopped wall. Any wall that is designed so that it has no corners is called a stopped wall. The second course of a stopped wall must begin on either end with a half block, in order to ensure that the mortar joints will be staggered throughout the course. You can use special corner blocks for this position, so that the end of the wall has a finished edge. As you build upward, alternate full and half end blocks to maintain the staggered construction.

A wall containing corners. Lay the first course on all sides of the project. For a building, you will have a square. Now build up the leads, just as you would for a brick wall. As discussed before, leads help to maintain straight and plumb courses and joint lines. Most masons like to build up these corners to five or six courses high before they start to fill in the stretcher blocks.

To lay the second course on the corner, cover the inside and outside edges of the base course with mortar. This is called face shell mortaring, and is usually done to join all courses but the first one. You may, if you prefer, apply mortar to the webbing as well. This technique is called full mortaring. Which method you use is a matter of personal preference. Face mortaring creates a sufficiently strong bond, and is the method most often used.

Mortaring for the second course. Lay a coat of mortar that is about 1 inch thick on the base course. Place a layer about ¾ inch thick on the end of the stretcher block you are about to place. Then build up the leads so that the mortar joints are staggered. Run the mason's line and use the line level to be sure that the corner blocks in the leads are level with each other, just as you did for the base course. Use the spirit level to be sure that each block is level in all directions. You also may wish to utilize the story pole at the corners to help gauge the block and joint height. As you work up the courses of the leads, shift the string line and continue to check for level and plumb.

Filling in Between Leads

Shift the string line up as you lay each course to provide a guide for positioning the blocks. Check with the story pole at the corners and along the wall to maintain the correct block and mortar joint height.

It is a good idea to scrape excess mortar that has oozed out of the joints. You can flip the mortar back into the mortar pan or board; quickly remix it back in place and use it again. If you wait too long, any excess mortar will set up and won't be reusable. Use the edge of the trowel as you would a knife to cut the mortar away. Then lift the mortar up with the top of the trowel as you work.

Location of Control Joints

On a small project, like a short, low garden wall, you may be able to avoid using control joints, but long stretches of wall do need control joints of some sort. As with concrete slabs, control joints are intentionally weakened sections designed to localize any cracking to areas where they are not visually conspicuous. There are too many variables to pinpoint the exact places where cracks will occur, so there are no meaningful rules that will apply to every wall. Experience shows, however, that cracks are likely to occur at changes in the height of the wall or the foundation (where the wall steps up or down a grade, for example) or at changes in wall thickness, such as at a pilaster. Long lengths of wall may crack because the wall contracts more than the foundation on which it sits. Therefore, it's common to see control joints at all points of potential stress. As a general rule of thumb, control joints fall about every twenty feet.

Types of Control Joints

There are several types of control joints, but in concrete masonry the Michigan type, the tongue-and-groove and the premolded rubber insert are those most widely used.

The Michigan joint. The Michigan control joint comes between two stretchers. Fold a strip of building paper and use it to cover all of the end of one stretcher. Lay the next stretcher in mortar, but do not butter it before positioning it.

Fill the core between the two blocks with mortar. Because of the building paper, the mortar bonds only to the uncovered unit. The mortar plug in the core prevents the wall from moving from side to side, but allows up and down movement. Regular block coursing is used for this method.

Tongue-and-groove joint. The tongue-and-groove control is made with special block units shaped as the name implies: one block is grooved and the other block has a tongue that fits into the groove. This coupling is not mortared. The construction of the joint holds the wall together, but it also allows for up and down shifting at the joint.

Premolded joint. Premolded control joints use rubber inserts shaped like a plus sign (+) that fit in grooves formed in specially made concrete blocks.

Caulking the Control Joints

All control joints should be caulked. When the mortar in the joint becomes stiff, rake it out to a depth of about ¾ inch deep. From a building supply store purchase concrete block sealers and bond breakers. Use the sealer to coat the sides of the joints; grease the back of the joint with a bond breaker. The caulk will adhere to the sides of the joint but will still slide up and down against the back of the joint.

The paper or felt must be wide enough to extend across the joint. This keeps mortar from bonding on one side and creates the joint.

Blocks with control joints cast into them are available. The tongue-and-groove ends shown give lateral support.

Striking Off and Finishing Mortar Joints

If you have kept the mortar cleaned up as you go, you can quite easily finish off the joints. This should be done when the mortar gets to the point that it will take a thumbprint. Check the mortar often, because if you wait too long you won't be able to get a smooth, even job. On the other hand, if you start too soon, you will drag more mortar out of the joint than you should and probably will have to repack the joint.

The most common method uses a concave or v-shaped tool to press the mortar between the blocks. This will create a mortar joint that is about ³⁄₈ inch deep. You should always tool the horizontal joints first; then tool vertical joints. Take care that you don't drag the lines out of the horizontal joints and cause "dug-in" places where the horizontal and vertical joint lines cross. After you have tooled the joints with the jointing tool, there will be slightly roughened edges left along the sides of the blocks. Remove these with the edge of the trowel.

Sometimes an extruded joint is left for a rustic appearance, but in most cases this joint is unsightly, and it catches rainwater and other moisture, which ultimately weakens the structure. Besides the traditional finish, you can choose one of the decorative joints illustrated for brick in Chapter 3.

BUILDING A CRAWL SPACE

Following the basic construction steps given, it is not too hard to construct a crawl space for a garden gazebo, a potting shed, a screen house, or even a home.

In most instances, a foundation wall for a crawl space is set on a footing sunk below frost level and stands at least four blocks above the footing. A crawl space requires at least two ventilation vents, as well as a crawl space opening. These are created with frames of 2x8 lumber or with ready-made steel framing pieces. The frame for a ventilation vent is normally about the size of one block; a crawl space opening is usually at least 2 blocks high and 2 blocks wide. The opening must be large enough to let you crawl through to get under the house or building if you need to.

At the end of each block-laying period, remove excess mortar from the blocks and place it down inside them.

The weight of the installation will force excess mortar from between the blocks. Remove the excess with the edge of the trowel.

A crawl space foundation requires ventilation (left) and an opening (right).

Then compress the mortar with the jointer. Do horizontal joints first, then vertical.

To tool the joints, first slice away the excess with the side of the trowel.

Frame in the crawl space opening just as shown. It should be at least 4 blocks high.

For the vent and crawl space openings, build the appropriately sized frame. These do not need mitered corners. Butt the pieces together and set them on the blocks and mortar. The mortar and the weight of the structure will hold the frames in place. The front edges must be flush with the outside edge of the block wall. The frames remain in place even after the wall has set. Attach metal vent coverings to the wooden framing around the ventilation openings. Fit a wooden door over the crawl space opening to keep small animals and children out.

Fastening the Sill Plate
Once the top course has been laid, the foundation is completed by filling the cores of each block with mortar. To prevent the mortar from dropping through into the holes in the lower blocks, either stuff the holes in the next to the last course with small pieces of rubble, or embed small pieces of screen wire in the mortar bed below the top course. If you use the wire screen, make sure it doesn't extend out far enough to protrude through the struck joints. Then pack the cores with the concrete.

Before the concrete sets, install L-shaped sill bolts. Let the concrete get just stiff enough to support the weight of the bolts so they won't sink into the concrete. Space the bolts about 3 feet apart and embed them in the concrete at least 6 inches. The sill bolts should have 2-inch washers or large nuts on the end embedded in the concrete. A threaded end extends above the concrete. This end secures the sill plate. The sill bolt must be long enough to go through the sill plate

(one or two 2x4s) and still allow enough room to seat the nut and washer that secures the sill plate. Select the bolt lengths accordingly. There should be a bolt no more than 12 inches from every corner, both directions from the corner. There must be at least 2 bolts per sill length.

BASEMENT WALLS
Constructing a house basement wall is done in the exact same manner as a crawl space. The wall should be at least 8 feet

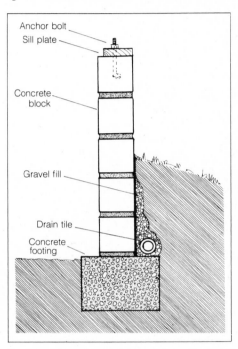

If a foundation does not have adequate drainage facilities, water buildup will ultimately destroy the wall. Use gravel fill and drainage pipes at the footing.

high. Allowing for a 6-inch pour for the basement floor, this height will provide a 7½ foot high basement if all pipes are run through and between the ceiling joists. If you plan on a dropped ceiling that covers heating ducts and pipes, make the wall 9 feet high.

How to Waterproof Foundation Walls
Once the mortar has had sufficient time to cure (at least 3 days) waterproof foundation and basement walls. This prevents later water seepage through the joints and the blocks and is done by applying a parge coat and then a waterproofing material.

Mixing a parge coat. The first step is to apply a plaster or parge coat of mortar. This is a smooth sealer spread over the outside of the wall. Use either the same mortar you used to set the blocks or a portland cement plaster, which consists of 1 part portland cement to 2½ parts sand, by volume. If you use the mortar, one parge coat is enough. However, two coats of the plaster application are necessary.

Applying the parge coat. Apply the parge coat in smooth sweeping strokes to about a ⅜-to-½-inch thickness. Allow the mortar to dry thoroughly.

Applying the waterproofing. Use an old trowel to apply a coat of waterproofing asphalt. The asphalt should be about ⅛ inch thick. You can apply liquid asphalt with a paint roller, although this is not quite as effective.

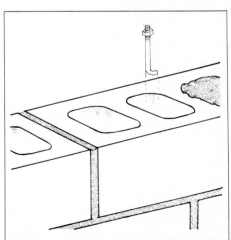

Anchor bolts hold a sill plate in place. Rubble or screens block the course below. Fill openings with mortar; install the bolts.

Before installing the drainage system, waterproof a foundation wall to seal pores in the block and help prevent leakage. The first is a plaster parge; the second is asphalt waterproofing.

Reinforcing Adjoining Interior Walls

Interior adjoining walls should be built up as you construct the main wall. To tie adjoining walls at the corners use the reinforcing designated by local building

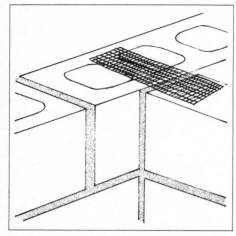

When interior and exterior walls meet, lay mesh webbing or other jointing hardware.

codes. The material may be metal lath or special metal bars. Both are inserted in the mortar joints to hold the wall intersections together. If you wish to add the adjoining wall later, merely insert the reinforcing material in place as you lay the primary wall, spacing the reinforcing every two courses. Later, when you build up the interior wall, lay the material into the mortar bed of the new wall.

Window and Door Openings

Window and door openings can be rough framed with wood and the blocks laid around them, just as for the ventilation and crawl space openings. You also can use special window and door unit blocks that provide a space in the blocks in which to set the frames. Window and door openings sometimes have a cast concrete header over the door and window units. Install cast concrete sills under all window units.

Finishing an Interior Concrete Wall

A block wall can be finished in several ways. The easiest method is to paint it with latex masonry paint. Use a special roller cover with a large nap. The heavy material will blend in the irregularities of the surface and cover the blocks well.

If you don't want to use paint, fasten down furring strips with masonry nails and then install wall board or paneling over the walls. In this installation, it's a good idea to install insulation between the furring strips, because a block wall doesn't have very much insulation value. Use panel adhesive to glue the paper side of the insulation right to the wall.

CONSTRUCTING A BUILDING OF CONCRETE BLOCK

You can build an entire building with concrete block. It will be sturdy and snug. Although such a project sounds like quite an undertaking, it's a good job for a

To finish off the exterior of a concrete block project, cover it with stucco. The surface can be finished in any number of styles.

do-it-yourselfer because the work can be done a little at a time. Basically the steps in creating the building are the same as those for wall construction.

Working Progression

The first step is to pour a combined slab and footing of concrete. Then construct the block building on the cured concrete. Insulation is strongly suggested. Openings for doors and windows are framed in and anchor bolts are fitted in the top course. The bolts hold a sill plate to which the ceiling joists and roof rafters are anchored.

APPLYING STUCCO TO AN EXTERIOR WALL

An exterior wall may be painted, but you will have a better finish if you cover the wall with cement, plaster or stucco. Stucco is actually a thin mortar-coat surface applied in three separate coats. The first coat is called the scratch coat, the second layer is called the brown coat and the last layer is the white or finish coat.

The Scratch Coat

Make up a mix of 1 part mortar cement and 4 parts sand, and add just enough water to make the mix workable. Use a steel trowel. Starting at the bottom of the wall, trowel on a coat that is about ¼ inch thick. Once you begin, you must complete the wall; otherwise there will be start and stop lines. A piece of cardboard held against window and door frames and at the corners helps create an even start and stop in those areas. As soon as you have covered an area, it should be scored with a scratch tool.

The Brown Coat

Apply the brown or second coat as soon as the scratch coat can hold up to it without cracking while the brown coat is troweled on. If you must wait longer, spray the surface of the first coat with a fine mist of water. Keep the delay between the scratch and the brown coat short; this results in a better bond and cure.

This second coat is mixed and applied in the same manner as the scratch coat. It is allowed to set for about 6 hours, and then is lightly moistened with a fine spray of water. Allow the wall to cure for about 2 to 3 days, gently moistening it every few hours or so.

The White Coat

For the last coat, moisten the brown coat with a water mist and apply a coat made up of 1 part white cement and 3 parts white stucco sand. This coat should be about ⅛ inch thick and is applied in the same manner as the first two coats. The white stucco coat can be textured in many different ways. If you flip the stucco onto

By applying the stucco in several layers, the final finish can be built up and textured. Select a texture that fits your landscaping scheme.

the finished surface, the surface ridges can then be troweled smooth or only slightly leveled down to create a roughened, pocked surface. You can also use the float to create unusual textures. After it has been installed, allow the stucco surface to cure by keeping it damp for a week.

CONCRETE PAVING BLOCKS

Long used in Europe, concrete pavers are one of the best materials for a durable

The beveled edges of concrete pavers guard against damage due to frost heave.

patio, driveway or walkway. Usually manufactured in the shape of a capital ''I,'' pavers interlock to make an almost solid surface that will rise and fall with frost cycles. The best ones have 45 degree beveled edges that allow them to ''roll'' with frost heaving, which prevents cracking.

Installing a Paver Patio

The pavers are set in a graded, tamped base of coarse torpedo sand which is very evenly-sized. The workman operates not from the base area but from the surface of the previously installed pavers. Cut pavers are split in the same manner as common brick.

Excavation. To figure the correct excavation depth, add the thickness of the paver and 4 more inches for layers of gravel and of sand. To that total add 2 extra inches to allow for creating a pitch.

Estimating quantities. Although the figure will vary with certain shapes of pavers, usually 2½ pavers will cover a square foot. So, for instance, you would need approximately 250 stones to cover a

patio that is 10 x 10 feet in size.

Filling in the base. First, add a 2-inch layer of tamped gravel. Then spread a base of torpedo sand at least 2 inches thick across the entire area. Tamp the sand thoroughly. Pitch the sand with a level and a long, straight 2 x 4. Add sand as needed to adjust the pitch. Once the pitch is set, do not step back on the sand. If you must do so, regrade the base and retamp.

Installing the pavers. Starting from a corner, lay four or five pavers in a line and work straight to the next corner, fitting the pavers together. Stand on the blocks you have laid, not on the sand. Then, working clockwise, turn the corner and continue laying the pavers until the patio has been filled in.

Finishing the installation. When the patio is completed, sweep fine mason's sand across the surface of the paving stones and dampen down the surface. Repeat the process. The pavers will now interlock to form a continuous, firm surface. Do not use portland cement mix on the pavers.

Concrete patio block can come in quite large sizes. In this installation, the large blocks were set in wood strip framing. This adds color and helps hold the blocks in position.

Placing the edging. When the sanding is done, finish the edges with railroad ties or end blocks. Some paver manufacturers make special end stones for this purpose. Then sweep the patio well and wash it down with the garden hose. Apply a coat of cement sealer to extend the life of the paver surface.

Specially-cast Concrete Paving Blocks

An alternative to an installation of the standard shaped concrete paving block is one that is made of individually designed blocks that you can cast yourself. Available from the Formlite Products Company are specially designed, reusable plastic molds for just this purpose. The pavers can be the color of ordinary concrete or can be colored in any number of shades with pigments available from your local building supply dealer. Colored pavers are created in two consecutive pours. The colored layer is added first; the base layer is then added.

First, coat the molds with 30W motor oil and place them on individual squares of ¾-inch plywood. Add the concrete. Tap the plywood board, not the form, to be sure that there are no air bubbles along the form edges. Allow the molds to cure for at least 10 hours before removing the pavers from the forms. Then set the pavers in a sand bed, just as you would ordinary concrete pavers. The joints can be either sand-filled or mortared.

USING DECORATIVE CONCRETE BLOCKS

Probably one of the most significant advances in the use of concrete blocks is the creation of decorative blocks. Blocks come with a great number of designs, either embossed on one face or pierced into the block. Decorative blocks can be used to create any number of unusual garden walls, room dividers or carport walls. Embossed blocks can be used to build solid walls and buildings, but pierced blocks often can't be used for load-bearing walls. Check local codes before using them in this manner.

Decorative pierced concrete blocks are typically 4 x 12 inches, although some sizes may vary with local manufacturers. These blocks are laid quite differently than standard building blocks. They are usually placed one above the other, so that the vertical joints align. This characteristic—keeping the mortar joints properly aligned both horizontally and vertically—is the most difficult aspect of a decorative block project. Use a straightedge as a guide, or preferably a 4-foot carpenter's level, for the vertical joints. Keep horizontal joints straight with the mason's string line, just as for standard concrete blocks.

Since the blocks are laid directly on top of each other rather than in staggered courses, there is no need to cut them to create the courses. In fact, you should avoid cutting altogether, unless you have the special powered masonry cutting saws required for this job. As long as the decorative block wall is not load-supporting, there is usually no reinforcing required in its installation. However, if the wall is a long one, you might wish to space solid block pilasters along the back and at the ends to provide more strength.

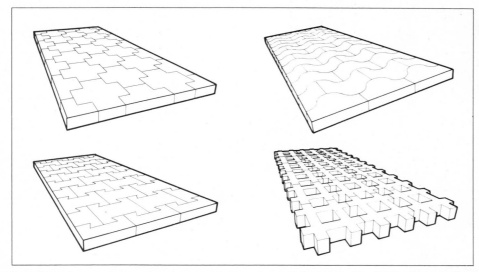

Decorative blocks are set similarly to regular blocks except mortar joints usually align.

To individualize a paver installation, try one of the projects available from Formlite Products. It offers forms for casting pavers in a number of designs, some of which are shown here.

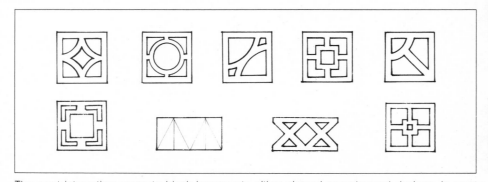

The most interesting concrete block incorporate either pierced or embossed designs. In most areas the pierced blocks cannot be used in load-bearing walls. Check local codes.

Build an entire structure, such as a screen wall, or combine with solid block.

6 PROJECTS THAT COMBINE MATERIALS

1x6 Nailer

The roof was extended out over the bathroom deck. Masonry anchor bolts in the wall held a sill plate for a new roof.

Many projects require skills in working with more than one type of masonry. For instance a mortared stone wall requires a concrete footing. More complex examples are such things as stone or brick fireplaces, garden pools, and sunken Roman tubs.

BATHROOM ADDITION

A decorator bathroom is a prime example of what a combination of masonry and concrete projects can do to modernize an older house. This original bathroom was quite small and in fairly bad shape. We remodeled it by enlarging the old bathroom in order to make the space more inviting and more varied. One entire wall is made of mortared stone. Sliding doors lead to a sunbathing deck enclosed by an outside garden wall. The room also features a ceramic tile covered sunken tub of poured concrete. The outer wall was created with stone masonry.

Although you may not have the exact same situation as the old farmhouse shown, you can utilize the ideas, perhaps to create a stone wall in a room of your

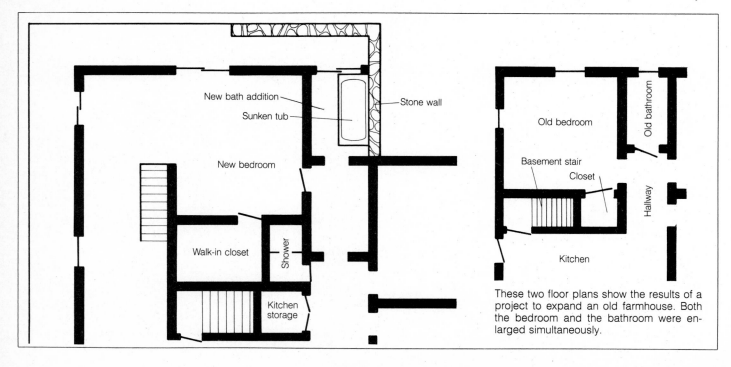

New bath addition — Stone wall

Sunken tub —

New bedroom

Old bedroom

Old bathroom

Basement stair

Closet

Walk-in closet

Shower

Hallway

Kitchen

Kitchen storage

These two floor plans show the results of a project to expand an old farmhouse. Both the bedroom and the bathroom were enlarged simultaneously.

home or even to build your own sunken tub. Remember to check with local codes and acquire building permits before construction of anything such as a room addition.

Laying Out the Room

The first step in construction of the bathroom was to lay it out using string lines and batter boards. Since the stone walls were quite heavy for this job, the footing in this instance was poured somewhat oversized. It was 2 feet deep and 2 feet wide to support the high wall.

Building the Stone Wall

Then the wall was constructed, just as described in Chapter 4. The mortar color was a charcoal gray to add color and to emphasize the fieldstone used in it. The high wall was completed to the ceiling height of the bathroom. After a layer of mortar was placed over the top course, L-shaped anchor bolts were positioned in place in the mortar. Then a 2x4 sill plate was bolted in place. Later, the ceiling joists and the rafters were anchored to the sill plate.

The end of the wall that joins the house was fastened to the siding using ripple-shaped metal wall anchors that commonly are used to anchor concrete block walls together.

The inside of the bathroom wall also features stone shelves used to hold towels and bath soap. These were formed utilizing large "lintel" stones placed over the top of the opening. In addition, a ¼x3-inch flat steel bar was placed in a bed of

mortar over these stones and then more mortar added on top of it before the rest of the wall was built.

Creating the Lower Wall

The lower privacy wall on the end of the bathroom deck was brought up at the same time as the full height wall. All corners were kept square and plumb. The top of this wall was finished off with flat cap stones, then the mortar joints broomed off smooth and flush with the stone tops. The difference in height of the two walls was solved by making a sweeping curve up from the lower wall to the top edge of the higher wall.

Supporting the Bathroom

To support a bathroom and deck floor that were level with the existing floors in the

house, we poured a high concrete shelf, 4 inches wide, all around the inner face of the stone wall. We inserted anchor bolts into the concrete, and when it cured, attached a sill plate. At the location where the deck meets the new outer bathroom wall, we poured a concrete footing and built a concrete block foundation, equal in height to the concrete shelf. Again we inserted anchor bolts and a sill plate. At the same time that we poured these footings, we also poured the footing and the concrete tank for the sunken tub, discussed more fully below. In that way we did not have to build the forms and work around floor joists. Instead we installed them once the tub was finished. The rest of the construction is one of a standard house frame. We had to frame in wooden walls, ceiling joists and rafters.

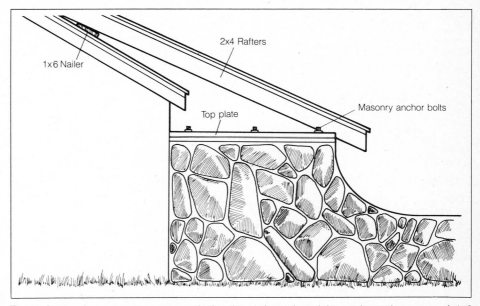

The roof extension covers the room enclosing the sunken tub and the outdoor privacy area. A 1x6 nailer fastened to the old roof helped to create the needed angle for the new roof.

The mortar in the stone wall wouldn't be enough to hold the wall to the house. Metal wall anchors were fastened to the studs; then the anchors were laid in the mortar.

Since the sunken bathtub extends along the stone wall, create openings for soap and towels. Lintel rocks support the wall above.

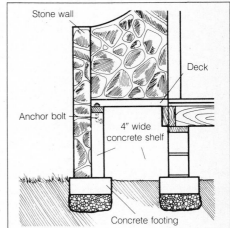

Footings support the weight of the stone wall. A concrete shelf and a concrete block foundation support the outer bathroom wall.

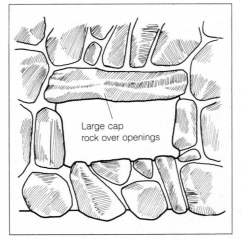

After the outer shell of the addition was finished, a hole was cut through the existing wall into the old bathroom. The old fixtures were removed to be put into the new bathroom. The sunken tub was finished in the bathroom extension.

ADDING A SUNKEN ROMAN TUB

You can build a sunken tub in your own home and it will bring many compliments. The tub is not only an unusual and beautiful addition; it also can be quite practical. You can size the tub to suit yourself. For instance, for a tall person, a 6-foot-long tub is more relaxing than most purchased tubs. This length also offers a good size area for the kids to bathe in without splashing water all over the floor. Constructing such a tub, however, is not a project to be taken lightly. Before you begin, check with local building codes to make sure you may build it.

Construction Alternatives

A sunken Roman tub is hand-constructed; then it is covered with ceramic tile. There are two common construction methods for this type of tub. The first, and the one that has been used for years, is to construct a metal tank, which is covered with a thick bed of mortar. Once the bed is properly cured, the tile is set in thin-set adhesive. The procedure is a fairly complicated one and requires a great deal of skill in the construction of the metal tank and the application of the thick bed of mortar.

The second method, and the one used by me in my home, involves building a watertight tub of concrete, much like one would use to construct a swimming pool. This method is now being used by several builders, and tubs so constructed do not suffer from the leakage problems that occur in metal tanks. The only structural requirement for a cast concrete tub is that the bottom of the tub be at ground level or just below it. You cannot suspend a concrete tub without a great deal of forming knowledge and special support construction.

Preparing the Base

Before you build a sunken tub, you must provide a suitably solid base on which it can rest. This keeps the weight of the structure from settling or causing drainage and heaving problems. The base is a concrete footing built in the same manner as described earlier. This footing must extend at least 6 inches farther than the tub on all sides.

The depth to which the footing must extend depends upon your location. Areas with little freezing require less depth than areas with a great deal of freezing. Layers of gravel and sand may be required as part of the base construction. To determine the best method for your particular environment, check the standards of your local building code. They will tell you how deep to excavate. Design your tub, complete with base specifications, plumbing schematics and wood formwork. Then have your community or county building inspector approve the plans before you begin work.

Digging the base. Once you know the necessary depth, mark out a stake-and-string outline of the area (6 inches larger than the tub on all sides) on which the tub will rest. Dig out all the soil within the stakes to the depth required. Then tamp the soil surface firmly. The floor of the hole must be level. Use a dragboard to check. Check the level in as many directions as possible, including diagonally. If the surface is not level, correct the situation by adding fill in those areas which are low. Tamp the added fill well. Otherwise you will have problems with moisture buildup below the base.

Formwork for the concrete footing. Dig trenches just outside the tub excavation area. They should be wide enough to accomodate the form boards and as deep as the hole dug previously. Place 2x12s on their edges in the trenches. The top edge of a 2x12 should extend above the level of the earth to the desired height of the finished slab—usually about 1-2 inches above ground level. To support, use 2x4 stakes fastened to 2x12s with duplex nails. Check that the form is square. Repeat this operation for the other form boards on the other sides of the hole. Stake 2x4s every 16 inches around the entire perimeter of 2x12s. Cut all stakes off just below form height. Having staked the perimeter, you have set the footing formwork. With the dirt that was removed during initial excavation, fill in around the outside of the boards. Tamp the dirt against the forms to prevent unwanted movement. On the inside of the form, tamp the earth so it is just below the bottom of the form board; if necessary, compact or refill to relevel and regrade the entire area.

Estimating material quantities. The dimensions of the tub here—81x41 inches—provide a good example of how to determine amounts. Since the base is 6 inches larger on all sides of the tub, the base measurements are 93x53. If the information received from the local building inspector dictates a 4 inch layer of gravel, double the depth requirement to 8 inches to allow for compacting. By multiplying 93x53x8 (length times width times depth) you learn that you need 39,432 cubic inches of gravel. To convert cubic inches to cubic yards, divide 39,432 by 46,656—the number of cubic inches in a cubic yard. The result tells you that you

The tub rests on a concrete footing. To ensure adequate working space, install the sunken tub before all of the floor joists are in place. Tiling is the final step.

You can design a concrete sunken tub in any number of shapes and sizes. The concrete tank is then covered with tile, which can be custom-made for special designs.

The tile can cover the tub only, or it can be extended to the surrounding floors and walls. Create a curved backing wall like this with 2x4 studs and kerfed Sheetrock paneling.

need less than one cubic yard of gravel. Use the same technique to determine the amounts of cement, gravel and required for the batches of concrete you mix later.

Filling the base. Place the gravel over the entire base floor in two layers of 4 inches each. Make sure that each layer is tamped thoroughly until firm. The gravel should be tamped down to at least two thirds of its original height. Then place the sand uniformly over the entire area in a 1 inch layer. Tamp the sand down. If the gravel shows through, add sand until the difference between the top of the sand and the top of the formboard will be approximately 4 inches. If the space is less, remove some sand. Then oil the form.

Mixing the Concrete

You can purchase premixed concrete, or you can mix your own. Use the basic formula for a concrete footing: mix 1 part cement, 3 parts sand, and 4 parts gravel. The maximum aggregate size should be 1½ inch. The amount of water required depends, as always, upon the sand (see Chapter 1). For the amount of concrete needed, a powered mixer is best. Test the mix to see if it is correct by making the slump test.

Making the Pour

Begin at one end of the form. Place the concrete mixture evenly from that end to the other. As you place the material, do not let it drop over 3 feet in height, because the drop from that height can cause segregation. "Spade" the concrete, especially at the corners of the form. Do not overdo this, however. If you do, the material could separate, causing the water to float to the surface.

Finishing and curing. Screed to attain the desired level of the completed pour. First, find a helper. Select a very straight 2x4 or 2x6 board that is longer than the form is wide. Place the screed across the upper edges of the form boards. Slide the screed back and forth as you move slowly down toward the other end of the form. Level all high spots and fill low spots. After filling in the low spots, go back and rescreed. Continue the operation until the entire slab has been leveled. This is the only finishing required.

Allow the concrete to set for about 4 or 5 hours; then dampen it with a fine mist from a garden hose. Make sure the water pressure is not too high—if it is, it will wash out the finish. Alternative methods of curing concrete are to cover it with burlap or old newspapers soaked with water.

Pouring the Tub

After the footing has cured, construct the inner and outer forms for the tub, as shown. Center the outer form on the foundation. To brace the outer form, cut 6 stakes of 2x4s to measure 24 inches long. Pound these in next to the slab, one at each corner and one at the half-way point along either long side. These stakes will support 2x4 braces for the outside form.

Fasten a 2x4 (on edge) with 8d nails so that one end supports the end wall of the form and the other end braces against the stake at that corner. The brace should form a right angle with the form wall and with the stake. Do this for all corners. The braces at the mid-points of the long walls push in against the walls. Finally cut 2 additional 2x4 braces that are 60 inches long. Nail one of these across the top of each short form wall for additional stability.

Once the outer form is secure, the inner form is suspended inside the outer form. The box-like opening in one short wall provides an open space through which the plumbing pipes are installed. This box rests on the footing. The rest of the inner form walls hang 3 inches above the footing. The open space thus created allows for the floor of the tub. Be sure to align the inner form so that the fixtures fall in the directions you desire.

Pouring the floor of the tub. If you do not use premixed concrete, use the following proportions to create the mixture for a watertight tank: for 1 part of cement, use 2¼ parts of sand and 3 parts of gravel whose maximum aggregate size is 1 inch. If you are using 1 bag of cement, use the following amounts of water for a given type of sand: dry sand requires 6 gallons, damp sand requires 5½ gallons, wet sand requires 5 gallons, and very wet sand requires 4¼ gallons. Again, hold to these proportions, even though you need less concrete than a full bag of cement will yield.

Before you begin the pour, insert reinforcing mesh supported by 1 to 2 inch rocks along the bottom. The rocks should be 6 inches from each other and from the sides of the tub. On top of these set a layer

To support the weight of the tub and of the wall between the bathroom and the deck, install doubled floor joists. The concrete forms will fit down between the joists.

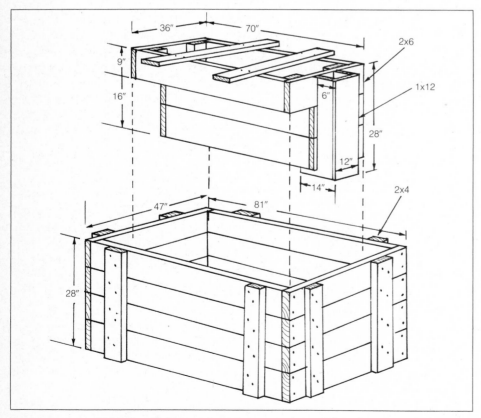

Don't pour concrete into the 12x14 in. rectangular area at the end of the inner form. Once the tub has cured, run the plumbing and drain pipes through this opening for easy maintenance.

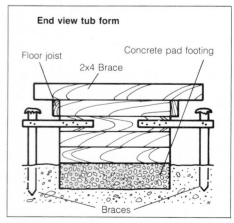

To prevent sliding on the footing during the pour, brace the sides of the form.

of 6x6 and 10x10 metal reinforcing mesh. Reinforcing mesh is sold in rolls. Cut the mesh with metal snippers. Be sure when you lay the mesh that none of the edges touch the forms themselves—you do not want the metal to stick out of the form once the concrete has set.

Then begin the pour. Spread the concrete carefully to be sure that there are no gaps between the mixture and the corners. Since the inner form walls are shorter than the outer form walls, carefully spread the concrete in the area below the inner form wall. Continue the pour until the mixture is level with the lower edge of the inner form. If the mesh has sunk down during the pour, hook it with something like a coathanger and lift it back up.

Now you must screed the floor so that it is level. Since the forms are in place, the screeding is more of a hand job than the screeding of the footing. Cut a short board that fits between the sides of the inner form. With the help of an assistant, pull the screed across the floor. Use a trowel to scoop out the excess concrete and level the section between the inner and outer walls. (Be alert, so you don't fall into the concrete!) Once the screeding

is finished, trowel the tub floor as smooth and level as you can. Let the tub floor cure for seven days.

Pouring the walls of the tub. After the floor has set, pour the walls of the tub. These must be reinforced; use ³⁄₈ inch reinforcing rods for the job. As you pour, insert vertical rods 6 inches apart all the way around the tub wall channel. Make sure that the rods are located halfway between the inner and outer forms. Otherwise the rods might show through after the concrete has set. Every time you have gone 6 inches up the side, lay a horizontal row of rods. By the time the entire tub has

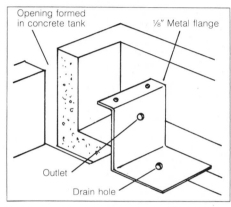

To house the plumbing, install a large metal flange over the open end of the tub.

been filled, you will have created a grid of reinforcing rods within the pour.

As the concrete is poured in the form, tamp the concrete to make sure that no air bubbles are trapped in the material. This is especially important next to the forms, since you will have to fill all air bubbles before you can install the tile. Keep the concrete damp and allow it to cure for at least seven days before removing the forms.

Installing the Flange
Covering the end of the tub that contains the plumbing is a large, ⅛ inch thick piece of sheet metal, especially cut and formed to cover the entire surface of the tub front wall. Unless you have considerable metal-working experience, have a professional form this flange for you. Measure the depth and width of the completed, cured front wall and have the flange built to fit. Then fasten it in place by inserting masonry anchors into the tub itself and screwing the flange in place with masonry screws.

Preparing the Surface
Remove all the form boards and supports. Use a hammer and chisel to break off any high spots or lumps created by the meeting of the form boards. Fill in any holes left by air bubbles that were not tamped out during the pouring. See Chapter 7 for repairing a concrete surface.

Leveling. Once the tub surface is repaired, cover it, including the metal flange area, with from two to four coats of portland mortar. These are intended to level out the surface. Apply each layer of mortar with a trowel to a thickness of ⅛ to ¼ inch. Allow each coat to dry at least 24 hours before laying the next. As you apply the mortar, hold the trowel as flat against the surface as you can. If the angle is more than 45 degrees, there will be ridges in the surface. By the time you are finished, your tub should have a level, smooth surface.

Waterproofing. Once the mortar has dried completely, you are ready to waterproof the tub. The key to the success of this tub installation is this step. Cover the entire tub—especially the flange area—with basement waterproofing sealer such as Thoroseal. Apply the sealer with a brush or a roller. The coat should be as thick as the manufacturer indicates. Let the waterproofing dry thoroughly. This

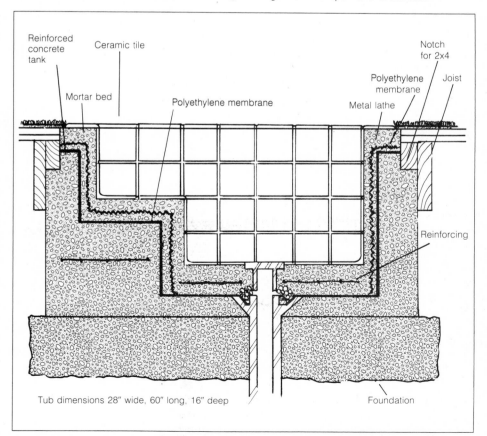

A second way to create a watertight tub is to install a water vapor barrier of 4 mil polyethylene. Fill about one half of the form, insert the film, and finish the pour.

will take about 4 to 6 hours, depending upon the humidity level in the air. Then sand the waterproofing smooth, using coarse sandpaper.

Repeat the entire process until you have applied four coats of waterproofing. Although this number might seem excessive, it isn't. Because of the attention paid, my tub has never suffered from the leakage problems often encountered with sunken tubs—even those based upon metal tanks.

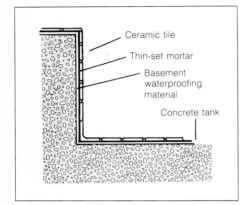

Four layers of basement waterproofing material create a watertight concrete tank.

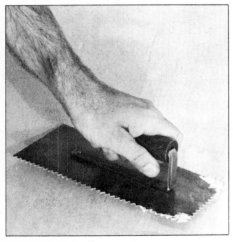

A prime coat is a moisture seal. It keeps the wall surface from absorbing moisture from the adhesive to weaken the bond. Apply the adhesive with the trowel's flat side.

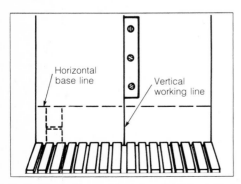

To tile the walls around a tub, establish vertical and horizontal working lines.

Plumbing. Now, in the opening provided in the forms and with the protection of the metal flange, run the plumbing connections into the tub. Vacuum away all debris and dust. Apply a prime coat of thin-set latex mortar adhesive. After the prime coat dries, you are ready to lay the tile.

Laying the Tile

Design considerations. The design of a sunken tub can aid the tiling process. Once the tile has been chosen, design the size of tub to correspond to the size of the tile so that no tiles need be cut. Think of the tub structure in terms of wall or floor surfaces rather than seeing the structure as a continuous whole. Plan to tile one section at a time. Tile the interior walls first; then the tub floor. Finish with the top of the tub walls.

Working lines. Before you begin, you must lay out working lines, so you will have a nice, neat, ''level-appearing'' job. Do not just start sticking tiles in place, although I admit that at this point it is tempting. A few basic guidelines will ensure a desirable final appearance.

(1) Plan the project so the starting point permits one continuous horizontal line across all the areas to be tiled.

(2) If you must cut tiles, set the tile in such a way that none of the cut pieces will be less than 2 inches wide.

(3) If you must cut a course of tile, make the cut on the row close to the base or bottom course.

(4) If tiles set with a thin grout line nearly fill the vertical or horizontal dimensions, try widening the grout line to avoid cutting any tiles.

Marking the horizontal and vertical lines for wall installation. Ceramic wall tiles are installed by starting at the bottom row and working upward. The first step is to establish a level horizontal base line. If you constructed your forms carefully, the joint between the bottom of the tub and the walls should be a level surface. This is your horizontal line.

To find the vertical line, dry lay a single row of tiles from corner to corner along the bottom. If you find that you will have to cut and lay one end tile that is smaller than half its normal size, move the tiles over so that larger cut tiles can be placed at each corner. At the approximate center, but corresponding to the nearest joint line, draw a vertical line on the wall from the bottom row of tile to the top row, where the tile will end. Use a carpenter's level to assure that the line is plumb. This is your vertical line.

Follow this procedure for all four tub walls. Extend the vertical lines up the walls and across the bottom of the tub. The lines on the tub floor should cross at right angles in the approximate center of the tub. The crossed lines will be the working lines of the floor layout.

Finishing wall corners. In my installation, I used no special corner tiles (cove tiles). Instead I just butted tiles on adjacent walls. However, you may use special

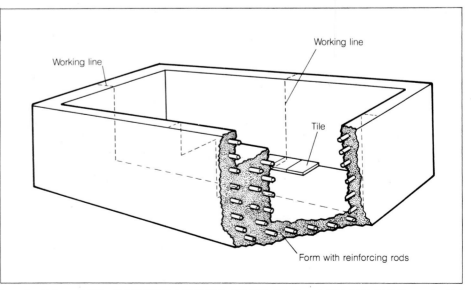

In order to have a tiling job that looks neat and well-planned, lay working lines before you spread the adhesive. Dry-lay tiles along the bottom; extend the lines up and across.

tiles to cover any corner or edge. These come in a number of styles, available from any tile dealer.

Applying adhesive to wall. Use portland-latex cement adhesive because of its water-resistant qualities. Critical water areas such as plumbing connections, corners in tub alcoves, voids in back of cove base, and joints between wall tile and floor tile should be prepacked with adhesive prior to spreading the bond coat.

Apply the adhesive with a notched trowel. Don't cover up the working lines; leave these visible until just prior to tiling in that area. Hold the trowel firmly against the surface at a 45 degree angle; spread the adhesive to cover the 10 to 20 square feet at a time. Don't cover a larger area; the adhesive will dry before all the tiles can be placed. The coat should be from ⅛ to ¼ inch thick. Bring the adhesive to within ½ inch of the point where the tile will end. If you are applying the adhesive with the correct amount of pressure, adhesive will appear only from the openings of the notches in the trowel. Each trail of adhesive will be called a "bead." The space between any two beads will be almost bare of adhesive. To check that you have applied the proper amount, position a tile in place and twist it back and forth a little. (Set all ceramic tile in this manner.) If adhesive squeezes out from under the tile, there is too much adhesive. If no adhesive squeezes out, remove the tile and look at the back. The spaces between the beads should have filled in to completely cover the tile back. If it is not completely covered, there is not enough adhesive.

Cutting the tile. A good rule of thumb about cutting tile is this: if one of two adjoining tile pieces must be cut, always cut the less complicated piece (a field tile, for example, rather than a cove). The cut will be easier to make, and, in case of error or breakage, the less expensive piece will have to be replaced.

First, determine the cut line. A typical installation would be as follows. You are filling in the bottom wall course. Work across until you can lay no more full-size tiles. Let the adhesive set. (You can continue filling in other rows during this time.)

Take two loose tiles (Tile A and Tile B) and a pencil, a felt-tip pen, or sharp, pointed tool like an ice pick or glass cutter. Place Tile A directly on top of the last full-size tile in the base line course, next to the corner. Place Tile B on top of Tile A; then move Tile B over securely against the wall. Using the edge of Tile B as a guide, draw or scribe a line on the surface of Tile A. This is your preliminary cutting line. If you use cove or corner trim, move Tile B over until it meets the edge of the cove tile, but doesn't cover part of the cove corner.

To find the final cutting line, figure in the width of two grout lines. If the line is ⅛ inch wide, two will be ¼ inch. You must make allowances for the grout lines before you cut the tile. Measure in on the tile; draw the final cutting line.

To apply adhesive, hold the trowel at a 45 degree angle to the surface; press firmly. Notches in the trowel will leave trails that show up as separate, distinct rows of adhesive.

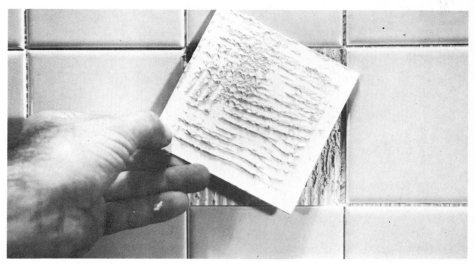

Press a tile in place. If you applied too much adhesive, it will squeeze out from the edges. Lift the tile. If the back is not filled in, you applied too little.

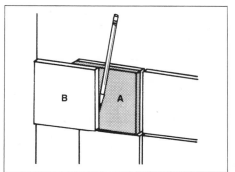

To find the cut line, place Tile A over the last full tile. Place Tile B over top of Tile A; slide Tile B to the corner; mark Tile A.

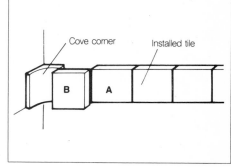

If there is a corner finishing piece, slide Tile B to the edge of the trim; mark Tile A. Allow for grout lines; then cut Tile A.

Tile can be cut with a rented tile cutter. Score the face of the tile as shown.

Instead of a tile cutter, you can score tiles with a conventional glass cutter.

Place the tile over a coat-hanger wire. Push down on both sides to snap the tile.

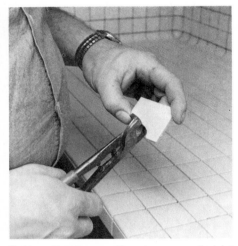

Cut irregular shapes with a nipper or a slip-joint pliers. Take ⅛ in. bites.

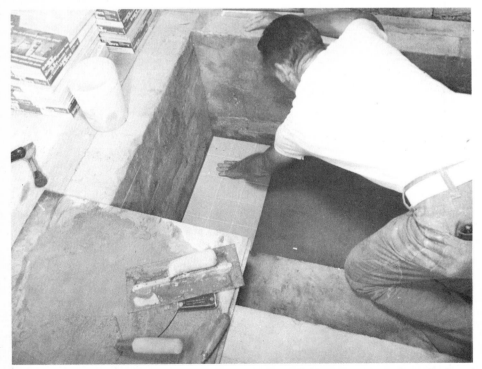

Simplify the tile job by using tile "sheets" containing several tiles fastened together with thread webbing or special silicone grout. Lay the sheets as you would regular tiles.

Using a tile cutter. The easiest way to cut straight lines on tile is with a tile cutter, which you either buy or rent from your tile dealer. It is a good idea to practice on several scrap pieces before you start the actual tiling job. Wear safety glasses whenever you cut ceramic tile—flying clay and glaze could injure your eyes.

A tile cutter is a large glass cutter with a carbide-tipped blade enclosed in a sliding frame. Clamp the tile into place, glaze side up. (If your tile has a ridged back, the ridges should lie parallel to the direction that the blade will cut. Re-mark the tile if this is not the case.) Score a line across the tile with the blade and remove the tile.

With the glazed surface still facing up, place the scored line over a piece of wire approximately ⅛ inch in diameter. (A coat hanger is an excellent choice.) Place one hand on either side of the scored line and press down. The tile will snap in two.

Using a tile nipper. Cut irregular openings for plumbing openings with a tile nipper. (You can also use an ordinary slip joint pliers.) Holding the tile with the glazed side up, take small, ⅛ inch bites with the nippers to break off tiny pieces at a time. Take your time. If you take too large a bite, the tile might break. You also could destroy the cutoff line or cut too much and have to start all over again.

Tile layout methods. For a small project such as this one, you probably can work from corner to corner to lay the tiles. Set them in place with a slight twisting motion. Leave space for the grout line. Usually this will be ⅛ to ¼ inch wide. Some tiles have built in spacers. If yours do not, either use manufactured spacers, or insert small wood splinters, such as toothpicks, between the

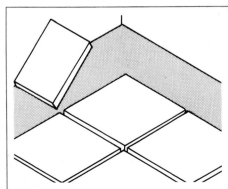

Lay tiles from the center of the tub out to the sides. Fill in as many full-sized tiles as possible. If needed, cut tiles to fill.

tiles. As you work, frequently check both the vertical and horizontal grout lines with a level.

Every so often, set the tile firmly in place by using a "beating block." This is a carpet-covered wood block equal in length to at least two tiles. Lay it across the tiles; gently tap the block with a hammer. Set all the tiles in this manner in order to eliminate any air pockets and to achieve a firm bond between the tile and the adhesive.

Installing drain cap, grout and plumbing fixtures. Let the adhesive set for at least two days. Then install the chrome drain cap. Seal this well with the waterproofing sealer. Finally, apply grout to all the surfaces.

Select a grout color that matches the project and the location of the tile. Today's colorful grouts can accentuate light, white or dark tile. There is no need to stay with traditional white grout. Grout color also helps hide soil buildup.

Mix or use the grout according to the manufacturer's instructions. Using a rubber float or squeegee, spread the grout diagonally across the joints between the tile. Make sure you pack the grout securely into every joint; watch for air bubbles. The time and type of cure will depend upon your type of grout. Some grouts require a dry cure; others need to be dampened periodically. The length of the cure also varies. Follow the directions for

your particular installation.

As soon as the grout becomes firm, use a wet sponge to wash the excess grout from the faces of the tiles. To shape the grout lines, run the handle of an old toothbrush along the joints. This process is called "striking the joints." Then clean

the tiles and smooth ("dress") the joints with a damp sponge. Allow the surfaces to dry, then polish with a clean cloth. It will probably take several washings to completely clean away all the excess grout. Finally, install the caps on the plumbing fixtures.

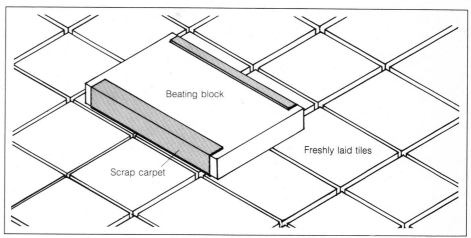
Use carpet to cover a wood block equal in length to 2 tiles. Tapping gently with a hammer, slide this "beating block" across the tiles to set them firmly into the adhesive.

Use a soft rubber squeegee to apply grout. Work the squeegee at an angle to the grout lines. This will completely fill the joints and leave no open air pockets.

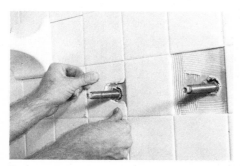
The areas around plumbing pipes must be fully packed with adhesive. Then place cut tiles.

Grout and cure the tub. Then finish off the installation with the plumbing flanges.

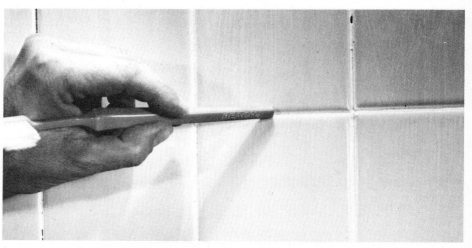
An old toothbrush is an excellent tool for shaping grout lines. Then use a sponge and clear water to clean the tiles and to smooth, or "dress," the lines.

BACKYARD PATIO AND FOUNTAIN

The patio on page 7 utilizes many masonry techniques. The patio, planters and benches are stucco-covered concrete. The fountain, created in the same way as the sunken tub, is covered with ceramic tile.

Planning and Excavating

A project this complex requires careful planning. Outline the patio with stake-and-string; set up batter boards; excavate for footings and base materials. Save topsoil to use later. Stake out the planters and benches. Allow for footings, set batter boards and excavate.

Finally set the stake-and-string outline of the fountain near water and drainage pipes. Allow for the footing, set batter boards and excavate. Connect water and drainage to the fountain. Then prepare the base and pour the footings.

Creating the fountain. After the footings cure, build a form of 2x6s. To create the octagonal shape, cut the ends of the formboards at a 45-degree angle. Butt tightly and brace with 2x4 stakes. Install top spreaders. After pouring the fountain walls, tamp to avoid honeycombing.

Finishing the fountain. Screed the top of the fountain walls; float level. After a seven-day cure, remove the forms. Install the drain and fountain head. Pour and float the floor to slope gently to the drain. Cure; then apply mortar to level and fill holes and cracks. Apply at least three coats of basement waterproofing.

Tiling the fountain. Using the methods discussed earlier, apply the tile with a portland-latex cement adhesive. Wait 24 hours; apply a grout designed for outdoor use.

The Patio and Accessories

Build forms for the planters, benches and steps. When building forms for structures on the upper patio level, allow for the extra height by using 2x12 formboards. Pour and cure the concrete. Then prepare the surface for tiling. The surface must be level, not smoothly troweled.

Creating the Upper Patio Level

Build and pitch the patio forms as in Chapter 2. The top of the formboards must come to the desired height for the two levels. If the upper level is substantially higher, place a bottom layer of

coarse fill that is thick enough to achieve the correct height. Follow this with a 1½-inch layer of gravel and 2 inches of sand to create solid fill.

Laying the brick and tile. Pour and cure a 4-inch slab. Lay brick on mortar for the bench seats and planters. Lay patio tiles in portland-latex cement adhesive; finish with portland-latex grout.

BUILDING A BARBECUE

A brick barbecue is an ideal masonry

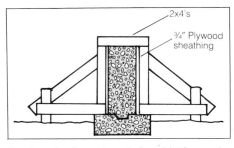

Small walls (less than 3 feet high) can be formed with sections of ¾ in. plywood. Support the sides with 2x4 braces. Secure the top opening with 2x4 strips every 2 feet.

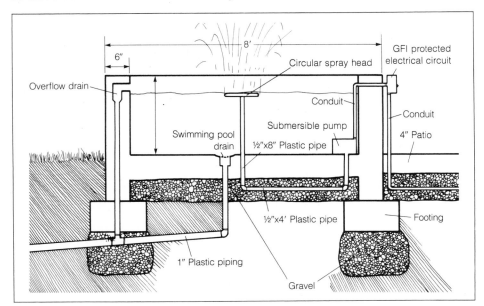

The pool layout is shown here. Install plumbing lines, if possible, below the footings. Special adapter pipe connects the overflow drain and pipe leading to the drainage lines.

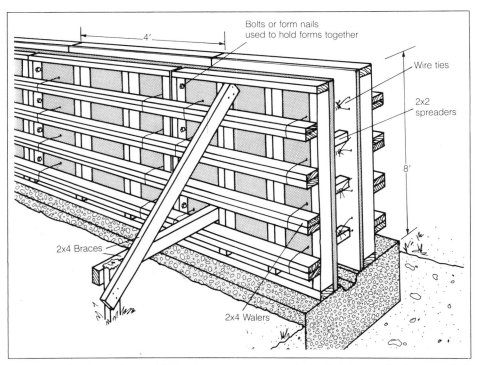

Use 4x8 prefabricated forms of ¾ in. plywood sheathing nailed to 2x4 frames. Set forms on their long or short sides; fasten together if needed. Hold forms in place with 2x4 walers connected with wire ties. Pass wire ends through forms and twist together inside. To ensure wall thickness, add 2x2 blocks inside forms. Brace the structure with 2x4 bracing and stakes.

project. It isn't particularly complicated, but requires attention to detail. Work a couple of Saturdays and the evenings between and you'll complete it in about a week.

The basic shape is a large U. Parallel to the sides of the U are two inner walls that enclose to create the barbecue's center section. The firebox and grill sit here. The center is filled with rubble and concrete so it absorbs heat and is more efficient. A chimney keeps smoke above table height. Maple cutting tops rest above storage areas.

Grill Alternatives

Purchased grill. This barbecue is fairly simple because of a metal firebox and grill unit that slides into place.

Built-in grill. This rests on pins set in mortar between courses. Use ½x4-inch bolts. About one inch should protrude. Provide several pin heights to adjust the distance between the grate and the coals.

Footing Specifications

Excavate for a 4-inch footing. This must be 4 inches larger than the barbecue, on all sides. Install 2 inches of gravel. Reinforce the footing with a grid of ⅜-inch rods, as shown on p. 108. Pour; cure for seven days.

Building the Barbecue

The bottom half. Using a nail, score the concrete to mark the outline of the barbecue; then draw in with a long straightedge and a carpenter's square. Dry lay the first course of bricks on the base. If possible, cut no bricks, but leave enough space for the grill.

Lay the first course for the outer U, then for the dividers. (If desired, close in the front face for a course or two.) Butt the first divider bricks against the back wall. Finally, lay the first course for the front enclosure wall. Build to the desired height. Because the walls are short, work course by course instead of building leads.

Filling in the center. After the center is high enough, fill it with rubble. Add enough sand to level, and end with a 2- to 3-inch layer of concrete. Use the tops of the walls as a screed guide. Trowel smooth.

Building the upper level and the chimney. Build up the outer and inner walls for three courses, or until the center

opening matches the grill. Then form the chimney with the back wall and shortened divider courses. Five courses create the firebox opening. Lay mortar on the fifth course; then embed a 3x3 angle iron for a lintel across the front of the opening. Lay mortar on the lintel; build up at least six more courses. Finish with a cap course.

Finishing the Barbecue

Maple cutting tops. The cutting tops are made of ¾x6-inch maple lumber. Your local lumber yard dealer will help you make changes to fit available thicknesses.

Purchase seven 9-foot boards. Cut them into 4½-foot pieces; then rip into

1½-inch wide strips, so you have 56 strips, 28 per top. Lay the strips so the ¾-inch side is up. Cut strips to fit the notch on each side of the chimney; then glue each top together with waterproof wood glue. Keep corners square.

To create an overhang, cut and glue pieces of 2½-inch-wide wood retaining strips to the front, back and outside edges of each top.

Storage doors. Attach two door hinges to the front edge of each top. Then cut and fasten ¾-inch Exterior plywood doors that will swing down to close off the storage area. To hold the doors closed, attach magnetic fasteners to the barbecue with masonry anchors.

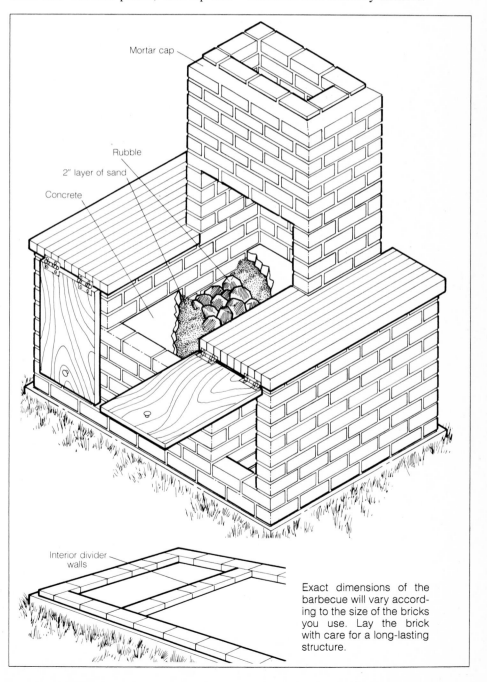

Mortar cap

Rubble

2" layer of sand

Concrete

Interior divider walls

Exact dimensions of the barbecue will vary according to the size of the bricks you use. Lay the brick with care for a long-lasting structure.

Barbecues Built Using Other Materials

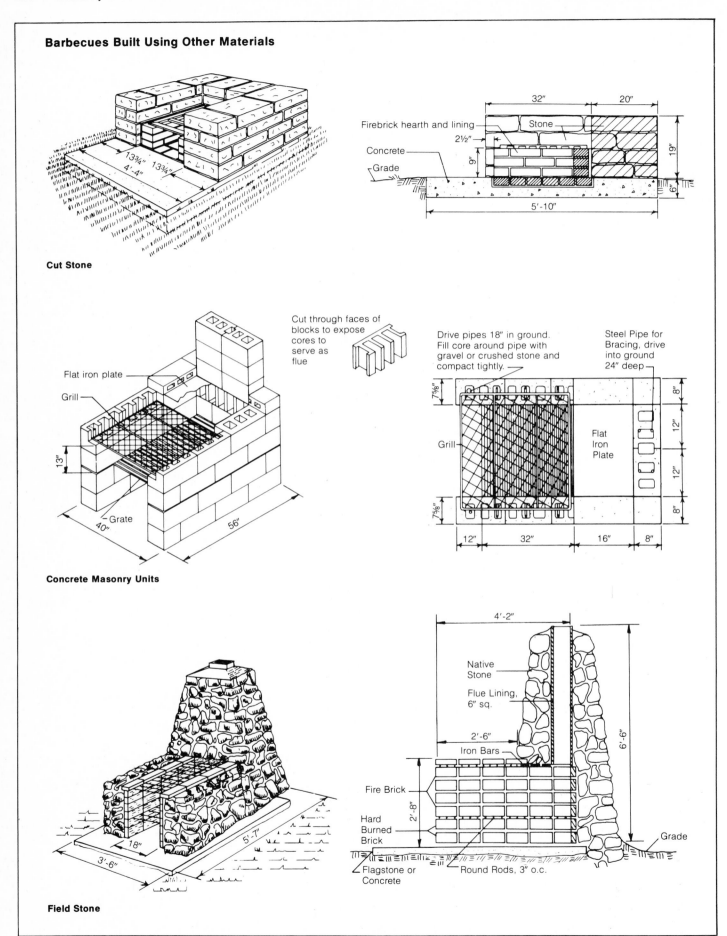

Cut Stone

Firebrick hearth and lining
2½"
Concrete
Grade
Stone
32"   20"
9"
19"
6"
5'-10"

Concrete Masonry Units

Flat iron plate
Grill
13"
Grate
40"
56"

Cut through faces of blocks to expose cores to serve as flue

Drive pipes 18" in ground. Fill core around pipe with gravel or crushed stone and compact tightly.

Steel Pipe for Bracing, drive into ground 24" deep

7⅝"
Grill
Flat Iron Plate
7⅝"
8"
12"
12"
8"
12"   32"   16"   8"

Field Stone

4'-2"
Native Stone
Flue Lining, 6" sq.
2'-6"
Iron Bars
Fire Brick
Hard Burned Brick
2'-8"
6'-6"
Grade
Flagstone or Concrete
Round Rods, 3" o.c.
18"
5'-7"
3'-6"

Barbecues built of materials other than brick follow similar procedures, and should rest always upon a concrete slab for adequate support.

BUILDING A STONE FIREPLACE

A fireplace is a very popular masonry project. It can be used to provide supplemental heat, or if the home is a small one constructed around a central fireplace, the fireplace can be used as the sole heat source. Fireplaces can be constructed of either brick or stone, depending on your particular taste and the style of your home. In almost all instances, construction of the fireplace is a masonry job that requires investment of both time and money. However, by doing your own work you should be able to save about half of the cost involved.

Planning Enough Support

Careful planning is a must for building a fireplace. Unlike a bookcase or cabinet, you cannot move a fireplace once it is in position. The weight of even a small natural stone fireplace will run many tons, putting quite a load on the ground.

In most cases you will need to submit a plan to the building authorities and acquire a permit.

Complex construction is required for a traditional masonry fireplace built on the outside with an opening through the wall on an existing home. A fireplace and chimney in the center of a room—or even in the center of a house—may be easier to build and is much more heat efficient. An advantage of a fireplace on the outside and built flush to the interior wall is that you do not use up as much floor space; cutting openings through the floor, ceiling and roof also is avoided. Assuring an adequate foundation for an inside fireplace can also be a problem in an existing home. The direction the floor joists run is another concern with an inside fireplace, requiring attention during the planning stage. If the joists run at right angles to the fireplace wall you will need a lot more supporting framing when cutting very far into the room floor. On the other hand, joists running parallel with the fireplace wall enable you to go farther into the room without as much support framing.

Figuring the Size of the Opening

You will have to determine your dimensions depending upon your room and available space. One of the most important considerations when designing your own fireplace is the size of the opening. Here is a good rule of thumb for matching the opening width to the room size: (1) add the room length and width together for a total number of feet; (2) allow one inch of fireplace opening per foot of the total—i.e., a 12x24 foot room would need a 36 inch wide (12+24=36) opening. The height of the opening will depend upon the width and the overall design of the firebox and the wall. (Refer to chart for recommended proportions.) A fireplace of this width can combine dramatically with other elements to create the dominant wall in the room.

An ideal advanced project using masonry and concrete is a fireplace. For safety reasons, careful construction is mandatory. Cover the front with a veneer of stone or brick.

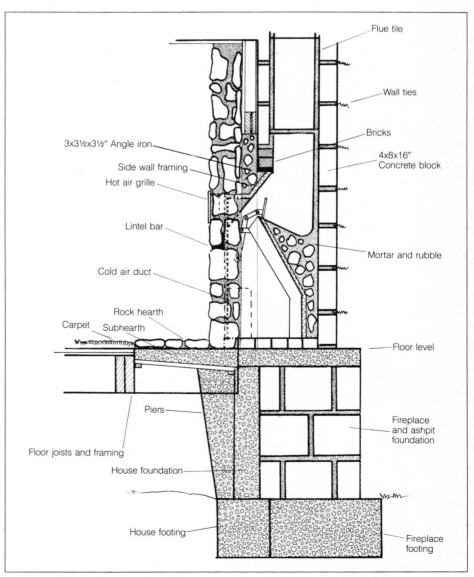

A vertical cross-section shows the stone fireplace described below. A prefabricated firebox was used. The entire structure rests on a new foundation just outside the house.

Using a Liner Unit

There are probably as many different ways to build fireplaces as there are masons, and there are many existing improperly constructed fireplaces, which are not only smoky, but dangerous. We recommend use of a preformed metal liner unit, whether you do the construction yourself or you hire a contractor.

Liner feature. The best types, such as the unit shown in this chapter, utilize an interior liner of ribbed boiler plate and an outside shell of metal. This provides an air-filled heat chamber around the firebox, which acts as a heat exchanger and sends the warmed air into the room. Side ducts bring in cool air, which is heated and then discharged into the dwelling. The ducts are fitted with fan motors to provide a more efficient exchange of air. The old-fashioned fireplace is only about 10 percent efficient, whereas this type is nearly 25 percent efficient. Heat can circulate to all corners of the room, and into other rooms, depending upon how the ductwork and vents are arranged.

There are additional advantages to use of a preformed unit. The double-walled steel unit comes complete with firebox, throat, smoke dome and a properly hinged and operating damper. Most also come complete with a construction guide that eliminates most confusion and should minimize installation errors.

Smoke shelf and damper. One of the problem areas when constructing a fireplace is the smoke shelf/damper, since these area dimensions and shapes are

critical. By using a preshaped unit, these details are already constructed for you. The units are properly engineered and built with correct angles and dimensions. This eliminates construction mistakes. The damper is pivoted at the proper point and swings backward to an open position, providing a well-designed smoke shelf (preventing downdraft and smoke problems).

Materials and Tools

A fireplace can be constructed from a wide choice of masonry materials, including many different kinds of brick as well as natural stone. This stone fireplace is actually a stone-enclosed, prefabricated fireplace installed outside the house on a new, separate footing and foundation with an ashpit. The house wall was opened—and reframed to meet the required clearances—so the face of the prefabricated unit could fit a few inches inside the room. This type of installation was required because of the mass and weight of the stone.

Builders frequently suggest a masonry surround for a prefabricated fireplace rather than a masonry fireplace built from scratch because it is easier, more dependable in engineering and is subject to fewer structural limitations. This stone fireplace could have been included anywhere in the house—if it were all new construction. However, placing this stone-faced fireplace and chimney on an exterior base meant that there was no need for major reconstruction of the basement floor,

floor/ceiling joists, or the roof.

This natural stone fireplace took about three months for the owner to build, working only an hour or two each day plus weekends. Because work began late in the fall, the fireplace itself was constructed first, as was the fireplace front on the inside. The block chimney was also completed early. However, the surrounding walls, raised rock hearth, air ductwork, and outside stone veneer were left until the following spring.

Using Natural Field Stone

To build a project as large as this takes a great many stones of many sizes—both large and small—of different shapes. Try to find stones 3 to 4 inches thick. The best stones have natural corners and good square edges, but a mixture of stones can also be used to create decorative effects. These also vary considerably in color; if properly selected they can create interesting effects. Use one type of stone primarily to keep the design from looking like a hodgepodge. Always have on hand plenty of square-corner rocks for use on corners. This makes the job much easier.

The main guideline is to stagger the courses; the rule is that two stones go above one, and one above two. They should all overlap to provide strength. In addition, the method of pointing the joints will be important to the project's strength.

Mortar and Sand

It is hard to estimate the amount of sand and masonry cement needed, so just start out with a fixed amount and purchase more as you need it. Cement is hard to store for a long period and over time will lose its strength. If you decide to color the mortar, such as in the fireplace shown, you will also need mortar color. (See also Chapter 5.)

Tools

The tools that are needed for building and stone fireplaces are not complicated. Naturally, a powered cement mixer will make mixing the mortar easier, but it is not very difficult to do by hand. You usually can rent a power mixer. However, because of the time involved in building a project such as a stone fireplace, it might be less expensive to purchase one. On the other hand, the small batches of mortar that are required for this type of construc-

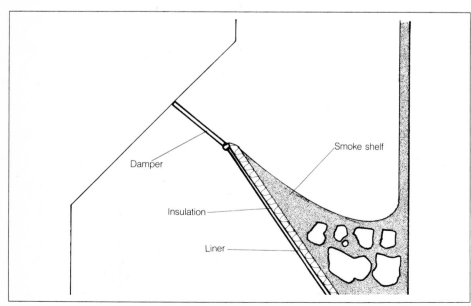

A liner unit is a complete firebox. Back and front walls slope to ensure heat reflection and to create the throat. Fill space behind the back and shape into the smoke shelf.

tion also can be mixed in a wheelbarrow, or in a mud box and shoveled into a wheelbarrow. If mixing in this manner, an old hoe with holes cut in the flat end makes a good mixing tool.

Mortar board. You will need a mortar board, which is nothing more than a board (approximately 16x16 inches) with a handle fastened in the center. You can create one easily from ¼ inch plywood. Cover it with a good paint to prevent moisture from being pulled out from the mortar by the wood. Attach a piece of a closet dowel, or 1¾x6 inch block, using a flathead countersunk wood screw. A small (24 inch x 24 inch) platform, resting on sawhorses or concrete blocks, also works well.

Because you will need a surface on which to set the mortar board while selecting stones, find an open-ended box, or even an old bucket, for this purpose. In addition, you will need a couple of pointed trowels, a carpenter's level, and carpenter's tools for framing in the opening, a hacksaw for cutting reinforcing rod, a whisk broom, steel brush and plastic buckets for cleaning up, and an old round head bolt for pointing the joints (or you can buy an inexpensive joint tool). You will need access to clean water, and scaffolding to enable you to work safely on the chimney as you build upward.

Opening the Wall

With all plans, materials and tools on hand, the first step is to lay out the wall opening or the floor openings, depending on fireplace locations. If your fireplace is built flush on an exterior wall, you can build the chimney along the exterior of the house and avoid any major cutting of the structural members that support the floor. Adjust the opening so you will not have to cut vertically down a wall stud. Locate the studs by tapping on the wall with a hammer. A hollow sound means no stud. A dull sound usually denotes a stud. Then either drive a long nail in place to determine if there is a stud, or use a portable electric drill to bore a hole through the wall to locate the stud. Lay out and plan the framing for the wall opening. The opening will have to be large enough to allow for clearances required by building codes as well as space for insulation and stone and mortar fill. Frame the opening to ensure that the structural strength in the wall is not weak-

ened. Double the side studs and install a double header across the top of the opening, securing the header to the cut studs with nails.

Supporting the Fireplace

Next, measure and mark the location of the foundation. If the foundation is not constructed correctly and on firm soil, the fireplace can settle, shift, and pull away from the house. A typical stone fireplace can weigh 20 tons or more; a larger fireplace can weigh much more. A fireplace must be built on solid rock, or on a foundation strong enough to support it.

Creating the Footing

The size of the footing will vary according to local ground conditions, frost conditions, and local building codes. It must be at least six inches wider than the dimension of the outside faces of the fireplace; on some soils it may need to be more. The depth will vary. The fireplace shown features an extremely high two-

story chimney, so the footing was poured two feet deep, even though the frost line is not that deep.

Excavation. The first step in creating the footing is excavation. First mark off the footing area, using stakes. Make this area at least six inches larger all around than the finished chimney and fireplace dimensions. Make the excavation quite a bit larger than needed; it's easier to work in an open excavation rather than having to try and fit boards and form stakes in too small an area. Then excavate to the proper depth. Be sure to remove all loose dirt. In case the fireplace is to be installed next to a concrete slab, excavate up to the slab and slab footing, but leave it alone. If the fireplace is next to a continuous foundation wall, you may wish to excavate under the wall foundation to add additional strength, but in most cases this won't be necessary—merely excavate next to the wall foundation. You can then utilize a cantilevered hearth on the inside of the house portion of the fireplace.

After stripping the house siding, cut through the sheathing with a circular saw. Don't remove the saw guard; wear protective gear.

Because an exterior deck was added behind the fireplace, the foundation was filled with rubble. As a result, there was no ashpit.

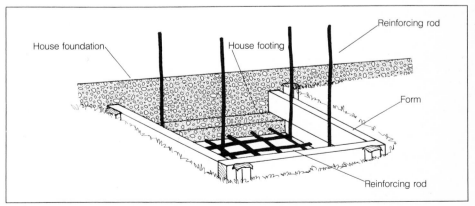

A fireplace requires a solid, reinforced footing and foundation adjacent to the house footing. Vertical reinforcing in each corner carries up through to the top of the footing.

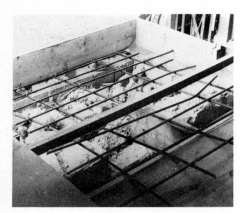

Lay reinforcement rods throughout the sub-hearth. Use wire ties at all junctures.

Building Forms

Once you have excavated the area, set up corner batter boards with leveled string lines to locate the corners of the footing corners. Use 2x6 form boards to construct a form to hold the footing concrete in place during the pouring. Brace the form with supporting 2x4s. A footing must extend at least twelve inches below the frost line in any particular area.

Reinforcing. Reinforce the foundation using ³⁄₈ or ¹⁄₂ inch reinforcing rods tied into a grid pattern and spaced about eight inches apart. Support this about halfway up from the bottom of the footing. Set it on rocks to hold it in place.

Vertical reinforcing rods should also be set into the footing while the concrete is still wet. These will help tie the fireplace to the footing. Set the vertical rods at each corner. of the fireplace chimney. Position them carefully, so they will be within the chimney walls yet not in the path of the preformed metal fireplace unit.

Placing the concrete. Pour and finish the footings as described in Chapter 2.

Reaching Correct Floor Level

One of the most important factors in planning the construction of the footing and foundation is determining proper heights. The floor of the hearth must come out level with the inside floor of the house. If the house floor is well above ground level, you will have to construct a rather high foundation; if the house utilizes a slab floor, the footing and foundation will be almost at ground level. In most cases you should measure down three inches from the desired firebox height (including firebrick); mark this level and build the masonry foundation to this height. If, as in the construction shown,

the floor is much above ground level, you may wish to construct a foundation of concrete or concrete blocks filled with rubble and mortar to reach the correct height.

Creating the Ash Pit

The foundation can also contain an ash pit. In the example given here, the ash pit was eliminated because an outdoor deck was to be installed around the chimney. Construct a masonry ash pit using concrete block and 2x6 forms. In this instance, the middle portion of the foundation or masonry-built-up foundation is left hollow, and the two sides are filled with rubble and mortar. A hole is framed with 2x6s for the ash pit door. The cleanout door is mortared firmly in place after the ash pit has cured and the 2x6s have been removed. The ash pit is poured at the same time as the subhearth. For an easy-to-clean ash pit, slope the concrete floor slightly from back to front so the

ashes will slide down toward the door as you clean them out. The vertical reinforcing rods will continue up through the ash pit. For more details, see p. 117–18.

Planning the Wall and Floor Openings

Once the foundation has been constructed, the wall opening can be made. Because it will probably be some time before the opening is closed off, it is a good idea to have a tarp or some other covering on hand. The opening must be framed properly to support the weight. The rough opening must be much larger than the planned finished opening to allow for installing framing. Place support beams and plate in below to hold up the ceiling and the wall until the framing can be completed.

Cutting the Exterior

Wood or stucco. Mark the location of the opening on the outside and inside

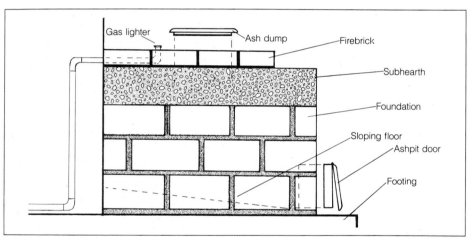

The foundation of a fireplace usually encloses an ashpit with an exterior cleanout door. One useful feature shown here is a gas pipe-fire lighter that will ignite any wood.

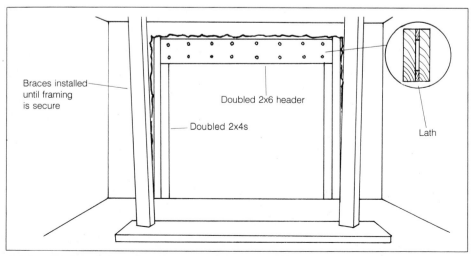

Install braces inside the house before you remove supporting ceiling studs. To restore support strength to the wall, install a doubled header across the top of the new opening.

walls. Use a brace and bit with a long electrician's bit to bore through at each corner, creating corner marks. Then use a straightedge or a level to mark around the boundaries to be cut. The same method can be used to mark the opening of a stucco house. Then use a metal cutting blade in a circular saw (watch for nails) for the initial outside wall cut.

Brick. This is not an easy process, and may require hiring a professional. To cut through brick you will need to first determine the location on the outside wall; then bore the holes using a masonry bit. Use a brick hammer and brick chisel to remove the bricks between the lines, and a little farther on all sides, remortaring the bricks in place after the chimney has been installed. In most instances you will not need reinforcing at the edges, but you should remove all bricks from floor to ceiling as you go up, to prevent sagging.

Making the Interior Cut

Remove the interior wallboard or plaster and lath (if in an old house) by first cutting the surface with a knife or key-hole saw and then pulling pieces away from the studs. Once the wall coverings on both sides have been removed, use a hand saw to cut out the studs at the top line. Pull the studs in and out to force them off the nails, which come up through the bottom plate. Using a hand saw and chisel, also cut through the plate on both sides, and remove it.

Build a new framing for the wall using double studs and a 2x6 double header as shown at the left and install it in place, carefully checking for plumb. Then toe-nail solidly in place.

Cutting the Flooring

After the wall has been opened and the opening framed properly, the next step is to cut away the flooring for the hearth. This also must be framed with double headers and joists, as shown. Steel joist hangers can be used instead to provide extra strength. In addition, you may wish to use concrete pier 4x4 posts to give even more support for the weight of the hearth and fireplace front. Since the fireplace shown utilizes natural stone for the side walls and cold air ducts, as well as the modified raised hearth, it was extremely heavy. Therefore, it was also supported with concrete piers poured against the foundation wall and down to the footing.

If the floor joists run at right angles to the wall rather than parallel to the wall, you will need to place a heavy support beam underneath them as a preliminary step. You won't need a steel beam on a concrete slab, but over a crawl space or a basement sometimes the use of a beam can help eliminate sagging and settling.

Creating the Subhearth

The actual hearth rests on a concrete subhearth. This is that portion over the foundation on which the fireplace unit sits, and which extends out into the room, underneath the hearth. The entire sub-hearth is poured concrete; the portion that fits into the room is most commonly cantilevered from the foundation. Again, make sure that the finished subhearth will allow for the firebrick portion of the hearth as well as whatever you use for the extension into the room. The ceramic tile, rock or brick used on the hearth should be flush with the floor, or come to the height you desire if building a raised hearth. The allowances are ¾ inch for tile and 2¼ inches for common brick. Dimensions for stone are based on your stone supply. Plan also on a bed of ½ inch mortar.

The subhearth should be at least six inches thick. Eight inches may be needed for a heavy fireplace. For a cantilevered forehearth, or the cantilevered portion of the hearth, install a wooden base form (see page 118) between the foundation and the doubled floor joists. This form may be left in place permanently.

Size. The size of the forehearth will depend to some extent upon how far into the room the fireplace unit will extend. The subhearth must provide support for a forehearth that extends a minimum of 16 inches in front of the fireplace opening. If the unit extends into the room 12 inches, the cantilevered subhearth must extend 28 inches from the house wall.

Frames and forms. For the construction shown, the outside edge of the sub-hearth was framed using wood. This was left in place so it could later be used as support for a deck which would extend out from the fireplace. However, in most cases the outside will be framed with brick or block. In either case, check that all framing is level. The preformed unit must be installed level.

The area over the clean-out ash pit can be formed using wire mesh to prevent

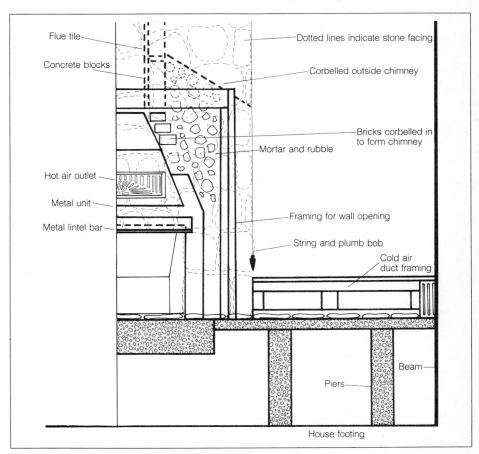

To support the increased weight on the floor joists, additional concrete piers were added to accept the stress of the concrete subhearth and the stone facing on the fireplace.

Lay firebrick on the firebox hearth area. Allow for the brick's thickness when you determine the required level of the subhearth.

Once you have laid the firebrick, set the prefabricated firebox in position. A mortar coat seals the firebox to the firebrick.

With the unit secured to the base, cover it with a layer of insulation to cushion expansion and to avoid cracking the masonry.

concrete from getting into that section. The subhearth must be reinforced with $\frac{3}{8}$ inch steel rods spaced from six to eight inches apart and tied securely. These should be placed about three inches below the top of the pour, and supported securely on rocks or chunks of rubble before the concrete is poured.

Pouring the Concrete

With a little work you can mix your own. The formula for this concrete pour is: one part portland cement, two parts sand, and three parts gravel or small stone. Add only enough water to make the concrete fluid; mix well.

Allow the concrete to cure for at least seven days, preferably longer. Keep it covered with damp sacks to prevent its drying out too quickly. Note that the reinforcing vertical rods must also extend up through the subhearth, placed carefully so they will be inside the outer chimney wall with enough room left for the installation of the metal fireplace unit.

If an ash dump is to be installed in the ash pit, the ash dump door must be framed in during the framing of the forms for the subhearth.

Laying the Hearth

After the concrete has set, you will be ready to lay the finished inside hearth. This must be installed using firebrick and special firebrick mortar which will withstand the heat of the firebox. Note that you need to install the firebrick only in the area of the firebox, and not entirely out to the sides; however, create a large firebrick-covered area on which the metal unit can sit. The firebricks are set onto a thin layer of mortar, with a thin layer in joints between bricks.

If you have planned to install an ash dump, the firebricks will be fitted around it. If you are including a gas log lighter, it also must be fitted in place at this time, using standard ½ inch gas pipe for a 20 inch log lighter unit with either natural or LP gas orifices. An on-off control valve may be recessed in the hearth or the fireplace wall.

Placing the Firebrick

First, measure the area of the metal unit and mark its outline, with a pencil, onto the hearth. You must make sure all the firebricks will extend out past the outside edges of the metal unit. The mortar used

is fireclay mortar, which is available at building supply dealers. Masonry cement mortar should not be used. The mortar seals the bottom of the heating unit to the firebrick, provides a means of leveling the unit, and prevents smoke from leaking out into the cold air ducts.

Mix the fireclay to the proper consistency as described on the mix package. Then trowel on the thin bed of mortar (approximately ¼ inch thick). Then start laying the firebricks in place, positioning them in the mortar bed and leveling them by tapping lightly with a brick hammer. Keep placing a level on their tops to make sure you keep them all level and their surfaces flush. Butter between each brick as you go, again leaving about a ¼ inch mortar joint. Once all the bricks have been laid, remove the excess with a trowel. Do not use a jointing tool to finish the joints or you will have depressions in the hearth that will be hard to clean. Instead, try to keep the hearth surface as smooth as possible.

Installing the Metal Unit

After the firebrick has cured properly (about 24 hours) set the unit in place, centering it over the firebrick and making sure it protrudes into the room the proper amount for your particular face design. The unit can protrude as much as a foot into the room, or as little as two to three inches, depending on how far out into the room you wish the face to be. The normal distance would be about eight inches. The hearth extension should be 16 inches into the room.

Placement of the larger units takes at least two people, so plan on asking for help. Be sure you install the unit level and plumb with the seal of fireclay mortar. This is extremely important; future construction will depend on the unit's being correctly positioned.

Adding the Insulation

Once the mortar has set, wrap fiberglass batt insulation around the entire unit. The insulation usually comes with the unit and is held in place with a thin coating of mortar. No metal surfaces should be allowed to contact the surrounding masonry. The insulation provides a cushion for the unit, handles expansion and contraction of the metal due to heating and cooling, and prevents cracks in the masonry. The procedure is a formidable one, but is stressed by the manufacturers of the unit. Apply regular or fireclay mortar firmly over the metal unit until the unit is covered. Then press the fiberglass matting in place over the wet mortar. All corners and edges are given a double layer of the insulation to provide more protection in those areas. This is no problem, because the second outside layer of insulation will stick quite readily to the first layer already installed. The overlap should be about two inches. Let the mortar dry before continuing work on this area of the fireplace.

Building the Chimney

Once the entire unit has been placed and thoroughly covered with insulation, you can begin building the chimney. In most instances the chimney lies against the exterior wall of the house. The only area needing additional cutting is the roof overhang. However, this can be and is changed in some instances to provide for the chimney to run on the inside of the exterior wall or totally inside if you should choose to build a center fireplace. This application does not provide nearly the structural support.

It is easiest to lay the chimney with four-inch-thick concrete block and then veneer it with four inches of stone. However, the chimney could also be laid entirely of stone.

Use a mortar mix of one part mason's cement, three parts sand and enough water to make the mortar buttery, but still able to stand up on its own.

Laying the blocks. The first step is to chalk an outline of the position of the outside line of the chimney, checking that it is square. Then place a bed of mortar around the perimeter of the chimney and on the foundation and, starting at each outside corner, set a block in place. Make sure these are level and plumb in all directions. Use a string line with mason's wooden corner blocks stretched from block to block, or a long level, to ensure that the corner blocks are level with each other as well. Then butter the ends of the rest of the blocks for the bottom course and position in place, again leveling in all directions. Once the first or bottom course has been laid, remove the string line and place mortar on top of this course. Again set the corner blocks, this time facing them in the opposite direction (perpendicular to the first course so that the block overlaps and offsets). Use a level to make sure they are plumb with the blocks below them as well as level in all directions. Attach a string line to the blocks and lay the second course. Continue laying courses in this manner.

Installing wall ties. As you lay the chimney walls, install corrugated wall ties approximately every third horizontal mortar joint space 24 inches apart to tie the stone to the block. When the stone veneer is applied, fill in the space between the inside of the chimney and the metal unit with mortar and rubble, bringing the filling up as you bring the chimney up. The proportion should be about 75 percent rubble and 25 percent mortar. Use a level to make sure the chimney wall is built plumb straight, and a string to keep the walls straight.

Facing the Fireplace Front

Once blocks for the exterior chimney have been laid, the stones for covering the fireplace front and surrounding the cold air ducts must be added. Wall ties also are used in the stone courses to tie them securely together.

Laying the stones. Choosing the correct stones is one of the most crucial steps in laying the stone for the fireplace front. Typically, they should be the largest you can fit into each space, and they should

Interior stone work begins when the unit is in place. Insulation around the unit buffers the stone work from any metal expansion.

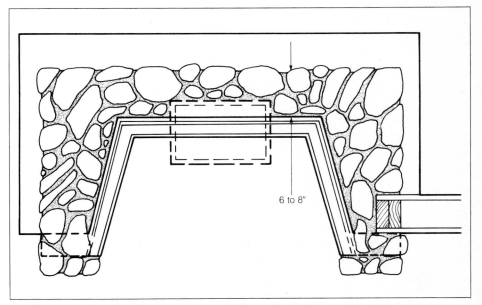

Lay concrete block around the unit. Then fill the space between the walls and the fireplace with rubble and mortar.

6 to 8"

You can build the entire fireplace surround of stone and mortar. Proceed slowly in order to allow the mortar to set. If you place too many courses at once, the stones will slip.

Install stones with a mortar joint between ½ and ¾ in. thick. Fit stones carefully.

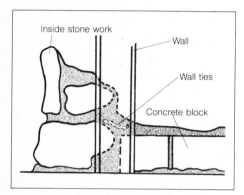

Wall ties are also used to join the interior facing and the block work. Embed the ties in the joints between blocks and stones.

Face ducts for cold air and heat circulation with stone. Pack the mortar carefully.

Bring stones up level with the top of the opening. Then set a level lintel bar.

have at least one sharp corner to delineate the inside edge of the fireplace sides. After careful selection of the stones, trowel on a bed of mortar, and place the first stone. Position the stone in place on the mortar bed; then force the mortar in around it. Starting at a corner is a good idea. Again, use a level to keep the corners as plumb as possible, although it won't be nearly as necessary as with straight-line materials such as brick or block. The mortar joint can vary; however, try for a 1 inch joint (which usually squeezes down to a ¾ inch joint when finished). Tap each stone gently to firm it in place and to eliminate air bubbles in the mortar joints. Lay the entire first course in this manner. The stones should overlap in all cases to provide a bonding joint.

To lay the next course of stone, dry fit the first stone to make sure you have chosen one that will fit properly to give a relatively uniform mortar joint. Choose stones that are alternately large and small. The shapes should fit around each other. Then butter up the bottom course with mortar and position the next stone course in place just as you did the first one. The mortar should be flush with the faces of the stones. Pack it in firmly, but not so that it will ooze out when the next course is laid. Once the stones are in position, tap them lightly to settle them in place. Always check to make sure that the faces of the stones are plumb and that they are not tilted out or in at the top. Place rubble and mortar in any holes behind or between stones. Wearing gloves, use your hands to force the mortar in and around the stones, removing all air pockets and filling all holes. Fill the gap between the chimney blocks and the exterior veneer as you proceed. Add wall ties to connect the stone fireplace front and the block chimney walls.

Helpful Hints

One important rule when doing stone work, particularly for walls and veneering, is to build only a little at a time. One course is a reasonable goal. Then wait and let the mortar set. Not only will too much stone laid at one time cause the mortar to slump, resulting in its squeezing out of the joints, but you can actually end up with the veneer falling apart. This did occur once during this project while the author was veneering the inside walls. After several courses were laid in rela-

tively quick succession, the entire wall slowly slid off onto the floor.

Supporting stones. If a stone has a tendency to tip out at the top, prop it in place with a stick or another stone until the mortar sets. Once the mortar has been applied to the top of the stone (in buttering the next course) and the next course has been installed, the stone usually will be locked in place. The exception is a stone with too round a surface, which may allow it to slip out of the mortar.

Correct alignment. Alternately work on each side of the fireplace a little at a time, bringing both sides up equally so you can keep them looking very much alike. This requires a large quantity of stones to choose from for the best results. Make sure you get the front faces of the stone fairly plumb and the side lines straight. A string dropped from a nail in the ceiling with a heavy weight can act as a plumb bob to set the exact location of the side lines.

Cold air ducts and inlets. On the fireplace shown, the cold air ducts and inlets for the heat exchanger were placed at either side of the room at floor level where they would be most efficient at picking up the cold air. The ducts were temporarily formed with ½ inch plywood next to the fireplace firebox. These were later removed after the stones had been set in place over them. Forms were nailed together with 4d finishing nails. Once the masonry had set, the forms were pulled out of the sides by hooking behind them with a crowbar and pulling.

Adding a lintel. After the two sides had been brought up to the underside of the top of the metal unit, a ⅜ inch x 4 inch x 4 inch angle iron was placed as a lintel bar across the sides at the top of the opening. To set the lintel, first build up the sides to an equal distance from the floor, just below the opening of the metal unit. Then position mortar in place on each end and lay the lintel bar across the opening, making sure it is kept level and embedded in the mortar on each end. Allow this to set up solidly. Then fill in on top of the lintel bar with a layer of mortar and start the stone course on top of it. The lintel must be absolutely level. Stop work and let everything set up, or head back outside and lay out some more of the chimney walls. Keeping yourself flexible, by going back and forth this way, can speed progress.

As noted above, once the lintel bar has been firmly set, place mortar across its top and lay some more stones. The stones directly on the lintel will probably have to be quite uniform in size. At this point, the work becomes a little more complicated because you will want to keep another level line just above the lintel bar for the warm air outlet. Pick out the stones carefully, working toward a level mortar line. Then, if using a purchased metal grille to provide the outlet cover, install it in place, keeping it level and plumb. Mortar it on both sides and bring the stone up next to it. Allow this to set thoroughly. Begin the next course; start on top of the metal grille and mortar the top securely in place. An alternative is to use stones in a "soldier" course—stones set up on end, spacing them about 1½ inches apart to provide the openings for the outlet. If you choose this arrangement, it is a good idea to add a small steel lintel over the top of the stones for more strength. When you have reached this point, it is merely a matter of continuing to place the stones until you reach within about four to six inches of the ceiling. Finish this space with molding if you wish. You will have difficulty finding stones that will fit in this small space.

Finishing the Mortar Joints

One of the most important facets of stone work is the cleaning up of the joints once the stones have been laid. With a little practice you will soon have a finished job that really looks professional and neat, and shows off the stones to their best advantage.

Pointing the joints. There are many different thoughts on how the mortar joints should look. In most instances you will wish to point the joints, or to remove a little of the mortar between the stones. This gives more light and shadow to help show off the stones. The amount of material removed is a matter of personal choice, but do not remove too much mortar (½ or ¾ inch maximum) or you will weaken the joint. If the veneer is thin (one inch), take out less mortar. It is very important to test the set of the mortar before you work the joints. If the mortar has dried too much before you begin work, you will not be able to clean out the joints properly. If the mortar still is too wet, you will force out too much mortar. Wait about half an hour to an

hour after applying the mortar., continually testing the mortar to see how it comes out of the joint. This operation can only be perfected with experience and by learning to recognize the feel of the mortar. Weather and temperature conditions will affect how fast the mortar sets.

For a rustic look, using the finger of a gloved hand does a good job of compacting and finishing a mortar joint. As an alternative, try a ⅜x6 inch round-head bolt. The large round head can be used to scrape the excess mortar out of the larger joints, while the smaller end of the bolt can be used to get into smaller spaces. Once you have scraped out the excess and have made a smooth, rounded joint, use a small whisk broom to remove any loosened mortar chunks. Smooth the

surface of any scrape marks left by the pointing tool, also using the whisk broom. The surface left after brooming gives an indication of how fast the mortar is setting; you should still be able to smooth the surface down with the whisk broom at this stage.

Follow the brooming with a steel bristle brush to remove any excess mortar that has gotten onto the faces of the stones. Later, after the mortar has set for several days, many stone masons like to clean the stone faces with water, to which a bit of muriatic acid has been added. However, if the mortar is cleaned as you go, a light washing with pure water and the steel bristle brush (a couple of days later) will clean away any mortar dust left from the first cleaning job.

Build cold air vents with plywood; cover with stone. Install metal grilles.

Tool the joints with a ⅜x6 in. bolt. Don't cut through to the mortar backing.

Clean the tooled joints to a rough finish. Use a small whisk broom.

Brush the joints with a wire brush to complete the tooling and clean the stones.

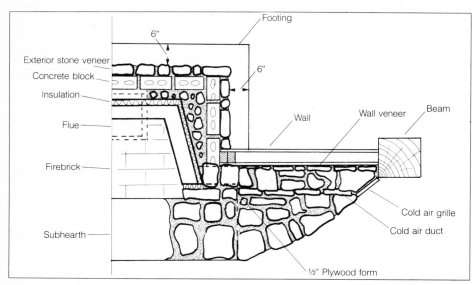

Cold air ducts reach to the edge of the wide forehearth and are covered with decorative grilles. The vertical beam at right was added for support and decorative unity.

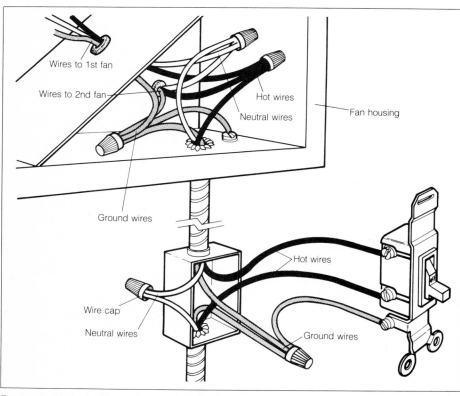

For greatest heat exchange, fans must pull cold air into the fireplace unit and blow out warmed air. The wiring isn't difficult. Shut off the power before connecting any wires.

Strengthen the bond between the veneer and the wallboard with metal wall anchors.

Providing Cold Air Ducts

In the fireplace shown, the next step was to construct a wooden frame for the cold air ducts which run to either side of the room. This was made of 2x4s nailed in place to the wall studs and to the floor joists. Then a ¾-inch plywood covering was installed.

Wiring. The fan motors on the metal grille units were wired by running a wire over the fireplace to the fan motors, then bringing a wire up through the floor for the incoming power lead and wiring to a switch box mortared in place on the adjoining stone faced wall. The wiring diagram is illustrated at left. A wooden channel was built on both sides to run the wires through; however, in some locations you may need to install conduit for the wiring to suit local codes.

After the wiring was completed, the framed air ducts were covered with stone and the metal grilles were mortared in place.

Veneering the Walls

Veneer the walls using thin, flat, field stones. This is probably one of the most difficult aspects of the job. Because of their thin shapes, the stones have a tendency to tip out or slide down out of position until the mortar sets. Concrete block wall ties were nailed up to each stud about eight inches in height to help hold mortar and stone veneer to the wall. An alternative would be to knock indentations into the existing plasterboard behind the stone veneer and to use these pockets to help lock the stones into place. A method often used by professionals is to first nail expanded metal to the wall. (Expanded metal is a specific material used in the trade. It is a form of wire mesh formed by stamping sheet metal into a pattern of open grids. Ask for "expanded metal"; otherwise, it might be confused with lightweight mesh such as chickenwire mesh, which is not recommended.) When the mortar has settled into this, the metal helps hold the stone and mortar in place.

If a stone tips and won't hold securely in place, use a wooden prop.

Building the Smoke Shelf Area

Now go back outside again for more work on the chimney. Fill the slanted area between the metal unit and the inside of the chimney wall with rubble and mortar as you bring up the walls. Place a wall tie into the inside as well as one to the outside, as shown. This rubble fill should reach to about six inches below the damper. Bricks or rocks should be used to corbel (offset) the sides in as shown.

Corbeling is a method of angling in the sides from the width of the fireplace opening to the width where the sides must meet the chimney flue. Corbeling is done by setting one stone over the other and extending it just a bit past the edge of the one below it. This is probably the hardest job in building the fireplace. You cannot work very quickly because the weight of the stones extending out over those below them can cause the wet mortar to sag, or the stones can even fall out before the mortar has a chance to set. Many masons like to use bricks for this job since they're easier to use. They won't show at all, so it really doesn't matter. The reinforcing rods also are bent around those corbeled sides at this time so they can be extended up through the corners of the fireplace chimney. On short chimneys you may only need to use one set of rods. However, on two-story chimneys you will probably need a second set, placing them right next to the ends of the first ones as you build up.

Construction of the masonry smoke shelf. This shelf ensures that air current downdrafts are sent back up the chimney and prevents downdraft smoking problems when the fireplace is being used. The shelf must be rounded and smooth, constructed of ordinary mortar, placed about six inches below the damper blade as shown at right. Use your hands to create a rounded surface. Then a small triangular trowel can be used for the final surface smoothing.

Let the downdraft shelf set overnight until the mortar has set up throughly. If you do not wait, any mortar or debris dropped onto the shelf will stick and create a roughened surface. Once the mortar has hardened you are ready to finish both the side and rear walls of the fireplace unit. You can continue to use concrete blocks on the outside chimney walls, but bricks should be used to form the corbeling, gradually laying them inwards on both sides of the metal unit to form a support for the tile flue liner. The corbeling in this case follows the outside shape of the metal fireplace unit, from the outside dimensions of the lower fireplace

section up to the location of the start of the chimney area. Again, bricks are substituted for stones, since they are much easier to use for the corbeling. They also create a more even area for attaching the stone veneer. Fill in with rubble and mortar, in a three to one ratio of rubble to mortar. Check as you go along to make sure the outside edges of the chimney blocks are plumb and straight. Continue laying the bricks in place until you can cover the top edge of the metal unit, as shown.

Placing the Flue Liner
Now install another $\frac{1}{4}x3\frac{1}{2}x3\frac{1}{2}$ inch angle iron to act as a support for the tile flue liner. Tile flue liners are used in the chimney because not as much creosote will stick to the tile as to brick, rough stones, mortar, or concrete blocks. The tile should be at least $\frac{5}{8}$ inch thick. This helps reduce fire hazard. Be sure to place the first tile of the flue liner so that it does not fall over a joint of the concrete block course. Otherwise you could have a crack through which a spark could leak back to the exposed woodwork of the house.

Flue tiles are quite heavy and require a great deal of support to hold them in place, so you can work only a little bit at a time. Butter up the edge of one tile; lift it in place carefully (this usually takes two people); check level and plumb.

Concrete blocks have already been laid to just below a flue tile joint. After the first tile has been installed, continue the concrete blocks on up around that tile, again filling the spaces between the tile and blocks with mortar and small pieces of rubble. Continue until you reach just below the next joint of flue tile, then mortar that flue tile in place and continue the blocks up around it. Install the blocks around the tile and fill between them with rubble and mortar. Allow it all to set up before installing the next flue-tile-and-block courses. The flue tiles are very heavy—as much as 65 pounds each—and the weight of one tile may force wet mortar out of the joint under the next lower tile. Professional masons are able to set several tile and block courses in a single day, but the homeowner building a chimney in this manner is better off doing one tile and block section a day—or two sets, one in the morning and one in the afternoon. Spacing the laying time will allow the mortar to set and give the

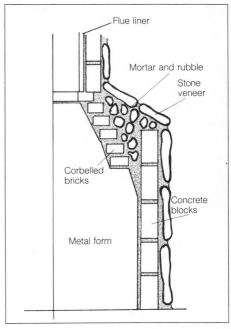

To support the flue tiles, corbel the brick up the sides of the firebox unit. Fill empty areas with rubble and mortar.

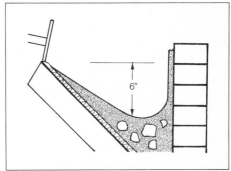

The smoke shelf curves below the level of the damper to a depth of 6 in. The shelf mixes downdraft air with rising smoke.

Flue tiles weigh 65 lbs each. Scaffolding aids exterior construction. Reinforcing rods are visible at each corner of flue tile.

homeowner a chance to regain his (or her) strength.

Avoiding mortar drips. One common problem when installing flue tiles is the mortar that drops down inside the chimney onto the downdraft shelf. To prevent this, fill an old sack with straw or rags, tie a strong rope to it and force it down inside the previously laid flue tile and up against the edge to be mortared. Then apply the mortar to the tile. Set the new flue tile in place, and smooth it. Pull the sack up, removing dropped mortar as you raise it. This also helps give smooth mortar joints on the inside of the flue tile liner. Make sure you have a strong rope on the sack, however—the author spent a great deal of time trying to fish out a sack from which the rope had broken.

Corbel the sides of the chimney. Once the tile flue liners have been installed, you will probably wish to corbel in the sides of the chimney (see page 118). Corbeling usually starts at the outside corners just above the smoke chamber and runs to just above the joint of the metal unit and chimney or flue tile. However, it could be started higher and run farther if desired, creating a better-looking chimney for a two-story house. Leave just enough space around the flue tile to fill with mortar, but work out the spacing so that you can cut the concrete blocks to fit. As mentioned earlier, you may wish to use brick instead, since it is easier to handle. Lay blocks; install flue tiles; fill between the two with rubble and

mortar until the top of the chimney is reached. As you go up, install additional metal reinforcing rods by setting them firmly in the mortar if the previously set rods do not extend to the top.

Chimney anchors should be used to help hold the chimney securely to the house. They may be required by some local building codes. The chimney anchor is a metal strap that wraps around the chimney blocks (between the blocks and the stone veneer). It is then brought into the house just above the ceiling joists through small holes bored in the sheathing (the siding will have already been removed in this area) and fastened to the ceiling joists, using lag screws in the holes provided in the straps. You can also use wall anchors, to anchor each course of block to the walls.

Preparing the Roof
The next problem occurs where the chimney reaches the roof overhang and starts

through it. Build the chimney up to the underside of the roof line, using a level. Then mark on the underside of the roof overhang, as well as on top of it, the exact location of the chimney as it comes through the overhang. Remove the shingles or composition roof to an area about six inches larger than the chimney opening. Mark the area to be cut away for the chimney on the roof sheathing; cut with a hand saw. This should be cut about two inches wider than the chimney dimensions for clearance. Cut through rafters and remove rafter pieces or ridgepole ends that may be in the way.

Rafter or ridgepole cuts. If a rafter or the ridgepole end has to be cut, first secure it on the inside of the house by nailing a brace to the end of the cut rafter and to the nearest ceiling joists.

Flashing. After the concrete block chimney has been brought through the roof, metal flashing is cut and installed around the chimney to seal off the area

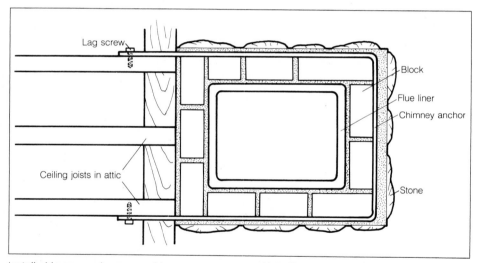

Install chimney anchors on a chimney over one story high. The anchors protect the chimney from excessive pressures during high winds and keep the chimney from pulling on the wall.

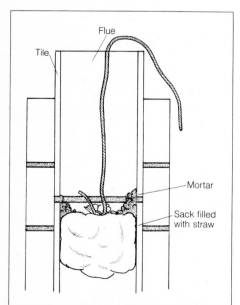

When the chimney is completed, lower a straw-filled bag. Pour mortar into the chimney; pull up the bag. This seals the joints.

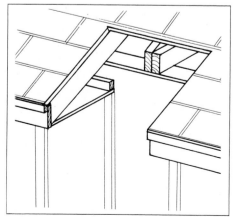

The flue is centered at the wall line and must extend straight up. Therefore, you must cut through the roof and eaves.

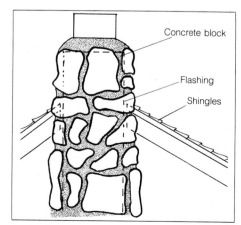

Build the chimney of flue tile, concrete block and stone veneer. Flashing at roof joint keeps water away from chimney.

from water. The flashing is installed in two layers. The first layer of metal is bent and installed on the wooden sheathing and against the blocks. Then the shingles and roofing material are laid down over the flashing and a second outside layer of flashing is installed over the roofing material. All this is cemented and caulked in place using roofing compound. After installing the chimney, lay the shingles back in place and seal with flashing as shown. Later, when the stone veneer is in position, this will complete the sealing job and keep out seeping water. Check with local building codes for the distance the chimney must protrude above the roof line. Normally this is a three to four foot minimum.

The cap. The last tile for the top of the flue liner extends up above the concrete or stone veneer to form a cap. To finish the cap, shape the mortar with your hands into a well-rounded form; then use a small fine trowel. An alternative would be a formed cap made by constructing a hollow wooden form on the top of the chimney and pouring mortar mix into the form. A cap not only has aesthetic value, but lets rain water run off rather than seep down between the blocks and the flue liner.

Veneering Outside Chimney

Veneer the outside of the chimney with stone, just as for the inside. In most instances the foundation would not be exposed—except in a case such as this, where the floor level is so high above the ground level.

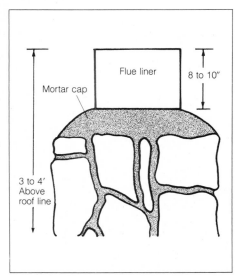

For safety. the liner should rise above the chimney veneer by 8 in. or more. A mortar cap directs water away from the tiles.

CONVENTIONAL FIREPLACE DIMENSIONS

Opening			Firebox			Throat	Flue Sizes	Lintel bar
Width	Height	Depth	Width	Flat wall/Height	Sloping rise	Width		Length
24″	24″	16″	11″	14″	18″	8¾″	8x12″	36″ (A)*
26	24	16	13	14	18	8¾	8x12	36 (A)
28	24	16	15	14	18	8¾	8x12	36 (A)
30	29	16	17	14	23	8¾	12x12	42 (A)
32	29	16	19	14	23	8¾	12x12	42 (A)
36	29	16	23	14	23	8¾	12x12	48 (A)
40	29	16	27	14	23	8¾	12x16	48 (A)
42	32	16	29	14	26	8¾	16x16	54 (B)*
48	32	18	33	14	26	8¾	16x16	60 (B)
54	37	20	37	16	29	13	16x16	72 (B)
60	37	22	42	16	29	13	16x20	72 (B)
60	40	22	42	16	31	13	16x20	72 (B)
72	40	22	54	16	31	13	20x20	84 (C)*
84	40	24	64	20	28	13	20x24	96 (C)
96	40	24	76	20	28	13	20x24	108 (C)

*A: 3x3 angle iron of ³⁄₁₆ inch metal; B: 3½x3½ x½ inch; C: 5x3½ x ⁵⁄₁₆ inch.
Information courtesy of Brick Institute of America

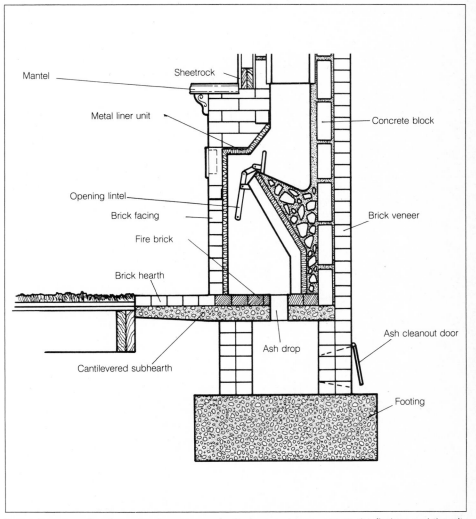

In most cases, a fireplace stands over an ash pit. An ash drop connects the firebox and the pit. A drop opening must be built into the form before the subhearth is poured.

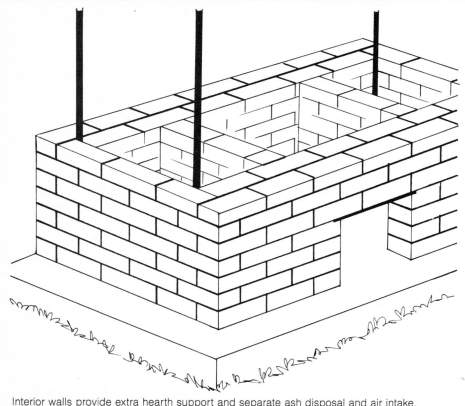

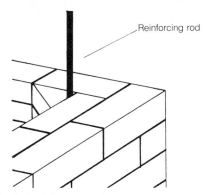

Vertical reinforcing rods run up through the corners of the construction. Allow enough space for the metal liner.

Interior walls provide extra hearth support and separate ash disposal and air intake.

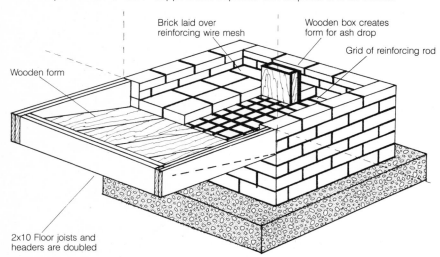

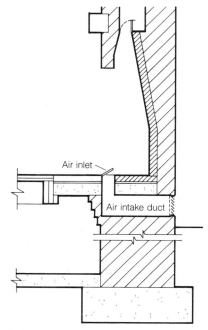

Include an outside air intake to provide combustion air directly to the fire.

It is easiest to create a poured concrete forehearth and hearth base. Or, you can set brick over reinforcing mesh in the main hearth area; only the forehearth is concrete.

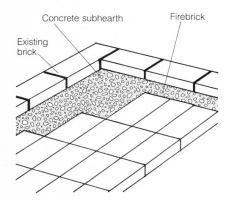

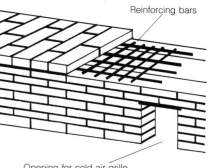

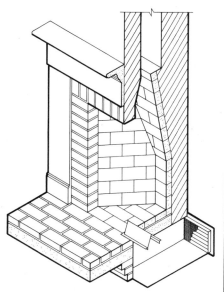

Outer walls serve as a form for the concrete subhearth; finish with firebrick.

To support bricks, set lintel over opening, reinforcing rods in upper mortar bed.

Cutaway: fireplace, subhearth, ashpit.

7 CONCRETE & MASONRY REPAIRS

Many masonry projects around the home involve no new construction, but call for repair of existing structures such as a cracked sidewalk or a leaking house foundation, or a chimney that needs repointing. Although masonry is probably the sturdiest material for building items, it can deteriorate over time from weather exposure or poor workmanship. All masonry surfaces will deteriorate to some degree from water and wind, and areas such as chimney joints can crumble eventually into sand, although it usually takes many years for this to happen.

The two chimneys in our old farmhouse are a prime example. The house was built 60 years ago, and one of the first things I did when we moved in was to inspect and repair the two chimneys. One chimney was constructed entirely of stone and mortar with a brick liner. The second chimney was built of brick. The mortar in the brick chimney had deteriorated to the point that the top half of the chimney was completely loose. On the other hand, the stone chimney was still solid. I can only guess that two different masons constructed the two fireplaces. Or, perhaps the

brick chimney—which was used not only as a heating flue for a woodstove, but for a cookstove as well—deteriorated more rapidly because it was subjected to a great deal more heat than the stone chimney.

REPAIRING CONCRETE

Patching Cracks
Probably one of the most common masonry repair jobs is patching cracks in concrete. Before attempting to patch the area, determine what is causing the crack. If it's a structural problem, you must correct it or otherwise the crack will simply keep getting larger. One situation occurs when a concrete slab settles.

Shallow cracks. The actual patching of the crack is normally quite easy to do. Using a hammer and a chisel, break away all old and crumbling edges from the crack, and if possible make the crack about 1 inch deep. The sides of the crack should be vertical; the hollow will form a sort of key for the patching material. Just make sure you don't end up with an area in which the new concrete must feather out very thin. This will only chip and

crumble away, resulting in a job that will probably have to be redone in a few months.

Use a broom or a shop vacuum to remove all dust and debris from the area. Flush the area well with clean water. Allow it to dry until there is no water standing in the crack, but the area is still quite damp. Then make up a mix of 1 part mortar cement and 4 parts sand. This

Widen a small crack with a star chisel. Make the opening 1 in. deep or more.

On larger cracks, widen the area with a brick chisel. Then flush with water.

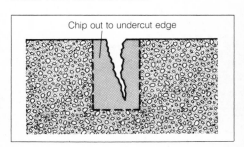
Chisel out so that sides are vertical. This will make a good seat for the patch.

Repair rather than replace concrete that has deteriorated to this point.

You can patch even large areas. First, clean away all dirt and loose debris.

Mix mortar with a fairly soupy consistency; it will pack the crack more easily.

Once you press the mortar into the crack, screed with a short 2x4.

Then use the trowel to smooth the surface to match the surrounding concrete.

Vertical cracks require thicker mortar. Apply it with the back of the trowel.

Working from bottom to top, force the mortar into the crack. Avoid air pockets.

Large patches must be anchored. Bore holes with a carbide-tipped masonry bit.

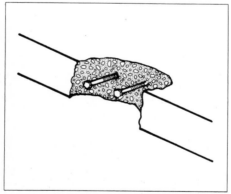

Then insert lag screws into the holes. The screws will help support the patch.

Prop a piece of plywood along the edge to create a temporary form for the patch.

Attach a second wood piece to create a form for the lip of an overhanging edge.

should be fairly thin and slushy. Fill in the crack or cavity with the concrete; use the edge of a board to screed the excess off. After the concrete material has set, use a steel float to float it smooth until it matches the existing concrete finish. If the patch is on a vertical surface you may have to use a slightly thicker mix. There are also special bonding materials that can be brushed onto the area and mixed with the cement to help hold the patch in place. Use whatever tool is necessary to trowel or float the final surface so it matches the existing surface as closely as possible. You won't be able to get the patch to match exactly because the new concrete will be lighter than the original.

Shallow holes. Patching a shallow hole in the top of a concrete surface is done in exactly the same manner. However, on larger surfaces the area should be roughened first with a cold chisel to help hold the patch securely in place.

Holes in new concrete walls. Quite often you will find holes in newly poured concrete walls due to poor tamping or because aggregates have lodged in center spots. For these holes, patch according to the steps given above.

Repairing Broken Corners and Edges of Steps, Walks, Curbs and Porches

The corners and edges of steps and walks, and other similar surfaces, are another common masonry repair problem. Their repair is actually quite simple.

(1) Brush off all crumbling and cracked edges, as well as any debris; wash the area.

(2) Use a carbide-tipped masonry bit in a portable electric drill, or a star drill and hammer, to drill ¼-inch-wide holes about 2 inches

deep into the edge, spaced about 1½ inches apart.

(3) Clean all debris from the area again, using a shop vacuum if possible.

(4) Force a bit of soupy mortar or epoxy glue into the holes.

(5) Drive lag screws or bolts in the holes, leaving the heads protruding about 2 to 3 inches. Do not position them too close to the edge.

(6) Build wood form to create a new corner or edge.

(7) Remove all dust and debris and hose down the surface.

(8) Mix up 1 part cement and 4 parts sand, with just enough water to allow the mix to pour into the form readily.

(9) Pour, tamp into place, and screed with the edge of a board.

(10) Allow to set for a little while, then float and trowel to suit.

For small chips, the pieces can often be glued back in place using epoxy glue.

Repairing Low Spots in Concrete

A low spot in the concrete follows much the same procedures as for patches. Again, use the chisel to roughen the surface and to undercut the edges. For more strength, you can also bore some shallow holes in the concrete depression. Use a masonry bit and an electric drill, or a star drill and a hammer. This will help lock the new masonry in place. Then mix a soupy mortar, pour, screed and float as before.

Fixing Broken Concrete

If an area is badly broken and unsafe it should be replaced. How much needs to be replaced will depend to a great deal on how bad the damage is. In all cases, the first step is to dig out the soil at the edge of the slab. Use a brick chisel and hammer to break away any crumbling edges until you reach the firm, solid concrete. Then insert reinforcing bolts in all edges and place the broken concrete pieces in the center of the area as ''fill'' stones. Pour in a standard concrete mix of 1 part cement, 2¼ parts sand and 3 parts gravel. On larger pours, also insert horizontal metal reinforcing rods across the bolts.

Raising Settled Slabs And Walks

One very frustrating problem is a settled walk or slab. This can be caused by the pour being made over soft fill materials, such as those around a new house. In most instances, you can relevel the slab or walk without breaking it up and making a new pour, unless it is too large to handle.

Raising walks. Let's take a walk as our first example, because that is the easiest with which to work. In most cases the walk will have cracked on the control groove cut in its top surface. If it hasn't, use a brick chisel and heavy hammer to crack it along that area. This gives you smaller sections to work with and results in an easier job.

Place a straight-edged 2x4 alongside the walk as a guide to indicate where you wish the top surface of the walk to be. Level it as needed to suit the terrain. Then use a steel pry bar and fulcrum, one on each side, to tilt and lift the lowest end of the slab up.

Supporting the slab. Prop it safely out of the way with 2x4s or pieces of rock. This is hard work and you will probably need several helpers.

Measure the height to which the slab should be brought; make sure it is propped up a little higher than the finished height will be. Place cut stones, and bricks under the slab to support it at the correct height. Then place pea size gravel around these stones or bricks for extra holding power.

Coping with roots. If there are roots in the area, cut as much as possible away with a mattock. They will continue to grow and to tilt the slab out of level.

Lowering the slab. Very gently, and with several helpers, lower the walk into place. Do the rest of the walk one section at a time, until the walk has been leveled to match the terrain.

Gridded patios. Slabs in a gridded patio are re-established in the same man-

To repair a sunken area in a concrete walk dig away the dirt along the edges.

With a helper, pry up the sunken section with heavy steel bars and a 4x4 fulcrum.

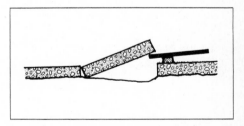
Be sure that the slab is secure before you insert gravel fill to raise the base.

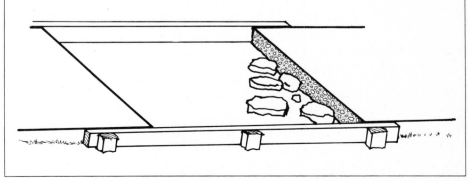
To repour a section of broken walk, remove the old section with a masonry chisel and hammer. Broken pieces can be used as fill, as long as they don't touch the sides of the form.

ner, using a steel bar and fulcrum to raise them. Use a steel bar or pipe to hold them up out of the way until you get the area underneath properly prepared.

One-piece slabs. A large, badly settled, one-piece slab that doesn't have control joints will usually have to be broken up and repoured. You can pour a new slab on top, after first roughening the surface of the existing slab.

Replacing a Broken Walk Section

If an entire section of a walk has broken too badly to be repaired, use a brick chisel and hammer at the control joint to break it away from the solid portion. Then, with a heavy sledge, break the sidewalk up into small enough pieces for it to be removed.

Remove all the larger debris and leave the smaller pieces in the bottom of the area as fill stones. Make sure the new sidewalk pour is as thick as the existing sidewalk.

Using a form. If you can't use the edges of the old concrete to support the new mixture while it hardens, you may have to build a form for the patch area for the fresh concrete. Use 2x6s for the forms. Align the forms so the top edges match the top surface of the adjoining concrete; you may need to level the forms

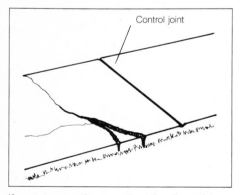

If you are removing a section of walk, work from control joint to control joint.

to achieve this match. Also, you will probably have to dig a small trench along the sides of the patch area in which to insert the form boards.

To support the forms, cut short lengths of 2x4s into stakes. Sharpen one end of these stakes so they are easier to drive into the ground. Once the forms are in position, drive in the stakes at 2-foot intervals so the tops of the stakes are about ½-inch below the top edge of the forms. Now, with double-headed concrete nails, spike the stakes to the forms. This gives the forms some stability when the concrete is placed.

Since the new concrete forms a patch, you probably won't need expansion or control joints between the old and new concrete. However, if control joints are necessary, make them by slicing through the fresh concrete with the edge of the trowel at the point where the new concrete meets the old. What you want to do is form a narrow gap so both sections can expand and contract without breaking each other. Or you can use an asphalt isolation strip between sections. The strip goes in before the concrete is placed between the form boards.

Keep the concrete damp with water for at least three days after it has been placed. This procedure cures the new concrete, making the patch harder. You can walk on the patch in about 36 hours; don't drive a car or truck on the surface for about 10 days or so.

About 2 weeks after the job is completed you can remove the form boards and replace any dirt and sod removed to make room for the forms.

Veneering the Old Walkway

"Veneering" can transform old, broken-down walks so they look new again. To veneer a walk you replace new con-

crete over the old walk, using the old walk as a base. The technique is simple; the work is hot and tiring. The cost of veneering is about the same as it would be for a new walk. The advantages are that you save some layout time, rock-busting, and digging.

Tools and materials. You will need a hammer or baby sledge hammer, crosscut saw, level, chalkline, hacksaw, 2x6 form boards, 2x4s for stakes, double-headed 10d concrete nails, 2x4 concrete screed, shovel, trowel, asphalt isolation joints, concrete groover, concrete edger, wooden float, rule, concrete, water, gloves, small reinforcement rods, and reinforcement mesh.

The concrete mix. Since this job usually is a large one, it's smart to either mix your own concrete to save money or buy the already-mixed to save time. Figure out how much material you'll need, using the chart given previously. The concrete veneer should be 4 inches thick.

Building the forms. Set the 2x6 form boards along the edge of the old walk so the bottom edges of the forms just touch the edge of the walk. Stake the forms with 2x4s that are pointed on one end so you can drive them into the ground easily. Nail the 2x4s to the forms—from the outside in—with double-headed concrete nails. As you set the forms, level them in place. To save time leveling, stretch a line along the edge of the tops of the forms. This will give you a guide while you set the rest of the forms. Also, don't forget to drive the stakes about an inch or so below the top edge of the forms. The 2x4 concrete screed has to move freely along the top edges of the forms.

Adding reinforcing. With the hacksaw, cut the reinforcing rods into lengths of approximately 1 foot. Then drive these rods into the surface of the walkway. Use

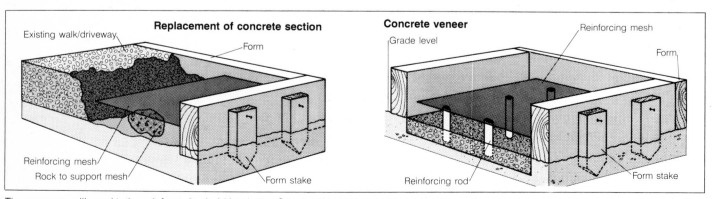

Replacement of concrete section

Existing walk/driveway
Form
Reinforcing mesh
Rock to support mesh
Form stake

Concrete veneer

Grade level
Reinforcing mesh
Form
Reinforcing rod
Form stake

The new area will need to be reinforced to hold its shape. Support the reinforcement mesh with small rocks. A concrete veneer over an old walk must also be reinforced. In this case, use reinforcement rods to support the mesh rather than using the rocks.

the cracks, holes, and other breaks to sink the rods so they protrude about 2 inches from the walk's surface. The rods will help hold the veneering in position. Space the rods about 2 to 3 feet apart in any configuration you want. Cut the reinforcing mesh to fit between the forms and tie it to the tops of the rods.

Placing the concrete. Work the mixture with a shovel to remove any air pockets and other voids in the concrete. Level the material as much as possible while it is being placed. At four to six foot intervals, insert an asphalt isolation joint. When about 12 feet of veneer has been placed, screed the top level with the 2x4, using a see-saw motion. If you find any low spots, fill them. If you find any high spots, remove the excess concrete and use it to fill the low spots.

When the water leaves the surface of the concrete, run the wooden float over the surface. If the float brings water to the surface, the concrete is not ready to trowel. Meanwhile, if the 2x4 screed hasn't leveled the surface to your satisfaction, you can use the float to level the surface. Floating should be done while the concrete is wet. After you use the float, you can trowel the surface.

For a rough surface, you can finish the concrete with the stiff broom. The broom's bristles will form little lines across the concrete for a nonskid surface.

WATERPROOFING MASONRY BASEMENTS

One of the most frustrating masonry problem is a leaky, wet basement. This can run the gamut from a small frustrating leak to a couple of feet of water in an old basement. It can often make the basement entirely useless and can ruin clothes and foodstuff, as well as wooden and metal items stored in the basement. The moisture also can cause a damp musty smell in the house. Several years ago, when I was an editor with *Workbench Magazine,* this was one of the most common home repair problems asked about by our readers.

Product Suggestion

There are several products on the market that can be used to help seal off a leaky basement. Our choice was one from Thoro System products. These utilize a product called Waterplug, which is used to plug troublesome cracks. It can even be used on cracks that have water squirting out through them. It hardens in about three minutes. This is then followed by a sealer that helps keep the water out.

Solutions. Depending on how bad the basement situation is, you can choose among several courses. If there is only a small crack or joint that permits water seepage, and if the basement is just used as a storage area, you probably will wish to patch only the crack—for this we suggest the Waterplug material mentioned above. If, on the other hand, you ultimately intend to create a finished basement—for example, for an all-weather play area for the children, or a game room for the teenagers, or a laundry or sewing room—then you probably will wish to add a sealer as well. The sealer comes in several colors.

A badly leaking basement may require the use of both the Waterplug and the sealer. Let's take a typical case of a badly leaking basement, because you can use any of the various techniques for other not-quite-so-bad situations. The first thing to remember is to make absolutely sure you follow the manufacturers directions for use of their particular projects.

Repair Steps

Surface preparation. Use a hammer and a star drill to create weep holes near the floor line to relieve the water pressure. Smooth any pieces of concrete using a brick, which serves as an abrasive. Then cut a groove at the junction of the floor line and the walls, with a minimum width and depth of ¾ inch each. Use a hammer and a chisel to cut all cracks and voids to a ¾ inch width and depth, with the exception of block and brick joints; cut these to about ⅜ inch. Undercut the crack in the walls, if possible. Remove any defective or loose mortar. Clean all loose materials from the joints and thoroughly wash the entire wall surface.

Inserting the plug. Mix the Waterplug according to manufacturer's directions using clean water and force it into the cracks, starting at the top of the wall and working downward. Use just enough water to form the material into a putty-like consistency. Do not mix more than you can place in three minutes.

Position the material in the wall, with a minimum of movement or rubbing, using a small trowel or putty knife. Force the material into the crack or hole by pushing firmly; apply as much pressure as possible. Do not brush or trowel the surface once the material is pressed in place; if you do, the crack will not seal. Keep the area damp for at least 15 minutes. If necessary, hand-hold the material in place for 3 minutes.

To seal the crack at the junction of the floor and walls, force the waterplug into the prepared crack with a round tool and smooth it out to form a cove at the junction. The tool can be a piece of ¾ inch pipe.

To use this material to stop running streams of water, start at the top of the crack and force the material in firmly. At points of greater pressure, do not immedi-

Thoroseal can stop leaks in a concrete wall—even one as damaged as this.

To use, merely push the material into the hole and hold in place for a short time.

Then smooth the material so that it is level with the surrounding surface.

ately place the Waterplug into the opening. Hold it in your hand or trowel until you feel a slight warmth, which indicates that the drying process had started. Then press the material very firmly into the opening. Exert pressure on the trowel or the hand over the material for a few minutes, just until material starts to set and the active water stops running. Shave the patch off even with the surrounding wall surfaces using the edge of the trowel.

Cut off the waterplug patches so they are flush with the surrounding surfaces. Leave the weep holes open.

To repair cracks when expansion and contraction are factors, first stop the running water with Waterplug. But do not bring the material flush with the surface. Allow a minimum depth of ½ inch. This can then be filled with a rubberized sealant.

Adding the sealant. Apply a masonry waterproofing sealer, such as the Thoroseal, a companion product to the Waterplug material; follow the manufacturer's directions (these will vary). However, first moisten the entire wall area with a light spray from a hose. Apply a coating of waterproofing material, using a brush or roller, according to coverage on the can label. Always keep the surface dampened ahead of application.

Sealing the weep holes. On the next day, plug the weep holes that you had cut to relieve the water pressure. Use the Waterplug and seal the holes with the appropriate sealer.

Cover minor leaks and seepage with a brush-on sealer. Then cover the entire wall.

Additional Products and Procedures

In addition to the waterproofing materials mentioned above, there are also several other materials that can be used to waterproof and to seal masonry.

Transparent sealers. Most of these are clear or transparent materials. There are several varieties, including clear silicone waterproofing such as that made by the Cabot's Stain Company, Thoroglaze, an acrylic sealer from the Standard Dry Wall Products, Inc., and Watco Dennis penetrating-oil masonry sealer. Almost all of these materials can be used for sealing brick, block, and even stone surfaces such as on mortared stone walls, as well as concrete surfaces such as exposed aggregate. Not only do they provide a durable, tough film that will expand and contract with the weather, they also offer a means of keeping the masonry materials clean. They can also help fill in and bridge small hairline cracks and open pores, preventing dirt from filling them in and water and weather from widening and deepening them. When used on exposed aggregate panels and mortared stone walls, transparent sealers bring out the natural colors of the stones and provide highlights to the stone surface.

Surface preparation. Regardless of which material is used, the surface must be clean and dry before the material can be applied. Remove all dirt, waxes, defective paint or coatings, efflorescence and other foreign substances. Use paint stripper or the appropriate cleaner. Then vacuum thoroughly.

Application. After the masonry surface has been properly prepared, the materials are then spread on the surface according to directions on the individual can labels. Some, such as the silicone and acrylic waterproofing, can be applied with a brush, roller or spray. If a penetrating oil finish is chosen, it must be applied with a brush or, preferably, a lambs wool applicator.

Hydraulic cement. You can try to patch interior cracks with hydraulic cement. Clean out the crack with a cold or brick chisel, driving these tools with a baby sledge hammer. Make the cut in the form of an inverted V, if you can. This will help hold the patch in place.

Press the hydraulic cement into the break and smooth it level with the surrounding surface of the foundation wall

Protect masonry and concrete projects with special sealers. Apply with a standard roller, brush or mop. The sealer dries in an hour and is impervious to harsh substances.

with a putty knife. You will have to work fast. Hydraulic cement sets very quickly. Wear gloves for this job, since hydraulic cement creates heat that could injure your skin.

REPAIRING BROKEN AND LOOSE PORCH RAILINGS

Metal and wooden railings are quite often fastened into concrete steps and porches. One frequent problem is broken or loose concrete around the fasteners.

One of the simplest methods of salvaging this situation is to use the Waterplug product (described above) to anchor the bolt or metal fixture back in place. Drill a hole whose length equals the bolt or fixture and whose width is greater than the fixture by 1 inch. Fill the hole with Waterplug, packing firmly, making sure every part of the hole is filled. Center the post or fixture in the material and force it in. Tamp firmly. Keep the area moist for 15 minutes. Do not apply any pressure to the railing or fixture for several hours.

A post or railing that is merely loose can often be tightened by tamping lead wool in around the fixture or bolt. This can be purchased at plumbing shops. Use a small rod and hammer to tamp the material firmly in place. You can also use special Epoxy concrete patching material to lock the bolt or fixture in place.

If a large piece breaks off at a point where the fixture is located, build a form around the area. Combine one part cement and three parts sand for a fairly soupy mix and pour it into the form. Screed, trowel, and then set fixture back in place. Smooth the surface around it with a trowel.

REPAIRING BRICK AND BLOCK

The steps required for repairing and maintaining brick and block are quite similar. There are basically two things that can go wrong with either material: The mortar can crumble and loosen in the joints, or the blocks or bricks can become loose, broken or cracked.

Tuckpointing Techniques

Loose mortar is fairly easy to fix. Repairing it, however, must be carried out periodically if the project is to have a very long life. Annually check all masonry joints to make sure they are still solid and in place. If you find loose or crumbly joints, then they must be tuckpointed to prevent further moisture absorption.

Constant expansion and contraction due to cold and heat, as well as to weathering caused by rain and wind, eventually erode and loosen almost all mortar.

Inspection. Deterioration is especially common in areas such as fireplace chimneys, which are subject to extremes in temperatures. Before each heating season, carry out a careful visual inspection of your entire fireplace system so you can repoint any loose or crumbly joints, replace any cracked bricks, and re-mortar loose bricks.

This includes not only the brickwork on the fireplace front, hearth and firebrick on the interior, but also the exposed brick or stone work on the outside—and the portion of the fireplace chimney that runs through an attic. Check these areas out thoroughly, looking for loose and crumbly mortar or for streaks of creosote running down the outside of the chimney

indicating loose joints. If you find the latter, you may really have some problems because a flue fire in an old chimney that has open holes, which can leak creosote, may catch the surrounding framing members afire. It is important to completely seal off the entire chimney with new masonry joints.

Cleaning out the brick. Using a cold chisel or an old 3/8 inch-by-8 inch-long stove bolt and heavy hammer, knock out the loosened and crumbling mortar. Anytime you are using the chisel and hammer, wear safety goggles and glasses. Don heavy leather gloves to protect your hands. Brush out any dust and debris using a small whisk broom. If possible, undercut the joints to create a good holding edge for the new mortar.

Moistening the brick. After completely cleaning all the mortar out of the old joints, use a hose on fine spray to moisten the entire exposed brick and joint surface. This prevents moisture from being drawn out of the fresh cement, causing the mortar to dry out too quickly.

Mixing the mortar. Make up a mortar mix of 1 part mortar cement and 3 parts sand. Add just enough water for a pliable mix so its consistency resembles that of ice cream. The mix should be able to hold its shape when pulled up into a pile with the mixing hoe. You can also use regular portland cement if you add about 1/4 part hydrated lime.

Repointing the joints. With a small pointing trowel, place the mortar in the joints, forcing it in well. Once all the joints have been packed, strike off excess cement using the edge of the trowel. With a jointer tool, compact the joints until the

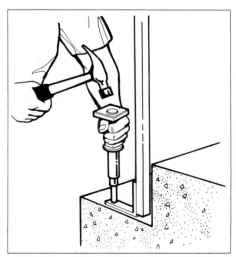

To replace a loose fastener for a railing, use a special drive-in fastener.

To repair brick mortar, remove with a star drill or a heavy bolt and hammer.

Then remortar the joints and tool to match existing joints. This is "tuckpointing."

A tool such as a brick chisel also can remove mortar. Cut down to firm mortar.

Pack in the new mortar so it is light. A jointing tool makes the job go quickly.

Before mortaring, fill a large crack with a piece of fiberglass insulation.

You can also fill large cracks with small rocks or rubble before you mortar.

mortar is firmly in place. You may also use a homemade jointer, made of a piece of ⅜-inch copper tubing. Be sure to match the new joints to the existing, surrounding joints. Finally, use the edge of the trowel to cut away the excess mortar that has been squeezed out of the joints.

Replacing Block and Brick

If damaged block or brick is over a window or door, under a window, or is stacked rather than staggered, it is better to call in a professional. These are critical load-bearing areas. If you were to remove the block or brick, the wall could sag or collapse.

Tools and materials. You will need a baby sledge hammer, star drill, cold chisel, brick chisel, premixed mortar mix, mixing container, trowel, tuckpointing trowel, and a joint strike. Wear safety glasses and gloves.

Surface preparation. With a star drill, brick chisel or cold chisel, break out the old brick or block. Use the baby sledge hammer to drive the cutting tools. You may have to use a combination of the tools to remove the old masonry. It is sometimes easier to start at the mortar joints and work the masonry unit out of the wall by prying and chipping on it.

This procedure reads quickly on paper, but it is actually a slow process that takes more patience than skill. Work slowly and chip away in small amounts.

When the old masonry unit is out, clean off any mortar debris with the cold chisel, but try not to disturb the mortar lines around the other blocks or bricks.

Mortar and brick preparation. Mix the mortar to a thick consistency. While you are at this, soak the new block or brick in a bucket of water. Let it absorb as much water as possible.

Adding the mortar and brick. Wet down the void in the wall where you will insert the new masonry unit. Then, with the trowel, lay down a bed of mortar on the bottom block or brick. Also butter the ends of the new unit with mortar and the top edge of the unit with mortar. Slip the unit into the hole. You will, of course, dislodge some of the mortar as the new unit slides into the hole. This is not a problem, as long as there is enough mortar left for a good bond. If not, rebutter the unit and give it another try.

When the new unit is in place, take a

tuckpointing trowel and force as much mortar into the joints as you possibly can. Don't skimp; pack the mortar in tightly. Now strike the joint with the tuckpointing trowel (strike means "to smooth") cleaning away any mortar that may have ended up on an adjoining block or brick. Rake the front of the masonry units with the edge of the trowel to remove any new mortar debris.

Striking the joints. Let the job set about 30 minutes. Then strike the new joint with a jointing tool or with the tuckpointing trowel. If possible, have the joint match the existing style. See Chapter Three for an illustration of common joint styles.

Hot weather. If you are working in hot weather, it is a good idea to wet that joint area with water. This will prevent the water from the mortar from soaking too fast into the masonry units and other mortar joints. Then strike the joints with the tuckpointing trowel or joint strike. In hot weather, keep the repointed area damp with water for several days. This produces a harder concrete.

Brick, Block or Stone Patio

Since paving bricks and stones are set on a sand base, both often tend to sink and tilt on the base. Normal settling of the ground, moisture (freezing and thawing) and weight can be blamed for the troubles.

Tools and materials. You will need rubber-headed or rubber-handled hammer, steel trowel, brick chisel or pry bar, level, stiff broom, and a bag of very fine sand.

Sand preparation. Remove the problem paving pieces using the brick chisel or pry bar to lift them off the sand base. If the units are too high, remove a little sand and replace a unit or two and check for

When a sand-bed surface sinks, a walk or patio becomes hazardous and requires repair.

level. Repeat this, adding or removing sand and testing, until the sand is level.

Setting the brick. As you set each unit, press it down in the sand and wiggle it back and forth very gently. This will properly seat the brick in the sand. Then tap the surface lightly with a rubber hammer or rubber handle of a regular hammer.

Once the job is finished, the units should be slightly higher than the surrounding surface: about ⅛ to ¼ of an inch. The units will settle to level in a month or two.

Filling sand joints. Sweep sand into the cracks between the units until the cracks are full. Then sprinkle the area with a fine spray from a garden hose. Sweep more sand into the cracks; sprinkle again. You will have to do this many, many times until the cracks are completely full. It is amazing how much sand seems to disappear down those small cracks.

Variation: cemented units. If the brick or stone paving units are cemented together, you will have to chip away the cement with a brick or cold chisel in order to raise or lower the units. Then follow the sand-leveling procedure described above. Recement the joints using a pointed trowel when the job is completed.

REPAIRING CHIMNEYS
Exterior Work

Quite often you will find that the top portion of the chimney has completely deteriorated, which means you may have to tear down part of it and rebuild it. If so, remove all loose bricks down to those that are solid. Clean all old mortar from the old bricks, using a brick chisel and hammer, while wearing safety glasses and heavy leather gloves.

Spray the still-solid portion of the chimney with water, mix up a batch of mortar, and lay the chimney bricks back in place. Keep blackened or stained portions of the bricks on the inside of the chimney. Clean excess mortar from the chimney, just as for standard brickwork.

Safety precautions. Since chimney work sometimes calls for a trip to the roof, take all safety precautions. Keep debris swept off the roof area where you are working, so you won't slip or slide on loose mortar. Wear tennis shoes or other rubber-soled shoes. Rig up roof jacks for steep roofs, and a safety harness if neces-

sary. Warn family members and neighbors; ask them to keep well away from the area below where you will be working, in case you drop a tool or a brick.

Fixing the chimney cap. If your chimney has a loose or broken chimney cap, first remove all the old pieces of the cap. Break it up into small pieces so you can easily take it off the roof. Soak the surrounding edges of the concrete so the old concrete won't draw all the moisture from the fresh concrete. Mix up a batch of mortar and apply it to form a new cap. Round the mortar to create the same shape as the old cap. In some cases, the cap may be a poured concrete one, which must be formed and poured, requiring a fairly soupy concrete mix.

If bricks are completely loose, such as in this chimney, tear down the courses until you reach solidly bonded materials.

Hose down the chimney. This will wash away the powdered mortar and dampen the bricks so they don't draw moisture from new mortar.

When working on a roof, keep all loose debris swept away from the project, and out from under your feet. Use safety measures.

In most cases, when you rebuild a chimney you must replace the chimney cap itself. This can be brick or preformed concrete.

Once the mortar has set so it will take a thumbprint, clean away any excess. Then tool the joints to the desired shape.

Replacing a loose brick or block. A loose brick or block in the middle of a wall usually indicates that the unit is not supporting any weight. Chip away a little of the mortar joint, then repoint the joint.

The mortar should be hard enough to take a thumbprint before you start finishing the joints. Tool the joints (but not deeply). Wait about 5 minutes; brush across the joints to remove excess mortar on the surrounding brick. Then tool the joints again. Loose and crumbling joints in concrete block walls are treated in exactly the same manner as for brick.

To prevent creosote or sparks from gaining access to the house, check for chimney leakage both inside and outside the building.

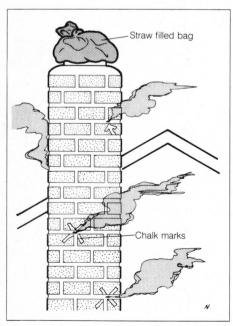

A leaking chimney is dangerous. To locate the position of any leaks, stop the chimney temporarily with a straw-filled bag.

However, loose block or bricks on top of a wall must be removed. All old mortar must be cleaned off the old bricks, and the surrounding area and the bricks or block carefully relaid in place in fresh mortar. Follow the brick-laying guidelines in Chapter 3.

Interior Fire Chamber

Tools and materials. You will need new firebrick, firebrick mortar, tuckpointing trowel, brick or cold chisel, baby sledge hammer, and a container for debris. Wear safety glasses and gloves.

Inspection. Examine the brick in the fire chamber for any damage. Broken and missing firebrick must be replaced. Also check the mortar between firebrick joints. If the mortar is loose and crumbling, the mortar lines should be tuckpointed.

Mortar for firebrick contains fire clay. The mixture (you will probably have to mix your own) is one part cement containing fire clay to three or four parts sand.

Follow the same procedures as for tuckpointing and replacing masonry units.

Sealing the Chimney

If there are air leaks in your chimney, seal them if they are minor. If the leaking smoke comes from major structural cracks, have a mason determine whether the chimney can be repaired or should be rebuilt. If your chimney is lined with flue tile, you can reseal cracks. This is not a one-person job. It can be done by two people, and three people will do a better job.

Adding a flue liner. Clean your chimney before repairing it. It is possible, of course, to seal the flue tile joints or to even install a metal flue liner if your chimney currently is only brick masonry—a possibility if your home predates current building codes. Inserting a metal flue liner is the same as installing stove pipe or a prefabricated chimney for a prefabricated fireplace. You will have to include a sealed collar at the base of the chimney flue (the top of the smoke chamber) so that smoke only goes up the pipe flue. These pipe liners often come with prefabricated sealer/collars. Check carefully before buying. Install according to directions. Purchase insulated pipe, which will keep heat inside the pipe and cut down on the buildup of soot and creosote.

Setting up the chimney area. First cover your smoke shelf and firebox floor with disposable drop cloths. Next, cut a piece of board or ¾ inch plywood so that it will be one inch smaller all around than the smallest part of your flue. This may involve some guess work, but it must be small enough to clear easily.

Adding the support rope. Drill holes in each corner and attach two lengths of sturdy hemp rope, running diagonally from opposite corners. Secure with knots on the underside of the board, leaving enough slack in each piece so that a third piece of rope—long enough to reach all the way from the chimney cap to the hearth—can be attached in the center, where the two pieces cross. Place a flat-bottomed rock or brick on the board under the pieces of crossed rope.

Creating a traveler bag. Line the bottom of a strong bag made of smooth canvas with straw. Lower the board into the bag and surround with straw. Tie the bag securely, around the long rope extending from the bag.

Lowering bag. Lower the bag until it rests on the smoke shelf; then pull it up to the bottom of the flue. A person kneeling in the firebox can see when the bag closes off all light coming down the flue and can

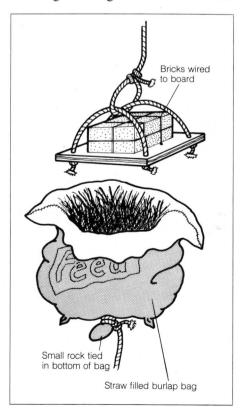

Bricks wired to board

Small rock tied in bottom of bag

Straw filled burlap bag

To seal an old chimney, first lower a "traveler bag" just large enough to fill the flue space. The bag smooths added mortar.

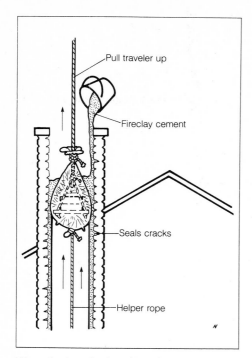

When the traveler bag is at the bottom of the flue, pour in mortar. Smooth by pulling up the bag. The mortar seals all cracks.

signal—by voice or by pulling a signal cord to the roof (not run through the chimney, of course)—when the bag has reached the base of the flue. If you cannot find a third helper, put a bright utility light in the firebox. When the bag reaches the smoke shelf, light should be visible; when the bag reaches the flue, no light should show.

Pouring in the mortar. Mix a batch of fireclay mortar to a consistency of cultured sour cream—it should flow, not run—and pull it or have it carried to the roof by the bucketful. Slowly and carefully pour the mortar down the sides of the flue.

Raising the bag. Have another person then slowly and carefully pull the weighted, straw-filled canvas bag upward. Repeat the process of pouring and pulling until the chimney flue is lined with a smooth coat of fresh mortar.

If the job goes easily, if your mortar is the right consistency, and if your bag does not get stuck, you should have a lining in your flue in a few hours. Some mortar will probably end up on the smoke shelf or firebox floor, which is why you put down the disposable dropcloths. If your mortar was too liquid, it has probably run off the walls and you will have to repeat the process. If your mortar was too thick, you probably needed a lot of help pulling the bag up. However, you now know how to do the job.

Curing time. Wait three weeks to be sure the mortar is completely dry before using the fireplace. Using it before this time will weaken the seal.

STONE OR BLOCK WALLS/PATIOS
Stone Laid Without Mortar

Dry-laid stone walls and patios and walks are repaired by repositioning the loose or fallen stones back in place. For sand-bed stone patios that have sunk, pry up the stones and pour sand under them.

To repair a dry-laid wall, reposition loose stones. If the top stones are particularly unstable, apply a mortar cap to strengthen.

Then place the stones back in position and level them, correcting as needed to bring up to the proper height.

Another problem that is often found with dry-laid stone walls is a loose top layer of rocks. The rocks can be knocked off easily by children or pets. In this case, you may prefer to install a mortar cap around the top of the wall to prevent a re-occurrence.

A Mortared Wall

A mortared stone wall is treated in much the same manner as a mortared brick or block wall. Loose and crumbling mortar should be removed with the chisel, bolt or screwdriver. Pack new mortar in around the stones. Strike the joints with an old bolt head. Broom the joints smooth and clean the wall.

If a veneer stone comes loose, you often can use epoxy masonry glue to glue it back in place. Prop it up with a wood prop until the glue sets up, or use the Waterplug system.

Broken flagstones can be removed and glued back together using epoxy. Then glue them back in place with epoxy or with a thin mortar bed.

How to Patch Stucco

Tools and materials. You will need a hammer, brick chisel, baby sledge hammer, nails, asphalt building paper (55 lb.), chicken wire, staples, latex-based cement, clean sharp sand, mason's trowel, wooden float, straightedge, notched trowel, wide paintbrush, rubber float, garden hose with a spray nozzle, masonry paint, paintbrush and a broom.

Surface preparation. Clean the damaged stucco area with a brick chisel, driving it with a baby sledge hammer. Brush away all the debris with an old broom. The area must be as clean as possible, and the damaged stucco cut back to the good, firm stucco.

Lining the patch. Line the patch with asphalt building paper, tacking it in position with a couple of nails. Over the paper, cut and fit a piece of chicken wire to match the shape of the patch. Nail the chicken wire to the sheathing in several spots—top, bottom, sides. Do not put in too many nails; the wire has to support the new stucco.

Applying the cement. Mix a small batch of latex-based cement (sometimes called bonding cement) with sand. Use one part cement to three parts sand. The consistency should be that of thick mud. With a mason's trowel, spread the mixture into the patch area, working from the bottom of the wire upward.

When the mixture starts to dry, lightly run a notched trowel across the patch. Try to give the surface of the patch a slight tooth so that a second coat of cement can be applied later over the first coat. Let the patch set for about ten days. Spray the first patch with water, but do not soak it.

Adding a second coat. Use the same type of mixture as for the first patch; apply a thin coat. With a straightedge that reaches across the patch, level the patch and then smooth it with a wooden float until you see tiny grains of sand on the surface of the patch.

Applying the last coat. Mix a third batch of patching cement, which should be thinned to the consistency of thick soup. This is a wash coat. Lightly spray the patch with water from the garden hose and apply this last mixture with a mason's trowel. Level the coat with the trowel as you work the mixture over the surface. Completely cover the second base coat with a thin layer of the cement.

Creating the finish. When the top coat starts to dry, lightly brush the surface with water. Then, using a rubber float, stroke the surface. Keep the unworked surface damp with water as you work the float. Since the mixture will be drying fast, you will have to work quickly. You have about 25 to 30 minutes in which to float the final surface on the patch. Blend the edges (feather them) into the surrounding stucco so the finish will match.

If the surface will be colored, you can add color to the top coat mixture. As an alternative, you can wait about three months and then give the patch and the entire siding a fresh coat of masonry paint.

To remove loose paint from brick, block or stucco, use a medium-stiff brush.

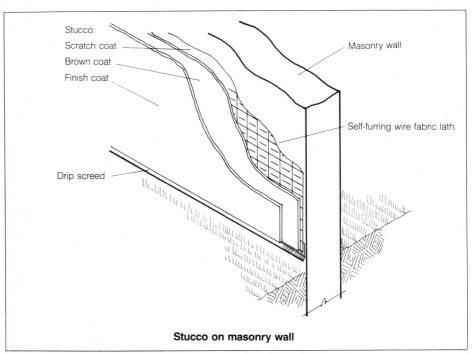

Stucco on masonry wall

Stucco:
Scratch coat
Brown coat
Finish coat
Masonry wall
Self-furring wire fabric lath.
Drip screed

To stucco an old masonry wall, nail down self-furring wire fabricating lath. Space the nails 8 in. on center; then apply the three coats of stucco as usual.

To repair broken concrete around a railing, cut out all crumbling concrete until a solid surface is reached. Make angle cuts.

Brush away loose concrete, chips and dirt. Hose down the concrete thoroughly with clean, cold water. The surface must be moist.

While the area is still damp, apply a grout coat of Thorite. Work it well into the area to be patched. Protect your hands.

Add cool water to the Thorite. Mix until the batch has a mortar-like consistency. Do not overmix. Add just enough to moisten.

Force the Thorite into the opening. Work from the corners in toward the center. Work in layers that are no more than 1 in. thick.

Thorite cures quickly, generating heat as it does so. Spray the first layer with cool water; scratch the surface. Cool as needed.

Follow the same procedure for all consecutive layers. Overfill the last coat so that it extends beyond the final outline.

Wait until the final layer sets up somewhat. This will not take long. Then shave off any excess; shape Thorite as desired.

Once the shaping is done, immediately apply a coating of Thoroseal to complete the bond. Cover the patch and the original concrete.

8 MAINTENANCE OF CONCRETE & MASONRY

Obviously when you have a structure or a surface that is made of stone or its equivalent, removing or replacing it presents very real problems. As a result, proper maintenance of concrete and masonry projects is very important. Very often, simple maintenance, easily performed, can prevent major repairs later on. By being aware of the conditions that can endanger your projects, and of the correct measures for each material, you can increase the longevity of any concrete and masonry project and spare yourself unnecessary expense later on.

STAINING A CONCRETE SURFACE

Very often a cement floor or wall will discolor or, even worse, crack, peel, or scale. Because the porous nature of a concrete floor or wall, and its moisture-absorbing properties, pose a real problem when it comes to painting it, you may wish to stain it instead.

Benefits

Staining provides a surface that will not crack, peel or scale. This type of finish will resist abrasion and moisture and will prevent the dusting that is characteristic of untreated concrete floors. Detergent and beverages will not mar the floor if the coating is properly applied. The cement floor stains may be applied with brush, roller or spray.

Waxing is not recommended. Dust and dirt will not penetrate a stained cement floor; you need only sweep or dust as necessary. Wash occasionally with a mild soap or detergent solution. In extreme traffic areas, floors can be renewed or spot-finished by applying a fresh coat of transparent sealer.

How to Apply the Stain

The best time of year in which to treat interior cement floors is in the winter, when the structure is heated and moisture condensation and humidity are at a mini-mum. Exterior staining is best done on dry, sunny, summer days. Cement should be age-cured before staining. This allows moisture to escape and reduces alkali problems. One to four months is recommended. Carefully follow the directions below to prepare the surface for the application of concrete cement stain.

Step one: cleaning the surface. The cement to be stained must be absolutely free of all foreign material such as paint, varnish, wax, grease or oil. To remove paint or varnish from the cement, use a good grade wax-free paint and varnish remover. It is mandatory that all paint and varnish be removed from the pores of the cement. Remove wax, grease and oil from the cement with special concrete cleaning solutions. Be sure to use enough to remove all the deposits.

Step two: etch the cement. All cement must be etched before using concrete stains. Use the etching material recommended by the stain manufacturer, following directions on the label.

The etching operation may also be satisfactorily accomplished with a solution of muriatic acid and water. In a non-metallic container, mix two parts of water with one part muriatic acid for a *maximum* solution, or five parts water and one part muriatic acid for a *minimum* solution. Apply the mixture to the cement with a straw broom or fiber brush. When the fizzing action has stopped (usually after 10 to 15 minutes) flush the surface with clear water. Allow the cement to dry at least twelve hours after the etching.

Step three: applying the first coat. Brush on first coat of concrete stain; use a brush or a flat applicator. Allow first coat to dry at least overnight.

Step four: adding the second coat. When the first layer of cement stain has dried, apply the second coat.

CAULKING AROUND MASONRY

The average home has many different places where masonry meets other mate-

To have a long life, a concrete structure such as a sidewalk or a dome home must be properly maintained. If not, temperature changes and weather conditions will take their toll.

rials such as wood. As a result of the differences in expansion or house settling, these joints will almost always eventually open. One of the most important home-maintenance chores is a continuing inspection and caulking of these joints.

Typically the joints might be between the fireplace and house siding, between a lower brick facade and upper siding installed over it, or between the chimney flue and the roofline. Another likely loca-

To prevent erosion, heat loss and rot, caulk the seams between both interior and exterior masonry surfaces and wood walls.

Slice off the tip of a tube of caulking at a 45 degree angle. Check the manufacturer's directions for the size of the opening.

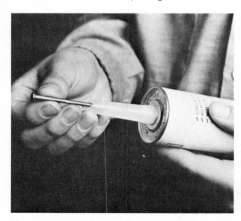

Use a long nail to puncture the seal between the tube and the nozzle. Otherwise the pressure of the applicator can split the tube.

tion is alongside the garage driveway or walk, where it meets a house or garage foundation. If these are not kept caulked to prevent water from entering, they can eventually cause real damage. Another problem area is between the wood of the window and the door frames in a brick or brick-veneered home.

In most instances a good silicone sealer applied with a caulking gun is the best means of caulking. However, in places where the expansion joint between a house or garage and walk or sidewalk has opened you may have to resort to asphalt caulking material to match the existing material.

Maintenance of Concrete Retaining Walls

For cracks in reinforced concrete walls, the treatment is similar to that for cracks in concrete driveways and walks. Clean out the break with a cold or brick chisel, cutting away the crumbling mortar to the good, hard concrete. Wet the crack with water and then fill the break with mortar mix concrete, mixed to a thick consistency. Smooth the surface with a triangular or tuckpointing trowel.

Make sure that all weep and drainage holes in any type of retaining wall are open. These weep holes let water buildup behind the wall escape, preventing damage to the wall.

If the wall does not have weep holes, you will have to make them with a brace and bit or a star drill.

Walk and Driveway Drainage Systems

The quickest and easiest way to stop erosion along walks and driveways is to install a concrete gutter system to carry

To protect steps leading to a sloping grade, install a drainpipe into the form for the steps. Place the concrete around the pipe.

away water. The gutters may be recessed into the ground so that they are hidden from view.

Tools and materials. You will need a chalkline, tile spade, trowel, 1x2 wooden stakes, premixed concrete mix (if the job isn't too large; if it is large, consider mixing your own concrete. See "Large Patches," this chapter); a 2-foot length of 3-inch plastic pipe, garden hose, a wheelbarrow or bucket for debris, 4-inch asphalt isolation strips, and small diameter reinforcing rods.

Preparation. Dig a trough along side of the walk or driveway. Make the trough about 6 inches wide and 4 inches deep. To guide your digging operations you can stretch a chalkline along the length of the area where the trough will be.

Just before you get ready to shovel concrete into the void, wet the freshly dug trough with a fine spray from the garden hose. If the earth is fairly damp, you won't have to sprinkle it. At the same time as you place the concrete, insert the asphalt isolation strips in the trough next to the walk or driveway. Then lay a reinforcing rod in the center of the trough and elevate it an inch or so with stones or small chunks of brick.

Placing the concrete. Pour the fresh concrete in the trough (you can work in 10-foot sections). Then use the plastic pipe as a screed to cut away the new concrete so you form a half-round "gutter" in the concrete. The hollow pipe will pick up excess concrete; you can empty the pipe when it gets full or heavy.

Finishing. Use the trowel to add any necessary touches to the newly formed gutter. Keep the concrete wet for about five days by sprinkling it with the garden hose.

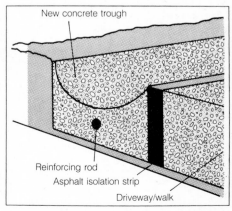

If you install a gutter along the edge of an existing walk or driveway, insert an isolation joint between old and new concrete.

Insulate all heating ducts that go through cold crawl spaces. Wrap carefully; seal the joints between the sheets with duct tape.

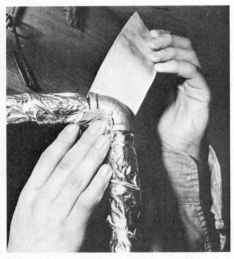
Some pipe wrap has a sticky backing that adheres directly to the pipe. The wrap prevents heat loss and moisture condensation.

PREVENTIVE MEDICINE
Cellar Waterproofing

In some older homes, the front porch floor serves as a roof for a fruit or root cellar. Although this slab is usually thick and well reinforced, it may crack under stress of temperature differential, shifting of the foundations, or even a mild earth tremor. These cracks are usually very fine because of the reinforcement. However, during extended periods of inclement weather, water may seep through the cracks. This will eventually cause a problem. The cellar area may become mildewed or the crack may become enlarged.

If the crack is very fine, you may be able to seal it with an annual or biennial application of cement-base waterproofing paint. This sealing paint is designed to be used on basement walls with pinpoint leaks and fine cracks. Applied to a clean surface, it also will seal the cracks on a concrete slab.

Brick and Block Maintenance

Other than occasional tuckpointing, brick and block need little maintenance. Here are some suggestions on how to keep these masonry materials in good shape.

Remove plants and clinging vines from masonry walls. This vegetation holds moisture that can crumble mortar joints. If you like the appearance of an ivy-covered home, then be prepared to tuckpoint the joints every few years. The joints should be inspected every year.

Mildew can be a masonry problem. You can buy mildewcides to remove the mildew. This involves washing the walls with the solution. You also can buy paint that contains a mildewcide, if the masonry surfaces have been painted.

If your masonry has an accumulation of grime, the best way to remove it is to sandblast the masonry. Some rental outfits offer small sandblasters for rent. But before you get started, make sure that local codes do not prohibit your doing the work. It is also a good idea to check with the neighbors before you begin.

If both neighbors and codes are amenable, the rental agency will furnish you with the necessary equipment and materials, along with instructions. We also recommend that you get bids from a professional sandblasting contractor. It may be to your advantage to have a professional handle this job.

Stains on masonry. Most stains on brick and stone can be removed with strong household detergent, water, and a good stiff scrub brush. If you can't get all the stain off with this treatment, mix 50% muriatic acid with 50% water and scrub this solution on to the surface. Rinse with clear water from a garden hose. Be sure to wear safety glasses and gloves when you apply the acid solution.

Foundation Drainage

Gutters and downspouts. Look for trouble here if your basement is leaking water. Often, faulty gutters and downspouts are serving as funnels to carry the water down against the foundation wall. The result is a damp or wet basement.

Weatherstrip concrete or masonry structures. Use the correct type: fiberglass and tape, pipe wrap with foil face, sponge rubber or felt door and window strips, rubber door sweep.

Flexible pipe, which bends to connect downspout openings and buried clay drainage tiles, is an excellent substitute for clay tile.

For serious drainage problems, hook the downspout to a section or two of perforated plastic pipe, which can be buried underground.

Special plastic fittings connect a downspout to a drain opening. Use it also to connect a downspout with a length of pipe or tile.

Bury the plastic pipe; tamp the earth tight around the pipe. Keep the earth sloped away from the foundation of the house.

Support a base of a downspout that doesn't reach the ground; this keeps the force of the water from dislodging it from the gutter.

Repairs or a new rain-carrying system may be the answer. However, in some cases the problem can be handled by adding an extension to the downspout pipe; it just slips over the end of the downspout. Another alternative is to hook a section of perforated plastic pipe to the downspout, and bury the plastic pipe underground.

Foundation Seepage

Tools and materials. Since the problem can involve gutters, downspouts, broken concrete joints, tools are related to each job as outlined below.

Hydraulic cement. First try patching

Maintain a tight seal between the chimney cap and flue lining to prevent water seepage. Watch for chipped areas in the chimney cap.

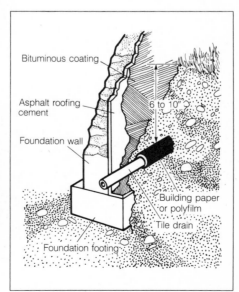

Install drain tile to carry rainwater away from the house footing and foundation, relieve water buildup and prevent water seepage.

any interior cracks with hydraulic cement. Clean out the crack with a cold or brick chisel, driving these tools with a baby sledge hammer. Make the cut in the form of an inverted V, if you can. This will help hold the patch in place.

Press the hydraulic cement into the break and smooth it level with the surrounding surface of the foundation wall with a putty knife. You will have to work fast; hydraulic cement sets quickly. Wear gloves for this job, since hydraulic cement creates heat that could injure your skin.

Waterproofing the foundation. If hydraulic cement does not work, and the rain-carrying system is not the problem, there is only one sure way to stop the leaking.

1. Dig a trench around the foundation, wide enough for you to fit in it, and deep enough to reach under the foundation footing.

2. Clean off the foundation wall. Use a wide scraper for this; scrub the wall down with water from a garden hose and a stiff broom or brush.

3. Make a 3-inch-thick bed of medium-sized gravel in the trench.

4. Lay a row of field tile on the gravel around the bottom of the foundation. The tile should have a slight pitch.

5. At one corner of the house, where the tile come together in the downward pitch, run a length of tile out into the lawn about 10 feet. You will need to dig a trench for this too. Lay the tile on 3 inches of gravel.

6. Coat the foundation walls, from the footing to grade level, with a thick application of asphalt roofing cement. You can apply this with a trowel and brush. Make sure all areas are covered thoroughly.

7. Embed a layer of black 4 mil polyfilm into the asphalt roofing cement. Overlap the joints of the polyfilm about 4 inches, sticking the joints together with asphalt roofing cement.

8. Give all the polyfilm a thin coating of asphalt roofing cement, brushing the cement onto the polyfilm.

9. Let the job dry for a couple of days. Then backfill the earth into the trench.

10. Save any leftover dirt. The ground will settle for some time and you will need this dirt to fill small voids.

Window Wells

Tools and materials. You will need a broom, plumbers' snake, asphalt roofing cement, hammer, pliers, screwdriver, nails, putty knife.

Prevention. Most window wells have French-type drains; i.e., the drain empties into a bed of gravel instead of a sewer. It may, however, be connected to the sewer. Keep the top of the drain free of gravel, grass, dirt, and other debris—an occasional sweeping with a broom is all that is needed.

Rusted drains. If the drain has become rusted shut, you can replace it with a new drain top. Remove the old one by remov-ing the screws or bolts holding the top and tapping off the top with a hammer.

Attaching loosened wells. Window wells often tip away from the house. You can secure them to the house with nails. If not, fill the gap between the flanges of the metal and the house with asphalt roofing compound. If the gap is a large one, you can force asphalt-impregnated isolation strips into the crack. Then cover the strips with asphalt roofing cement, using a putty knife as a trowel.

FASTENING ITEMS TO MASONRY

A wide variety of items can be fastened to masonry, ranging from a heavy-duty porch or step railing to lightweight brackets to hold flower planters and such. There are also many different methods of fastening items to masonry, depending on what the masonry material is and what type of item must be attached. Some items are fastened in place during forming of the masonry project, while for others, holes may be drilled later on.

Installation During Construction

A typical example is the installation of holding bolts for sill plates on foundation walls. Another example is the bolt pins that hold posts in place on concrete piers.

Several manufactured fasteners can be utilized to hold different items, such as the U-shaped anchor plates for fastening heavy posts to a concrete pier or foundation.

In most instances, items that are fastened in place during forming of masonry projects are quite simply installed. Merely insert the item into the mortar joint. Be absolutely sure you have the unit positioned exactly where it is needed. Then allow the mortar to set up thoroughly before using them.

Fastening to an Existing Surface

The difficulty of fastening items to an already existing masonry surface depends on the project and the materials involved.

Gluing. The simplest way to attach an item to a masonry wall is to merely glue it in place using epoxy and special adhesives, such as panel adhesive. However, this can only be done for lightweight

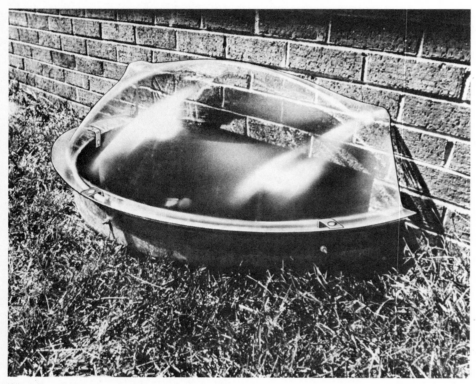

Window wells at ground level collect rotting leaves and hold rainwater or snow. These can damage or ruin the foundation. Well covers such as this prevent such problems.

REMOVING STAINS FROM EXTERIOR MASONRY

Type of Stain	Removal Technique
Smoke	Ammonia and water; apply with stiff brush.
Soot	Household detergent and water, or 1 part muriatic acid to 1 part water (commercial chemicals available).
Crayon	Remove with case knife, then use stiff wire brush or wire brush attachment for a portable electric drill.
Mud/dirt	Mild household detergent and water; apply with stiff brush. If area is large, work from bottom up. Rinse thoroughly.
Mildew	Use good commercial prep. If repainting, use paint formulated with mildewcide. For small areas, try mixture of lemon juice and water.
Moss	Use hydrated lime and water. Wear heavy gloves; protect face and arms. Scrub with stiff brush; flood the area with water.
Lime salts	Use commercial solution.
Grease	Remove with a case knife and a soft, absorbent cloth. Then wash with mild household detergent and water. Rinse thoroughly.

Plan ahead. If you know that you are going to fasten something to a concrete surface, insert masonry anchors into the pour itself.

projects or those that won't be subjected to any stress. Make absolutely sure you read manufacturers' directions on the glue container to see if it works on masonry surfaces.

Nailing. The next simplest method of fastening an item is to merely nail it on. This is often the most common method used when installing furring strips for wallboard or paneling and other wall coverings over a masonry surface.

The nails used are special masonry nails. These nails are not driven with a regular woodworking hammer. Instead, a ball peen or small sledge should be used. Because the nails are extremely hard, they are also quite brittle and can snap off with great force. When driving these nails, always wear safety goggles or a shield and wear heavy gloves to protect your hands.

Driving masonry nails isn't easy at all and in fact can be quite frustrating, but there are several ways to make the job easier. The first is to hold the nail with a pair of pliers with a good grip, not with your fingers. (Mashed fingers are quite often the rule with these nails.) Instead of using heavy blows, use a light tapping blow of the hammer. If you are having trouble, you might consider predrilling the holes for the nails. If installing them in brick or block walls, use the nails in the mortar rather than the block, as you might crack the block or brick. These nails shouldn't be used when a stress or shear load is placed on them, such as when installing heavy shelves.

Several companies make special driving tools to make driving masonry nails much easier. The most common one is a hand-held tool that positions the nail in place. To drive the nail you strike the top of the tool, which has a shield to protect your hands. On the other hand, professionals use a tool that is powered by blank 22 cartridges to drive the nails in quickly and easily. If you have an extremely large job these can sometimes be rented in larger cities.

Types of Masonry Fasteners

In most instances, a better approach to fastening items to masonry is to prebore holes and insert masonry fasteners. On hollow walls, such as block, these inserts expand behind the wall surface to hold the items in place.

Regardless of what type of fastener is used, the first step is to bore a hole for it. In most instances the manufacturer of the fastening item will specify what size hole should be bored for their particular fasteners and for a good, safe holding job you should adhere to their suggestions.

Tool usage. The hole can be drilled in one of two ways, using a star drill and hammer or a portable electric drill with a masonry bit. Using the star drill and the mason's heavy hammer is the old-fashioned method. It is rarely used today because it takes quite a bit of time and not

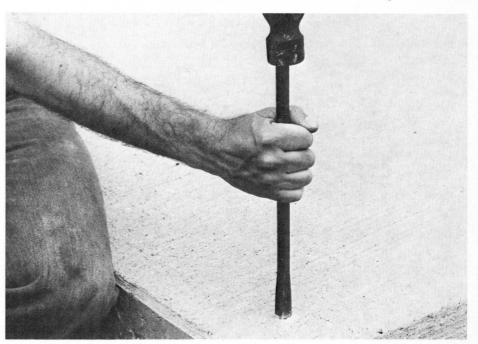

Use a star drill rather than a normal screwdriver to insert holes into a concrete slab. Rotate the drill as you hit it with a mason's hammer. This chips away the surface.

a little expertise to create a good, straight-sided hole. Using the star drill isn't particularly hard, but it does take practice. The drill, which looks like a long steel chisel with a star point on the end, is held in place against the masonry surface and tapped with a heavy hammer; at the same time it is rotated to produce a rounded chipping action. On large holes it's a good idea to first make a smaller hole, then follow with one drill larger.

The problem lies in making the hole the correct size and with straight sides. Most

Holes can also be drilled with a carbide-tipped masonry bit in a portable electric drill. Select a bit that is large enough to allow for the size of the anchor, not the screw.

people tend to get the mouth of the hole much larger than the back, which doesn't allow the masonry fasteners to expand properly. In this case, you must patch around the masonry item or fill in with epoxy to help hold the item in place.

A much quicker, easier and usually better job is done using a portable electric drill and a carbide-tipped masonry bit. Choose the bit of the correct size to make the hole size needed.

The trick in proper masonry boring with a masonry bit is to have plenty of power and a slow speed. For this reason, the more economical ¼ inch portable electric drill does not work well because it turns too fast and doesn't have enough power once the bit gets deep into the material. A ⅜-inch variable speed drill is best for light boring jobs; a ½-inch variable speed is ideal for boring holes in masonry. This is because the ½ inch bit has a lower rpm. Whatever the tool you use, wear safety goggles while boring in masonry.

After the holes have been properly bored there are any number of fasteners that can be installed. In almost all instances they are driven or pushed into the holes.

Toggle bolt. This bolt is used when hanging something on a hollow wall or a concrete block wall. The toggle bolt consists of a machine screw with a pair of collapsible wings. Once inside the wall, the wings will pop open.

The toggle bolt screws are available in various lengths so that you can buy the size suited to the thickness of the material you are hanging. The screw must be long enough to go through the wall thickness and the item to be hung.

Expansion shield. Expansion shields are often used in masonry. To use one, drill a hole in the wall that is as wide as the diameter of the sleeve of the device, and as deep as the sleeve length. The sleeve may be lead, fiber or plastic depending on the manufacturer; the lead sleeve is the best. Drill a corresponding hole through the item. Slip the sleeve into the hole drilled in the wall. Slip a screw in the sleeve; the screw should be long enough to go through the back of the item to be hung and halfway into the sleeve. Then tighten the screw. As you do this the sleeve will expand, locking itself against the sides of the hole by friction and pulling the item against the wall.

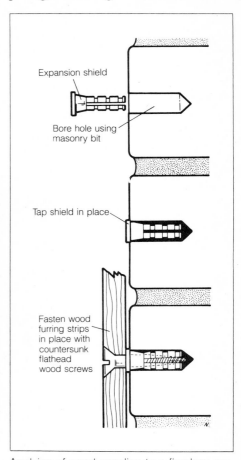

Applying of wood paneling to a fireplace surround requires expansion shields and screws. These must not punch through the masonry.

Sand-bed walks and patios must be re-sanded yearly. Otherwise erosion and foot traffic will result in sunken areas in the surface.

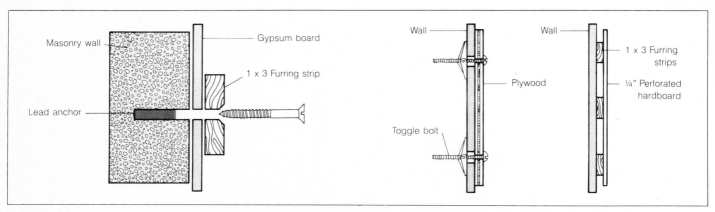

Use the correct fastener for a given setting. Synthetic brick installations require toggle bolts. The "wing" in back of the bolt spreads to add extra support. Masonry walls, on the other hand, require lead, fiber or plastic anchors that hold a screw.

Metric Conversion Charts

LUMBER

Sizes: Metric cross-sections are so close to their nearest Imperial sizes, as noted below, that for most purposes they may be considered equivalents.

Lengths: Metric lengths are based on a 300mm module which is slightly shorter in length than an Imperial foot. It will therefore be important to check your requirements accurately to the nearest inch and consult the table below to find the metric length required.

Areas: The metric area is a square metre. Use the following conversion factors when converting from Imperial data: 100 sq. feet = 9.290 sq. metres.

METRIC SIZES SHOWN BESIDE NEAREST IMPERIAL EQUIVALENT

mm	Inches	mm	Inches
16 x 75	⅝ x 3	44 x 150	1¾ x 6
16 x 100	⅝ x 4	44 x 175	1¾ x 7
16 x 125	⅝ x 5	44 x 200	1¾ x 8
16 x 150	⅝ x 6	44 x 225	1¾ x 9
19 x 75	¾ x 3	44 x 250	1¾ x 10
19 x 100	¾ x 4	44 x 300	1¾ x 12
19 x 125	¾ x 5	50 x 75	2 x 3
19 x 150	¾ x 6	50 x 100	2 x 4
22 x 75	⅞ x 3	50 x 125	2 x 5
22 x 100	⅞ x 4	50 x 150	2 x 6
22 x 125	⅞ x 5	50 x 175	2 x 7
22 x 150	⅞ x 6	50 x 200	2 x 8
25 x 75	1 x 3	50 x 225	2 x 9
25 x 100	1 x 4	50 x 250	2 x 10
25 x 125	1 x 5	50 x 300	2 x 12
25 x 150	1 x 6	63 x 100	2½ x 4
25 x 175	1 x 7	63 x 125	2½ x 5
25 x 200	1 x 8	63 x 150	2½ x 6
25 x 225	1 x 9	63 x 175	2½ x 7
25 x 250	1 x 10	63 x 200	2½ x 8
25 x 300	1 x 12	63 x 225	2½ x 9
32 x 75	1¼ x 3	75 x 100	3 x 4
32 x 100	1¼ x 4	75 x 125	3 x 5
32 x 125	1¼ x 5	75 x 150	3 x 6
32 x 150	1¼ x 6	75 x 175	3 x 7
32 x 175	1¼ x 7	75 x 200	3 x 8
32 x 200	1¼ x 8	75 x 225	3 x 9
32 x 225	1¼ x 9	75 x 250	3 x 10
32 x 250	1¼ x 10	75 x 300	3 x 12
32 x 300	1¼ x 12	100 x 100	4 x 4
38 x 75	1½ x 3	100 x 150	4 x 6
38 x 100	1½ x 4	100 x 200	4 x 8
38 x 125	1½ x 5	100 x 250	4 x 10
38 x 150	1½ x 6	100 x 300	4 x 12
38 x 175	1½ x 7	150 x 150	6 x 6
38 x 200	1½ x 8	150 x 200	6 x 8
38 x 225	1½ x 9	150 x 300	6 x 12
44 x 75	1¾ x 3	200 x 200	8 x 8
44 x 100	1¾ x 4	250 x 250	10 x 10
44 x 125	1¾ x 5	300 x 300	12 x 12

METRIC LENGTHS

Lengths Metres	Equiv. Ft. & Inches
1.8m	5' 10⅞"
2.1m	6' 10⅝"
2.4m	7' 10½"
2.7m	8' 10¼"
3.0m	9' 10⅛"
3.3m	10' 9⅞"
3.6m	11' 9¾"
3.9m	12' 9½"
4.2m	13' 9⅜"
4.5m	14' 9⅓"
4.8m	15' 9"
5.1m	16' 8¾"
5.4m	17' 8⅝"
5.7m	18' 8⅜"
6.0m	19' 8¼"
6.3m	20' 8"
6.6m	21' 7⅞"
6.9m	22' 7⅝"
7.2m	23' 7½"
7.5m	24' 7¼"
7.8m	25' 7⅛"

All the dimensions are based on 1 inch = 25 mm.

NOMINAL SIZE (This is what you order.)	ACTUAL SIZE (This is what you get.)
Inches	Inches
1 x 1	¾ x ¾
1 x 2	¾ x 1½
1 x 3	¾ x 2½
1 x 4	¾ x 3½
1 x 6	¾ x 5½
1 x 8	¾ x 7¼
1 x 10	¾ x 9¼
1 x 12	¾ x 11¼
2 x 2	1¾ x 1¾
2 x 3	1½ x 2½
2 x 4	1½ x 3½
2 x 6	1½ x 5½
2 x 8	1½ x 7¼
2 x 10	1½ x 9¼
2 x 12	1½ x 11¼

PIPE FITTINGS

Only fittings for use with copper pipe are affected by metrication: metric compression fittings are interchangeable with Imperial in some sizes, but require adaptors in others.

INTERCHANGEABLE SIZES		SIZES REQUIRING ADAPTORS	
mm	Inches	mm	Inches
12	³/₈	22	³/₄
15	½	35	1¼
28	1	42	1½
54	2		

Metric capillary (soldered) fittings are not directly interchangeable with imperial sizes but adaptors are available. Pipe fittings which use screwed threads to make the joint remain unchanged. The British Standard Pipe (BSP) thread form has now been accepted internationally and its dimensions will not physically change. These screwed fittings are commonly used for joining iron or steel pipes, for connections on taps, basin and bath waste outlets and on boilers, radiators, pumps etc. Fittings for use with lead pipe are joined by soldering and for this purpose the metric and inch sizes are interchangeable.

(Information courtesy Metrication Board. Millbank Tower. Millbank. London SW1P 4QU)

WOOD SCREWS

SCREW GAUGE NO.	NOMINAL DIAMETER		LENGTH	
	Inch	mm	Inch	mm
0	0.060	1.52	³/₁₆	4.8
1	0.070	1.78	¹/₄	6.4
2	0.082	2.08	⁵/₁₆	7.9
3	0.094	2.39	³/₈	9.5
4	0.0108	2.74	⁷/₁₆	11.1
5	0.122	3.10	½	12.7
6	0.136	3.45	⁵/₈	15.9
7	0.150	3.81	³/₄	19.1
8	0.164	4.17	⁷/₈	22.2
9	0.178	4.52	1	25.4
10	0.192	4.88	1¼	31.8
12	0.220	5.59	1½	38.1
14	0.248	6.30	1³/₄	44.5
16	0.276	7.01	2	50.8
18	0.304	7.72	2¼	57.2
20	0.332	8.43	2½	63.5
24	0.388	9.86	2³/₄	69.9
28	0.444	11.28	3	76.2
32	0.5	12.7	3¼	82.6
			3½	88.9
			4	101.6
			4½	114.3
			5	127.0
			6	152.4

Dimensions taken from BS1210; metric conversions are approximate.

BRICKS AND BLOCKS

Bricks

Standard metric brick measures 215 mm x 65 mm x 112.5. Metric brick can be used with older, standard brick by increasing the mortaring in the joints. The sizes are substantially the same, the metric brick being slightly smaller (3.6 mm less in length, 1.8 mm in width, and 1.2 mm in depth).

Concrete Block

Standard sizes

390 x 90 mm
390 x 190 mm
440 x 190 mm
440 x 215 mm
440 x 290 mm

Repair block for replacement of block in old installations is available in these sizes:
448 x 219 (including mortar joints)
397 x 194 (including mortar joints)

NAILS

NUMBER PER POUND OR KILO

Size	Weight Unit	Common	Casing	Box	Finishing
2d	Pound	876	1010	1010	1351
	Kilo	1927	2222	2222	2972
3d	Pound	586	635	635	807
	Kilo	1289	1397	1397	1775
4d	Pound	316	473	473	548
	Kilo	695	1041	1041	1206
5d	Pound	271	406	406	500
	Kilo	596	893	893	1100
6d	Pound	181	236	236	309
	Kilo	398	591	519	680
7d	Pound	161	210	210	238
	Kilo	354	462	462	524
8d	Pound	106	145	145	189
	Kilo	233	319	319	416
9d	Pound	96	132	132	172
	Kilo	211	290	290	398
10d	Pound	69	94	94	121
	Kilo	152	207	207	266
12d	Pound	64	88	88	113
	Kilo	141	194	194	249
16d	Pound	49	71	71	90
	Kilo	108	156	156	198
20d	Pound	31	52	52	62
	Kilo	68	114	114	136
30d	Pound	24	46	46	
	Kilo	53	101	101	
40d	Pound	18	35	35	
	Kilo	37	77	77	
50d	Pound	14			
	Kilo	31			
60d	Pound	11			
	Kilo	24			

LENGTH AND DIAMETER IN INCHES AND CENTIMETERS

Size	Inches	Length Centimeters	Inches	Diameter Centimeters*
2d	1	2.5	.068	.17
3d	1/2	3.2	.102	.26
4d	1/4	3.8	.102	.26
5d	1/6	4.4	.102	.26
6d	2	5.1	.115	.29
7d	2/2	5.7	.115	.29
8d	2/4	6.4	.131	.33
9d	2/6	7.0	.131	.33
10d	3	7.6	.148	.38
12d	3/2	8.3	.148	.38
16d	3/4	8.9	.148	.38
20d	4	10.2	.203	.51
30d	4/4	11.4	.220	.58
40d	5	12.7	.238	.60
50d	5/4	14.0	.257	.66
60d	6	15.2	.277	.70

*Exact conversion

INDEX

Adhesive, ceramic tile, 98, 99, 102
Air-entraining agent, 9, 12
American bond, 44
Anchor bolts, 11, 28, 61, 77, 87, 89, 93, 136
Apron (driveway), 35
Ash dump, 110
Ash pit, 106, 107, 108, 118
Ashlar, 65, 70

Backer stones, 70
Backfill, 32, 37, 135
Bank-run sand, 11
Barbecue, 40, 46, 102-104
Base materials, 24, 25, 32
Basement, 63, 87-88, 123-125; *repair, 123-125*
Basketweave, 41, 56, 59
Bathroom addition, 92-94
Bathroom patio, 30-31
Batter boards, 39, 81, 93, 101-102, 108
Bond-on-bond, 81
Bond patterns, 44-45; *brick, 44-45*
Bond stones, see Tie stones
Boulders, 28
Beaded joints, 48
Bearing surface, 51
Beating block, 101
Bed joints, 49
"Birdbaths," 16
Brick, 32, 38-64, 102, 105, 108, 109, 115, 125-129; *characteristics, 38-41; corner leads, 46; dry run, 44; firepit, 60-61; fireplace, 105-118; free-standing leads, 46; mortar, 43-44, 47-48; one-wythe walls, 46-51; patio, 56-60; patterns, 45-46; pier-and-panel walls, 48-49; preparation, 44; repair, 125-129; sand-bed, 57-60; screen wall, 51; serpentine wall, 50; size, 40; techniques, 46-48; terminology, 42; terraces, 56-60; tools, 38-40; two-wythe walls, 51-56; types, 40; veneer (exterior), 61-63; veneer (interior), 63; walks, 56-60*
Broken walk, repair 122-123
Brick hammer and chisel, 41, 47, 67, 80, 119, 127
Brick, types, 40
Building brick, 40
Building contractor, 36, 37
Buildings, 77, 79
Buttering, 47, 82, 83, 110, 111, 112, 126
Buttressed wall, 37

Cantilevered hearth, 107, 109
Cantilevered retaining walls, 36-37
Capping, 54, 55-56, 61, 72, 74, 80 *brick, 54, 55-56, 61; concrete block, 80; stone, 72, 74*
Caulking, 85, 132-133; *control joints, 85; masonry joints, 132-133*
Cedar edging, 33, 57
Ceiling joists, 87, 89, 93, 116
Ceramic tile, 92, 94, 98-101, 102, 109; *adhesive, 99; cutting tile, 99-100; design, 98; finishing, 101; Working lines, 98-99*
Chalkline, 44, 51, 53, 54, 82
Chimney, 108, 111, 112, 114, 116, 119, 125, 127-130; *repair, 127-130*
Chimney anchors, 116
Chimney cap, 117, 126, 128, 135
Chimney veneer, 111
Closure block, 83
Closure brick, 42, 44, 47
Coarse aggregates, 9, 10, 11, 13, 14, 15, 16, 17, 18, 19, 20, 21, 28, 60, 77, 95, 96
Colored concrete, 21; *coloring agents, 21; dry powders, 21*
Common bond, 45

Common brick, 40
Concave joints, 47, 48
Concrete 8-37; *abrasions, 33; air-entrained, 12, 15; amount required, 12-13; edging, 17, 18, 20; finishing, 10, 16-17; jointing, 17, 20; materials, 10-11; mixing, 14-15; pouring, 16; proportions, 11-12, 13, 14; ready-mix, 13, 15; spading, 16; stains, 33; transit mix, 15-16; tools, 9-11; See also Footings, Foundations*
Concrete block, 57, 61, 78-91, 108, 111, 112, 116; *amount required, 80; basement, 87-88; bond patterns, 81; buildings, 88-89; characteristics, 78-79; chimney, 108, 111, 112, 116; control joints, 85-86; corner leads, 82-83; crawl space, 86-87; cutting, 83-85; finishing, 86; mortar, 80-81; pavers, 90-91; placement, 81-82; repair, 125-129; stucco, 89-90; tools, 79-80*
Concrete block bond breakers, 85
Concrete block sealers, 85, 91
Concrete block, types, 79
Concrete mix test, 14; *settling, 14; slump, 14*
Concrete tub tank, 93, 94-98; *base, 94; footing, 94-95; forms, 96; pour, 96-97*
Construction joint, 24-25, 34; *buttered, 24, 34; keyed, 25*
Construction key, 25
Control joints, 17, 24, 26, 32, 35, 37, 85, 122; *concrete block, 85*
Coping, 49, 77
Corbel, 115
Corner block, 79, 82
Corner stones, 67
Cove tiles, 98, 99
Crawl space, 86-87
Creosote, 115, 125, 128
Crown, 34, 58-59
Crushed stone, 11, 58, 102
Curb, 24, 30, 131; *for ramp, 30*
Cure, 15, 18, 21, 32, 94, 97, 102; *colored concrete, 21; grout, 101*
Cutting technique, 47, 83-85, 68-69, 98, 99-100; *brick, 47; concrete block, 83-85; stone, 68-69; tile, 98, 99-100;*
Cypress edging, 33, 57, 58

Damper, 106
Deck, 24, 28, 92, 108
De-icing treatments, 12
Downdraft, 106, 115
Dragboard, 26, 58, 59, 69, 94
Drain tile, 37, 76, 87
Drainage, 28, 32, 76, 94, 96, 102, 133, 134-135
Dressing grout lines, 101
Driveway, 13, 15, 18, 34-35, 90, 133; *base, 35; design, 34; finishing, 35; forms, 34-35; pour, 35*
Dry-laid stone wall, 70-72, 129
Dry-laid stone, 67-68, 69-72, 76-77; *patio, 68-69; repair, 129-130; retaining walls, 76-77; steps, 72; walks, 67-68; wall, 69-72*
Ducts, cold air, 106, 109, 110, 111, 114
Dutch bond, 44

Earth-and-stone retaining wall, 76
Edge stiffener, 32, 33
Edging (concrete), 10, 17, 18, 30, 36
Elevated patio, 32
English bond, 44, 45, 52
Erosion, 25, 26, 32, 66
Excavating, 22-23, 24, 32-33, 40, 57, 69, 70, 90, 94, 101
Expansion shield, 138
Exposed aggregate, 16, 20-21, 22, 33, 34
Extruded joints, 48

Face brick, 40
Face-shell mortaring, 84, 85
Fascia, 62
Fieldstone, 65-77, 93-94, 106-117
Fill stones, 70, 73, 110, 111, 114, 115; *mixed with mortar, 110, 111, 114, 115*
Finished grade, 50
Finishing, 56, 61, 72, 74-75; *brick wall, 56; firepit, 61; stone wall, 72, 74-75*
Firebox, 105, 108, 110, 128
Firebrick, 40, 60-61, 108, 109, 110, 125
Fireclay mortar, 40, 60-61, 110
Firepit, 60-61
Fireplace, 9, 40, 46, 72, 92, 105-118, 133; *ashpit, 108, 118; creating openings, 107, 108-109, 116-117; ducts, 114; excavating, 107-108; fireplace front, 111-113; flue liner, 115-116; hearth, 110; materials, 106; metal liner unit, 106; mortar, 106-107, 113; opening size, 105; smoke shelf, 114-115; subhearth forms, 108, 109; support of, 107; tools, 106-107; (see also Chimney)*
Fireplace cap, 116, 127
Fireplace front, 112, 125
"Flagstone" (concrete), 19
Flagstones, 67, 130; *repair, 130*
Flange, 97; *tub, 97*
Flanges (concrete block), 79, 82-83, 84
Flashing, 55-56, 61, 117
Flemish bond, 44, 45
Floating, 16, 17, 18, 19, 20, 28, 29
Floor joists, 93, 94, 96, 105, 109
Floors, interior, 16, 17, 91
Flue liners, tile, 79, 115, 119, 128-130, 135
Flush joints, 47, 48
Footings, 13, 24, 28, 32-33, 36, 40, 42-43, 44, 46, 57, 63, 67, 69, 72, 81, 87, 92, 93, 94-95, 96, 101-102, 106, 107, 108, 109
Form-building, 8, 13, 25, 28; *lumber, 13; tools, 8*
Forms, 15, 16, 17, 21, 24, 25-26, 32, 33, 34-35, 36, 81, 93, 94, 96, 102, 108, 112, 120
Forms, curved, 32, 34
Foundation, 11, 24, 25, 48, 70, 72, 78, 79, 80-85, 93, 94, 105, 106, 107, 108, 109, 119-123, 134-135, 135-136; *concrete block, 79, 80-85; drainage, 134-135; repair, 119-123; seepage, 135-136*
Fountain and pool, 92, 101-102
Fountain pump, 102
Free-form patio, 31-32, 57
Frost heave, 9, 21, 22, 25, 28, 33, 42, 90, 94, 107
Frost line, 24, 37, 42, 70
Full mortaring, 85
Furring strips, 77, 88, 137

Garden wall, 46, 65, 85, 91
Gas log lighter, 110
Granite, 65
Gravel, 10, 11, 20, 28, 32, 35, 57, 58, 76, 87, 95, 102, 121
Gravity retaining walls, 37
Green concrete, 21
Ground cover, 27, 32
Grout, 101, 102
Grout lines, 98, 99, 100
Gutter, 133

Hand mixing (concrete) 12, 14-15
Handrails, 30, 125-127; *repair, 125-127*
Header (brick), 42, 45, 46, 51, 54, 61
Header (lumber), 107, 109
Hearth, 108, 109, 125, 128
Heat chamber, 106
Heat exchange, 112

Herringbone pattern, 58, 59
Hydraulic cement, 123-125, 135

Infilling, 56
Insulation, 88, 107, 110-111, 126, 134
Isolation joint, 24, 26, 29, 33, 35, 136

Joint styles, brick, 47-48

Landing, 26, 27, 28
Layout, ceramic tile, 100-101
Leads, 46, 52-54, 62, 74, 82-83; *brick, 46, 52-54, 62; concrete block, 82-83; stone, 74*
Lime, 43, 80-81, 125
Lintels, 63, 80, 93, 112
Load-bearing walls, 42-43, 45, 63, 79, 91, 126
Local building codes, 22, 24, 33, 34, 36, 40, 42, 44, 49, 51, 60, 61, 70, 72, 79, 81, 88, 91, 94, 107, 114, 115, 117
Lumber sizes, 13

Masonry anchors, 92, 97, 120, 136
Masonry nails, 137
Masonry screws, 97
Masonry, stains, 134, 136
Mason's brush, 41
Mason's mortar cement, 43, 89, 105, 106, 110, 111, 112
Mason's string line, 41, 46, 52, 70, 72, 74, 79, 82, 85, 111
Measuring box, 8-9, 13
Metal liner unit, fireplace, 106, 109-111
Metal tub tank, 94, 98
Michigan joint, 85
Moisture absorption, 10, 15, 44, 81, 125-127; *brick, 44, 125-127; cement, 10; concrete block, 81; subgrade, 15*
Moisture barrier, 62
Moisture treatment, 56
Mortar, 19, 40, 42-43, 52, 60, 74, 80-81, 87, 97, 102, 106, 110-112; *brick, 42-43; concrete block, 80-81; stone, 74*
Mortar bed, 22, 41, 46, 57, 82, 126
Mortar cap, 49, 72, 117, 129, 130
Mortar color, 93, 106
Mortar, fireclay, 40, 60-61
Mortar hawk, 44, 46, 79, 82, 85, 107
Mortar joints, 43, 44, 45, 46, 47-48, 52, 55, 79, 80, 81, 82, 93, 112, 119, 125-126
Mortar mix, proportions, 43, 73, 80-81, 96, 110, 119-120, 121, 125, 129; *brick, 43; concrete block, 80-81; fireplace, 110; repair, 119-120, 121, 125, 129; stone, 73; watertight tank, 96*
Mortar mix, test, 43, 72, 81; *brick, 43; concrete block, 81; stone, 72*
Mortar mixes, concrete block, types, 80-81
Mortared stone walls, 72-72, 92-94, 130; *repair, 130*
Muriatic acid, 75, 113

Nominal vs. actual size, 13, 39-40, 79; *brick, 39-40; concrete block, 79; lumber, 13*
Non-load-bearing walls, 43, 63
Notched trowel, 99

Ornamental concrete block, 79, 91

Painting concrete, 21
Panel and pier wall, 48-50; *design, 49; reinforcement, 49*
Parge coat, 56, 87
Partially mortared wall, 75
Partition, concrete block, 79
Patio, 13, 15, 16, 17, 20, 21, 22, 28, 29, 30-33, 38, 40, 41, 52-60, 65, 67-68, 90-91, 101-102
Patio block, concrete, 90

Patio, brick, 52-60; *design, 56-57; mortar bed, 60; sand-bed, 52-60*
Patio, combination, 101-102
Patio, concrete, 30-32; *design, 30-32; location, 30-31*
Patio, stone, 65, 67-68, 69
Pavers, brick, 40, 57-60
Pea gravel, 19
Permanent edgings, 57, 69
Permanent forms, 21, 32, 34
Pier-and-panel brick wall, 48-50, 55
Pier footings, 24, 109
Pilaster, 85
Pitch, 26, 29, 33, 34, 35, 58-59, 69, 90, 102
Pitted concrete, 18-19
Placing, 52, 73-74, 82-83, 99, 101; *brick, 52; concrete block, 82-83; stone, 73-74; tile, 99, 101*
Planters, 20, 38, 56, 65
Plastic concrete, 11, 12, 17, 18, 19, 33
Plaster, 56, 87
Plumbing, 94, 96, 97, 98, 99, 101, 102
Pointing trowel, 41, 73
Polyethylene, 62, 97
Posthole footings, 11, 24
Portland cement, 10, 11, 14, 15, 59, 69, 72, 95, 96; *storage, 10; types, 10-11; see also Masonry mortar*
Pouring concrete, 16
Power mixing, 9, 12, 13, 15
Premolded control joint, 85
Prime coat, 98
Privacy wall, 30-31, 93

Quarried stone, 65, 66

Rafters, 93, 116
Railroad ties, 21, 28, 32, 33, 57, 91
Raked joints, 48
Ready-mix concrete, 15
Redwood edging, 33, 58, 69
Refractory mortar, 60
Reinforcement, 11, 24, 26, 28, 35, 36, 37, 49, 55, 88, 96-97, 108, 110, 111, 116, 117, 118, 121, 122, 133, 134
Repair, basement leakage, 123-125
Repair, brick or block, 125-129; *chimneys, 127-129; replacing, 126; sand-base, 126-127; tuckpointing, 125-126*
Repair, concrete slab, 119-123; *broken corners and edges, 120-121; broken section, 122; low spots, 121-122; shallow cracks, 119-120; shallow holes, 120; veneer, 122-123*
Repair, dry-laid stone walls, 129-130
Repair, loose railings, 125
Repair, stone walls, 129-130
Repair, stucco, 130
Repointing, see Tuckpointing
Retaining walls, 27-28, 32, 36-37, 56, 65, 67, 70, 72, 76-77
Rise, 28-30
Risers, 26, 27, 28-30
Rock gardens, 27, 32, 76
Roof opening, 116
Roof rafters, 89
Roofing compound, 117, 135
Rowlock header, 42, 51, 52, 54, 55, 56, 58, 74
Rowlock stretcher, 42, 52, 54, 58
Rounded joints, 47, 48
Rubble stone, 66, 126
Run, 28-30
Running bond, 41, 44-45, 52, 54, 56, 81

Sailor, 42
Safety glasses, 47, 67, 100, 125, 127, 137

Sand, 10, 11, 12, 13, 14, 15, 21, 32, 35, 43, 80-81, 89, 90-91, 95, 96, 126; *moisture in, 12*
Sand bed, 22, 42, 57-60, 67, 69, 90-91, 138; *filling joints, 59-60; repair, 126-127; setting, 59;*
Sand-mortar joint, 59-60, 69, 90
Scaffolding, 107
Screeding, 16, 17, 20, 24, 29, 30, 35, 95, 97, 120
Screen wall, 51, 78
Segregation, see Separation
Separation (concrete), 11, 16, 95
Serpentine wall, 50
Settling test (concrete), 14
Sharp sand, 11
Sill plate, 77, 87, 89, 92, 93, 136
Silt test, 11
Single-wythe wall (brick), 46-51, 61-63
Skimmers, 72
Slab, 11, 12, 13, 17, 19, 20, 21, 24, 25, 32; *specifications, 11*
Slab footing, 24
Slip-forming, 77
Slope, 29-30, 32, 34, 36, 76-77; *driveway, 34; patio, 32; walk, 29-30; see also Pitch, Drainage*
Slump test, 14, 95
Smoke dome, 106
Smoke shelf, 106, 114-115, 128
Soffit, 62
Soil types, 24, 25, 34, 35, 58; *clay, 24; dry-packed, 25; hard, 25, 34; loose, 58; poorly drained, 25, 58; sand, 24; sand-and-gravel, 24; well-drained, 35; wet, 25*
Soldier, 42
Sona Tube, 24
Spacers, 44, 46, 82, 100
Spading, 16, 35, 95, 117
Special-purpose concrete blocks, 79
Spray cure compound, 21
Spreaders, 102
Square patio, 31
Squeegee, 101
Stack bond, 44, 45
Staining concrete, 21, 132
Stake-and-string line, 25, 31, 32, 68, 93, 101
Stamped designs (concrete), 19-20
Stepped walks, 29-30
Stepped-back walls, 28
Stepped ramps, 28, 29-30, 32
Steps, 16, 21, 24, 26-30, 32, 72, 125; *base, 28-29; design, 26-28, 29-30; excavation, 28; form, 28-29; reinforcing, 28; stepped walks, 29-30*
Stone, 65-77, 105-117; *acquiring, 65-67; cutting, 68-69; dry-laid, 67-68, 69-72, 76-77; fireplace, 105-117; mortared, 72-76; partially mortared, 75; retaining walls, 76-77; slip-forming, 77; techniques, 67-77; tools, 67; types, 65; veneer, 76*
Stone shapes, 66-67
Stopboard, 24, 25, 33, 34, 35
Storage, concrete block, 81
Story pole, 41, 46, 53, 79-80
Striking grout lines, 101
Stretcher (block), 79, 82-83, 85
Stretcher (brick), 42, 44, 45, 46, 51
Striking mortar, 52, 126
Stucco, 88, 89-90, 101, 108-109, 130; *brown coat, 89; repair, 130; scratch coat, 89; white coat, 89-90*
Studs, 93, 95, 107, 109
Subgrade, 15, 23
Subhearth, 108, 109
Subsurface, 24
Sunken Roman tub, 92, 93, 94-102; *base preparation, 94; flange, 97; footing, 94-95;*

Sunken Roman tub continued
  pouring tub, 96-97; tiling, 98-102; tub
  forms, 96; waterproofing, 97-98
Support, fireplace, 105-110
Support framing, 107
Surface finishing, 10, 16, 17, 18, 19, 20, 21,
  28, 33, 34, 35; broomed, 10, 16, 18, 28, 35;
  exposed aggregate, 16, 20-21, 33, 34;
  "flagstone," 19; floated, 16; pitted, 18-19;
  timing of, 17; troweled, 16
Synthetic brick, 63

Tamping, 14, 16, 21, 23, 26, 29, 33, 35, 58,
  72, 94, 97
Terrace walls, 36, 56-60, 76-77
Throat, fireplace, 106
Tie stones, 67, 70, 71, 72, 74, 75
Tile cutter, 100
Tile nipper, 100
Toggle bolt, 138
Tooling joints, 47-48, 55, 60, 74-75, 86, 110,
  113
Tools, brick, 40, 41, 44, 46, 47, 48, 55; chisel,
  41, 47; hammer, 41, 47; jointing tool, 41,
  47, 48, 55; level, 46; mason's brush, 41;
  mason's string line, 41, 46; pointing trowel,
  41; spirit level, 41; story pole, 41, 46; string
  level, 46, 48; tongs, 40; trowel, 41, 44, 46,
  47; see also Tools, concrete
Tools, concrete, 8-9, 10, 12, 13, 14, 15, 16,
  17, 18, 19, 20, 21, 25, 28; anchor bolts, 28;
  bristle brush, 16; broom, 10, 20; bullfloat,
  10, 17, 18; darby, 17, 20; duplex nails, 25;
  edger, 10, 17, 18; float, 10, 17, 18, 19, 21;
  groover, 10, 17; hoe, 10, 13, 14, 15; knee
  pads, 18, 20; measuring box, 8-9; mortar
  box, 13, 14; power mixer, 9, 12, 13, 15;
  power trowel, 10; rake, 9, 16; rubber
  hipboots, 8, 16; scaffolding nails, 25;
  screed, 9, 16; shovel, 9, 16; tamper, 19;
  trowel, 10, 18, 21, 30; vibrator, 9, 16;
  wheelbarrow, 9, 13, 14, 15
Tools, concrete block, 79-80, 83, 85, 86, 91;
  gloves, 79; jointing tool, 80, 86; level, 80,
  91; mortar hawk, 79; safety glasses, 79, 83;
  story pole, 79-80, 85; string line, 79, 83, 91;
  trowel, 79
Tools, general, 8, 26, 30, 44, 52, 58, 60, 67,
  82-83; chisel, 30; cross-cut saw, 8;
  crowbar, 8; electric saw, 8; hammer, 8;
  level, 8, 26, 58, 60, 67, 82-83; rasp, 30;
  sabre saw, 30; sledge, 8; square, 8, 52;
  straightedge, 44, 58, 60, 67
Tools, stone, 67, 68, 74; broom, 69; gloves,
  67, 68, 74; line level, 67; pry bar, 67; raking
  board, 69; safety glasses, 67, 68;
  sharp-bladed shovel, 67; tape measure, 67;
  wheelbarrow, 67
Tongs, brick, 40
Tongue and groove control joint, 85
Topsoil, 101
Transit mix concrete, 15-16
Traveler bag, 128-129
Treads, 24, 26, 27, 28-30
Tree well, 57
Trench footings, 24
Troweling, 17, 18, 19, 22, 28, 36, 46, 52, 56,
  60, 73-74, 82, 84, 86, 107, 110; brick, 46,
  52, 56, 60; concrete block, 82, 84, 86;
  stone, 73-74
Tuckpointing, 119, 125-126
Two-wythe walls, 42, 45, 51-56

Used brick, 40
Utilities, 22

Vee joints, 48
Veneer, stone, 73, 76, 105, 112, 114

Veneer, brick, 44, 45, 61-63, 105; exterior,
  61-63; interior, 63
Veneer, concrete, 122-123
Vertical joints, 49

Walks, 15, 16, 17, 18, 20, 22, 24, 25-26,
  27-28, 56-60, 67-69, 119-123, 133; repair,
  119-123, 133
Walks, brick, 39, 42, 56-60; base, 58-59;
  design, 56-57; edging, 58; excavating,
  57-58, 60; finishing, 59-60; mortar-bed, 59,
  60; sand-bed, 57-60
Walks, concrete, 25-28; base, 25-26; design,
  25; excavating, 25; form, 25-26; reinforcing,
  26; stepped, 26, 27-28
Walks, stone, 66, 67-69; dry-laid in sand,
  69-70; dry-laid in sod, 67-68
Wall anchor ties, 53, 62-63, 76, 93, 111, 112,
  115
Walls, 13, 20, 39, 40, 42, 44, 64, 65, 78, 80,
  90, 128; brick, 46-56; concrete block, 78,
  80, 81-85, 86, 87, 88, 89, 90, 91; stone,
  70-77
Warm air outlet, 113
Water 11, 12, 13, 15, 43, 81, 96, 111; in brick
  mortar, 43; in concrete mix, 11, 12, 13, 15,
  96; in concrete block mortar, 81, 111
Waterplug, 123-125
Waterproofing, 87, 97-98, 101, 102, 123-125,
  134; basements, 123-125, 134; concrete
  tub, 97-98, 101; foundation exterior, 87;
  fountain, 102
Waterproofing sealer, 124
Water seepage, 87
Weathered joints, 48
Weepholes, 36, 62, 123, 124
Weight, concrete block, 79
Whisk broom, 107, 113
Window sills, 63, 80
Window wells, 136
Wonder-Brix, 63
Wood (pressure-treated), 21, 32, 33, 57, 58
Working lines, 98
Wythe, 42

Z-Brick, 63

CONTRIBUTORS ADDRESSES PICTURE CREDITS

We wish to extend our thanks to the individuals, associations, and manufacturers who graciously provided information and photographs for this book. Specific credit for individual photos is given below, with the names and addresses of the contributors.

Grateful recognition must be given to Mr. Frank Randall of the Portland Cement Association, 5420 Old Orchard Road, Skokie, Illinois. Both he and the Association were generous and helpful with information, tables and photographs for this book.

American Olean Tile   2583 Cannon Avenue, Lansdale, Pennsylvania 19446 95 bottom, 100 top left and middle center

BQP Industries, Inc.   4747 Ironton Street, Denver, Colorado 80239 136 top left

Michael Bliss, Landscape Architect   222 Sunset Drive, Encinita, California 92024 5 top, 6 bottom left, 53 bottom left

Brick Institute of America   1750 Old Meadow Road, McLean, Virginia 22101 38 upper, 48-49

California Redwood Association   One Lombard Street, San Francisco, California 94111 95 top

Rick Clark, Photographer   10843 North 45th Lane, Glendale, Arizona 85304 138

Ted Dayton Photography   2643 Manana Drive, Dallas, Texas 75220 2, 5 bottom, 6 top and center right, 7 bottom right, 43, 64 top

Ego Productions, James M. Auer   1849 N. 72nd Street, Wauwatosa, Wisconsin 53213 50, 66 top left

Formlite Products, Inc.   2 Hughes Avenue, Rye, New York 10580 91 top left

Goldblatt Tool Co.   511 Osage, Kansas City, Kansas 66110 9, 10, 40, 60 top right

Lied's Green Valley Gardens   N63 W22039 Highway 74, Sussex, Wisconsin 53089 64 center right

William Manly, Interior Designs   6062 North Port Washington Road, Milwaukee, Wisconsin 53217 41 center right

National Concrete Masonry Association   P.O. Box 781, Herndon, Virginia 22070 57 center, 78, 88, 89, 90 bottom, 132

Richard V. Nunn, Media Mark Productions   Falls Church Inn, 6633 Arlington Boulevard, Falls Church, Virginia 22045 121, 126, 130, 133, 134, 135

Portland Cement Association   5420 Old Orchard Road, Skokie, Illinois 60077 19, 20, 29, 33 upper left, 34

James E. Russell   1656 Vinton, Memphis, Tennessee 38104 6 center and bottom right, 41 bottom right, 44 bottom left, 49 left, 51 top, 52 upper left, 54 upper left, 55 lower right and upper, 56 upper and center right, 57 bottom right, 58 top and center left, 59 bottom left

Thoro System Products   7800 N.W. 36th Street, Miami, Florida 33166 87, 123, 124

Z-Brick   Woodinville, Washington 98072 (synthetic brick) 63

Tables on pg. 12, reprinted from *Concrete for Small Jobs* (IS174T) Portland Cement Association, Skokie, Illinois

Information on pp. 36-37 reprinted with permission from MWPS-21, *Home and Yard Improvements Handbook,* 1978, Midwest Plan Service, Ames, Iowa 50011.